AFTER THE REVIVAL

After the Revival

Pentecostalism and the Making of a Canadian Church

MICHAEL WILKINSON
and
LINDA M. AMBROSE

McGill-Queen's University Press
Montreal & Kingston • London • Chicago

ISBN 978-0-2280-0364-9 (cloth)
ISBN 978-0-2280-0365-6 (paper)
ISBN 978-0-2280-0523-0 (ePDF)
ISBN 978-0-2280-0524-7 (ePUB)

Legal deposit third quarter 2020
Bibliothèque nationale du Québec

Printed in Canada on acid-free paper that is 100% ancient forest free (100% post-consumer recycled), processed chlorine free

This book has been published with the help of a grant from the Canadian Federation for the Humanities and Social Sciences, through the Awards to Scholarly Publications Program, using funds provided by the Social Sciences and Humanities Research Council of Canada.

Funded by the Government of Canada | Financé par le gouvernement du Canada | Canada | Canada Council for the Arts | Conseil des arts du Canada

We acknowledge the support of the Canada Council for the Arts.

Nous remercions le Conseil des arts du Canada de son soutien.

Library and Archives Canada Cataloguing in Publication

Title: After the revival: pentecostalism and the making of a Canadian church / Michael Wilkinson and Linda M. Ambrose.

Names: Wilkinson, Michael, 1965– author. | Ambrose, Linda McGuire, 1960– author.

Description: Includes bibliographical references and index.

Identifiers: Canadiana (print) 20200266810 | Canadiana (ebook) 20200267213 | ISBN 9780228003656 (paper) | ISBN 9780228003649 (cloth) | ISBN 9780228005230 (ePDF) | ISBN 9780228005247 (ePUB)

Subjects: LCSH: Pentecostalism—Canada—History. | LCSH: Pentecostal Assemblies of Canada—History. | LCSH: Canada—Religion.

Classification: LCC BR1644.5.C3 W55 2020 | DDC 280/.40971—dc23

This book was typeset by Marquis Interscript in 10.5/13 Sabon.

Contents

Tables

Acknowledgments

The idea for this book took shape over extended conversations about Pentecostalism, usually at conferences but also online in different forums. We met each other for the first time in June 2008 at the annual meeting of the Canadian Society of Church History in Vancouver when an efficient program chair logically arranged a session that would include the two proposals he had received with the word "Pentecostal" in their titles. Since that time, we have collaborated on a number of initiatives, and we have presented material from this book project (separately and together) at several different academic conferences, including GloPent, the Society for Pentecostal Studies, the Canadian Historical Association, the Canadian History of Education Association, the Canadian Society for the Study of Religion, the Association for the Sociology of Religion, and the Society for the Scientific Study of Religion. Comments and questions from respondents and colleagues who attended the sessions where we tested our ideas helped us to think through our approach to this material. We wish to thank all of our conference friends and colleagues for their comments and recommendations.

We want to thank Kyla Madden, senior editor at McGill-Queen's University Press, for working with us on the project. Kyla's support was constant, even when we were not sure the book would ever be completed. The entire team at MQUP have expedited this book, and we are grateful for the expert guidance every step of the way. Dorothy Turnbull's careful copy editing is much appreciated. Catherine Plear is an indexer extraordinaire, and it was a pleasure to work with her.

Peter Althouse read an early draft of our manuscript, and we thank him for his insightful observations. The anonymous peer reviewers provided us with comments that helped us to clarify our argument and sharpen our focus. Jim Craig from the Pentecostal Assemblies of Canada Archives in Mississauga helped us to locate material that we would have never found on our own, and he helpfully and efficiently suggested additional items he thought we would find useful. Laurie Van Kleek gave complete access to the archival collection of Bernice Gerard papers housed at the Lorne Philip Hudson Memorial Library at Summit Pacific College in Abbotsford.

Funds from the Laurentian University Research Fund (LURF) supported the excellent work of conscientious research assistants, including Patrick Beaudry, Jacob Belcher, Alissa Droog, Nathan McCoy, Stephanie McPherson, Laura Robinson, David Scott, and Ellen Sheppard.

We acknowledge that this book has been published with the help of a grant from the Federation for the Humanities and Social Sciences, through the Awards to Scholarly Publications Program, using funds provided by the Social Sciences and Humanities Research Council of Canada.

Finally, we want to acknowledge our families, who offered their generous support allowing us to research, attend conferences, and write.

AFTER THE REVIVAL

Introduction

It happened to all kinds of people in Canada, starting in 1906. She was a recent British immigrant, a wife and mother of four, running a rest home in Toronto, and when she prayed for strength to carry on, "it" happened to her. She was the first one. A few weeks later, a Holiness preacher from the Ottawa Valley, who was holding meetings in rapidly growing prairie towns, took the train to Los Angeles because he wanted to see and receive "it" firsthand. He was the second. Then more and more people experienced "it." A Winnipeg real estate man sent word to his family that he did not know when he would be home from Chicago because he planned to stay there until "it" happened to him. A precocious high school student in rural Ontario defied her parents' wishes by spending the night in town with people who introduced her to "it" and to her future evangelist/missionary husband. The stylish and successful owner of an Ottawa haberdashery was heartbroken over the condition of his bedridden wife, so he took a chance that "it" might be their only hope. A student from Sarnia, Ontario, bored with her studies at McMaster University, decided to go to Toronto to check out the place that everybody seemed to be talking about, and that is when "it" happened to her. Shortly afterward, she became a missionary to India. "It" was the Pentecostal experience associated with a series of revivals in the early twentieth century. Speaking in tongues was a sign that one had been filled with the Holy Spirit. In Pentecostal meetings, the gospel was preached and signs and wonders followed, especially experiences of speaking in tongues, physical healing, and a call to missionary work.

These six vignettes represent a cross-section of some of Canada's earliest converts to Pentecostalism. The first was Ellen Hebden, who came to Canada in 1904 with her husband James and opened the Toronto East End Mission at 651 Queen Street East. Ellen Hebden was the first one in Canada known to speak in tongues, and after that experience in November 1906, the Hebden Mission quickly became the hub of Canadian Pentecostal activity. The second story is that of the Reverend R.E. McAlister, one of thirteen children born to a farm family in the Ottawa Valley in 1880, who would play a leading role in formulating the largest Pentecostal denomination in Canada after he experienced the baptism of the Spirit at the famous Azusa Street Revival in Los Angeles. The real estate agent was A.H. Argue, a highly successful Methodist building his wealth in the booming markets of Winnipeg. Having heard about the Pentecostal experience, he resolved to "tarry" under the ministry of William Durham in Chicago until he "came through" to his personal Pentecost. He stayed for three weeks before returning home to hold prayer meetings for "tarrying" in his home. The high school girl in Ingersoll, Ontario, was Aimee Kennedy, who spoke in tongues after attending a revival meeting led by the evangelist Robert Semple. "Sister Aimee" would become the infamous Aimee Semple McPherson, the most widely recognized name in North American Pentecostalism of the twentieth century. The haberdasher was C.E. Baker, whose wife was miraculously healed of cancer at a downtown mission in Ottawa. Baker would soon give up his career in fashion to enter full-time ministry and establish the largest Pentecostal church in Montreal. The McMaster student was Barbara Johnston, who received the baptism of the Spirit at the Hebden Mission in 1907 and went on to become Canada's first Pentecostal missionary to India. These individuals were instrumental in establishing Pentecostalism in Canada.

What followed these initial modern-day experiences of the Holy Spirit, however, was not always straightforward, and over time there were various debates about the meaning of these encounters. Pentecostals themselves spent time defending these experiences through preaching, testimonies, tracts, and magazines. Camp meetings were held to encourage people to seek the Holy Spirit for empowerment in mission work. Conventions with key leaders were held to promote the Pentecostal message and form networks that spanned around the world. Worship services were organized with large orchestras that played with a Pentecostal zeal. Over time, as Pentecostals came together, questions were raised about whether or not to organize, and it would take more than a decade before the Pentecostal Assemblies of Canada (PAOC) would form. The organization of Pentecostals was controversial, but it served to create and sustain an organizational identity that expanded throughout the country. Pentecostal identity formed around the central question about who they were as an organization and how that identity would be worked out through the expansion of congregations, doctrinal statements, departments, programs and ministries, missionaries, Bible colleges, policies, and leaders who worked tirelessly to manage the organization. In spite of the popular notion that Pentecostals were only about experiencing the Holy Spirit and not theology or organization, with the PAOC we observe that there was an incredible amount of energy spent on organizing Pentecostals in an orderly manner. When that order was challenged, the PAOC responded with clear views of what kind of organization they were and what it meant to be part of that organization. Those who challenged the organization faced a leadership that claimed authority to lead. Boundaries for the denomination were forming. Those boundaries not only defined who was inside but also the way the PAOC would relate to other spheres of society. Experience, identity, and boundary-making are central to our cultural analysis, and we place our book in the context of existing Pentecostal studies and its various debates, especially among historians and sociologists.

Pentecostalism is also complicated. For that reason, Pentecostal studies demands multidisciplinary research to draw upon a wide range of disciplines for observing and interpreting Pentecostalism. For example, theologians have focused on a series of issues, including assessing and critiquing doctrinal views and constructing Pentecostal theologies. Biblical scholars have examined the text to understand how the Bible informs Pentecostal interpretations. Linguists have explored the understanding of glossolalia as a type of language. Religious studies scholars have focused on assessing the nature of religion among Pentecostals. Historians have examined a wide range of issues around Pentecostal origins, historical development within specific countries, biographies of key figures, and the relationship of religion to areas like gender. Social scientists, from anthropology, political science, and sociology, have examined the culture of Pentecostalism, its role in politics, and its relationship to institutionalization and secularization. Key scholarly societies and research groups have brought researchers together to explore specific questions in a multidisciplinary fashion, including the Society for Pentecostal Studies and its journal, *Pneuma*, GloPent in Europe and its journal *PentecoStudies*, and the Canadian Pentecostal

Research Network with its journal, *Canadian Journal of Pentecostal-Charismatic Christianity.*[1] There are other key research groups in Asia, Africa, Latin America, and Oceania that have contributed to a growing worldwide literature on Pentecostalism. In some cases, the scholarly work is interdisciplinary and draws upon two or more disciplines.

This book, whose authors are trained in history and sociology, is shaped by our mutual research interests on Pentecostals in Canada. While historians and sociologists have specific research methods and theoretical orientations that shape their academic work, there are many areas that overlap and shape our cultural analysis of the PAOC. We argue that the history of the PAOC is characterized by a series of interactions with Canadian society that demonstrates the flexibility of religious organizations to negotiate their place in the religious landscape, sometimes reflecting broader cultural patterns while at other times in conflict with them. After the revival, Pentecostal leaders established organizational structures that were animated by a subculture that navigated the denomination through external social and cultural shifts as well as internal challenges to its authority. Drawing upon a specific cultural repertoire, the PAOC established boundaries that defined a particular type of Pentecostalism that moved from the margins of twentieth-century Christianity to its current central place among Protestant Christians. This historical development was not without some conflict and pragmatic response but in no way is predictive of its future. What we are interested in are the questions that highlight the social processes of religious organizations – specifically, how the PAOC organized, established its identity, and constructed a subculture that served the organization.

We develop our argument by asking: How does Pentecostalism come to shape the identity of the PAOC and its congregations, policies, practices, activities, and sentiments? What is the nature of Pentecostalism as a cultural repertoire, and how does it animate the PAOC while serving as a cultural narrative about who they are and how they envision their role in Canadian society and the world? How does the PAOC provide some coherence to the Pentecostal experience for individuals and congregations in relation to other spheres of society like politics, education, and law? What role do the organization and its leaders play in telling the narrative, shaping the way in which participants understand it and experience Pentecostalism? What are the limits to cultural cohesion, and what happens when the subculture's system of meaning no longer makes sense either to insiders or outsiders? How does the PAOC reconcile itself with social and cultural change? How does the PAOC think of itself and its practices in relation to other Christians like evangelical Protestants, mainline Protestants, Eastern Orthodox, and Roman Catholics? What is the impact of feminism on the PAOC, and does it offer insight into the changing views of women in ministry? How does the PAOC respond to an organizational bureaucracy that is structured around a specific life course model prominent in the 1950s that expects everyone to follow a certain path from childhood to youth, marriage, and family when this life course model no longer makes sense in the twenty-first century when many people do not marry, do not have children, or are in same-sex marriages? How does the PAOC respond to social change since the 1960s on issues like abortion, homosexuality, multiculturalism, and the increasing immigration of non-Christian religions?

These are the types of questions that shape this book, and what we explore are the various ways in which Pentecostalism, as represented by the PAOC, engages with Canadian society. This allows us to observe and assess the multiple practices and experiences that shape its identity and the discourse that highlights the questions about Pentecostal authority, both internally among Pentecostals themselves and externally in relation to other social institutions. More specifically, this is a study of one denomination and how it has interacted with particular social and cultural shifts in Canada. Drawing upon a range of sources, including archival data, census data, interviews, primary documents, and observations, we demonstrate how the PAOC sometimes reflects Canadian social institutions and cultural patterns and at other times is in conflict with them.

With these assumptions in mind, this book takes the following form. Chapter 1 places our work in the context of existing scholarship on Pentecostalism, which tends to be multidisciplinary in nature. Coming from two different disciplinary backgrounds ourselves (sociology and history), we recognize the value in cross-disciplinary approaches and the fruitful exchanges that such studies can bring. The historical work we highlight includes both popular and academic works. Because our book traces one denomination over the twentieth century, we are also interested in the popular histories that the PAOC has published about themselves to observe the different emphases that those books have made over time and offer explanations for those historiographical differences. There is a growing body of academic history about Pentecostals, including not only American scholarship but more and more Canadian studies too. We draw on those works but bring a greater attention to questions of organizational culture and gender dynamics than previous studies have done. Theories from the sociology of religion and culture helped us to frame this book, and therefore, we take time in the first chapter to discuss the prevalent sociological theories that have informed Pentecostal studies to date. In the end, we adopt a cultural frame as our analytical orientation, allowing us to consider how the PAOC has faced questions of authority, engaged in boundary-making to create a particular organizational subculture, and interacted with the broader Canadian culture by invoking a Pentecostal cultural repertoire.

Chapter 2 focuses on the activities, events, and spiritual experiences that came to be known as Pentecostalism prior to the official organization of the PAOC in 1919. We give attention to the social context of Canada and the optimism of the new century around industrialization and urbanization with new economic and religious opportunities because this establishes our thesis about the importance of paying attention to how the PAOC interacted with the broader Canadian context. Pentecostalism was controversial as it emerged and attempted to gain some sense of legitimacy. That legitimacy was not derived from a particular set of doctrines but from spiritual experiences that were signs of continuity with its Methodist and Holiness experiences from the nineteenth century, as well as reports of "something new" in the form of renewal from other sectors, including the Keswick meetings in England and other worldwide revivals in Wales, Los Angeles, Korea, and India. The process of establishing a symbolic boundary to define Pentecostal identity in Canada was characterized by "disorder," not only between Pentecostals and non-Pentecostals but especially within the movement. Debates centred on the meaning of the experiences and whether or not "ordering" the Spirit in some type of Pentecostal organization was the best way forward. What we observe is that while Pentecostalism was emerging and crystallizing, the development of a Pentecostal organization, including its identity and subcultural qualities, was not a smooth process.

In Chapter 3, we turn our attention to the organizational aspects of the PAOC, its structure, polity, and leaders. We are particularly interested in the way in which the fledgling organization interacted with the Canadian economic context of expansion and, more specifically, how a business model became embedded within the PAOC very early in its formation. The organization also faced conflict and tension within as it sorted out its mission and vision, responded to leaders with different views, and created a stronger boundary that defined its organizational identity. The process reflected the broader culture's modernist impulses, including the development and expansion of policies as well as statements about spiritual experiences around worship, healing, spiritual gifts, and missionary work, in response to internal pressures. Organizing also involved the development and expansion of Pentecostal theological education through the PAOC's Bible schools and colleges, which served to socialize leaders around a core curriculum that contributed to their Pentecostal identity. The two world wars forced the PAOC to address questions about its relationship to the Empire (and, later, the Commonwealth) and to Canada, creating some tension especially when the PAOC held to a pacifist position but also included individuals who wanted to serve to show loyalty to the British Empire and the Dominion of Canada. We highlight how leaders of the Latter Rain movement in the late 1940s forced the PAOC to articulate its position on organizational authority when those boundaries were tested and threatened by competing expressions of Pentecostal experience.

Chapter 4 considers how the PAOC consolidated and expanded its organization with a wide variety of new programs and activities following World War Two. Here again, our argument about the PAOC interacting with the surrounding culture is reinforced because developments in the broader Canadian context were at the heart of the PAOC's evolution. While the country was enjoying strong economic growth and the baby boom was in full swing, the PAOC was also enjoying that prosperity with congregations bursting at the seams. Some of the most significant growth for the PAOC took place between the 1950s and 1970s. And like Canadian society at large, Pentecostals were redefining appropriate roles for women in the midst of postwar economic growth and rising birthrates. In the early period of Pentecostalism, women had been missionaries and pastors who started new congregations and led successful ministries. As men returned home from war, conservative ideas about appropriate roles dominated Canadian public opinion, and new programming initiatives by the PAOC reflected those cultural norms. The PAOC created the types of programs and structures that could meet the changing nature of the family with new expanded programming for children and youth. This chapter critically evaluates the institutional embeddedness of a family development model within the PAOC, how that shaped its identity, and the challenges for the PAOC to adjust to the social and cultural changes in a particular postwar understanding of the nuclear family, including the role of women in ministry.

Chapter 5 focuses on the social changes that emerge in the 1960s, most notably the Criminal Law Amendment Act, 1968–69 and questions for Pentecostals about abortion and sexuality. It is during this period, when Canadian social mores were liberalizing, that the PAOC engaged the political realm with a growing sense of confidence but also moral panic about the proposed legal changes. Pentecostals responded to social and cultural change in a particular way that called upon a discourse of concern and threat that had to be addressed. During the 1970s, the PAOC mobilized its clergy and congregations to take action. The PAOC also developed a Social Concerns Department that was politically active until the beginning of the 1990s when the denominational leadership called for a course correction, believing that political and social issues were not their primary mission. They called for a return to spiritual renewal, evangelism, and discipleship. During this period, ongoing questions were raised about LGBTQ issues as the body became a site for cultural questions and new boundary-making, both in the broader culture and within the PAOC.

In chapter 6, we turn our attention to the view of Canada as a mission field in the PAOC and the role of the Home Missions Department. What we are particularly interested in here is the focus of the department on two groups in Canada – French-speaking Roman Catholics and Indigenous peoples. These two themes dominated Canadian public debates during Quebec's Quiet Revolution and as Indigenous cultural renewal and activism were emerging. The assumption that Canada is a mission field is shaped by a particular cultural view that Roman Catholics and Indigenous peoples need to be evangelized and converted. The role of story and testimony are cultural tools that are employed by Pentecostals to justify a certain course of action. However, the tension between English and French Canada extends beyond Protestant and Roman Catholic to controversy among English and French sectors within the PAOC. This is also the case between Indigenous and non-Indigenous Pentecostals. This chapter focuses on the complexity between cultural interaction, conversion, and Pentecostalism.

Chapter 7 examines the relationship between the PAOC as it intersects with multiculturalism, ethnicity, and religious diversity. The view of Canada as a multicultural society is one that is fluid and has changed since the 1970s from a largely pan-European society to one that is increasingly shaped by new migration patterns with people from Africa, Asia, and Latin America, solidifying Canada's reputation and identity as a welcoming and eclectic immigrant-receiving society. The response of the PAOC in the 1930s and 1940s was to form organizational structures known as Branch Conferences with Pentecostal immigrants from Europe, mostly German, Slavic, and Finnish peoples. As immigration patterns shifted to non-European countries in the 1970s, the PAOC viewed immigrants as sources of church growth. The transplanting of Pentecostals from non-European regions, however, presented to the PAOC a new set of tensions with a range of uniquely organizational, cultural, and ethnic patterns. At the same time, there were also questions about immigrants who identified with non-Christian religions like Islam, Hinduism, and Buddhism that challenged Pentecostal assumptions about the religious and ethnic identity of Canada and raised issues about inclusion and exclusion as new boundaries were imagined by the PAOC.

Overall, a cultural analysis of Pentecostals in Canada allows us to focus on questions about how the PAOC negotiated its place in Canadian society while developing a Pentecostal subculture and organizational identity through the types of experiences and practices they promoted over time. The organizing of Pentecostals into the PAOC highlights the organizational nature of the denomination, the role of its leaders, policies, finances, and interaction with social institutions like the family, politics, and economics. Our cultural lens allows us to focus on the fluidity of Pentecostal identity and the way it changes over time as it engages other social institutions while questioning its own authority and that of the public realm. Finally, we observe how Pentecostals adjust their symbolic boundaries in relationship to changing ethnic and religious diversity in Canada and, in doing so, how they redefine what it means to be Pentecostal while utilizing available cultural tools from their religious repertoire.

1

Experience, Identity, and Boundary-Making

INTRODUCTION

In 1919, the Pentecostal Assemblies of Canada (PAOC) received its charter from the government to officially exist as a religious institution. With its new charter, the PAOC was granted authority to establish local congregations and schools of religious instruction and to conduct missionary work in Canada and throughout the world. Pentecostals first appeared in the Canadian census in 1911, with 515 people identifying with Pentecostalism (see table 1.1). The growth of Pentecostalism was quite substantial throughout the twentieth century, reaching a high mark of 478,705 in 2011. Pentecostalism represents one storyline within the broader narrative of religion in Canada. Religion in Canada is largely shaped by five key storylines, including the significant decline of mainline Protestantism, most notably the United Church of Canada; the relative stability of Roman Catholicism with which nearly half of all Canadians identify; the increase in religious and cultural diversity with ongoing migration from Africa, Asia, and Latin America; the growing numbers of Canadians who do not identify with any religion; and the relative vitality of evangelical Protestantism, including Pentecostals. The vitality of evangelicalism is rooted in congregational life, which plays an important role in shaping the subculture. Evangelical congregations are characterized by an emphasis on clear mission and vision statements, high levels of weekly attendance, active youth and children's programs, leadership well-being, and large financial contributions that support evangelical work.[1] While congregations are key for understanding the regular activities of the subculture, denominations play

Table 1.1
Pentecostals in Canada, 1911–2011

Year	*Total*
1911	515
1921	7,012
1931	26,349
1941	57,742
1951	95,131
1961	143,877
1971	222,390
1981	338,785
1991	436,435
2001	369,475
2011	478,705

Sources: Derived from Dominion Bureau of Statistics, 1953, 1963; Statistics Canada, 1973, 1983, 1993, 2003; Household Survey, 2011.

an important role in establishing policies, priorities, and resources for congregations and their leaders.[2]

The PAOC has grown to be the largest evangelical denomination in Canada, with weekly attendance rates that exceed those of the United Church of Canada, which was at one time the largest Protestant denomination.[3] The PAOC, however, is not the only Pentecostal denomination in Canada but is one of about twelve older or classical Pentecostal churches that include the Apostolic Church in Canada, the Apostolic Church of Pentecost, the Canadian Assemblies of God, the Church of God, the Church of God in Christ, the Church of God of Prophesy, the Elim Fellowship of Evangelical Churches and Ministries, the Foursquare Gospel Church of Canada, the Pentecostal Assemblies of Newfoundland and Labrador, the Pentecostal Holiness Church of Canada, and the United Pentecostal International Church. The PAOC is the largest of these, representing roughly two-thirds of all of the classical Pentecostals. Pentecostalism, however, is not limited to these older Pentecostal denominations, and in Canada there are charismatic Christians in the historical Protestant churches as well as among Roman Catholics. Furthermore, there are numbers of neo-Pentecostals that are largely independent. According to Todd Johnson and Gina Zurlo, in 2015 there were 2,602,805 Pentecostals,

Charismatics, and Independent Charismatics in Canada (see table 1.2), growing by about 300,000 since 2000.

Since its beginnings as an officially recognized religious organization in Canada, the PAOC has grown quite substantially in all areas, including numbers of clergy, congregations, colleges, finances, and missionaries. For example, in 1920 the PAOC claimed to serve 3,101 adherents in twenty-seven congregations with thirty-nine clergy (see table 1.3).[4] The growth was quite substantial, with significant increases over each decade so that after fifty years of ministry, the PAOC reported in 1970 that they were serving 91,894 adherents in 743 congregations with 1,933 clergy in Canada and around the world. By 2017, the numbers had increased to 247,042 adherents, 1,060 congregations, and 3,685 clergy.

Financially, revenues for the PAOC were also growing (see table 1.4). In 1919–20, the PAOC reported total revenue of $2,241, which grew within the first fifty years to $2.2 million in 1969–70. The most substantial increase was from 1980 to 1990 when total revenues grew from $8.6 million to $20.4 million. Reports submitted to the Canada Revenue Agency (CRA) from 2000 to 2017 show some significant changes (see table 1.5). First, the rate of growth begins to change with a decrease in total revenue between 1990 and 2000 from $20.4 million to $17.6 million. Second, in the decade following, the total revenue begins to increase again but only reached $20.3 million in 2009, about the same figure as in 1990. Since 2009, the total revenue begins to grow again, reaching a peak of $25.2 million in 2017. CRA reports also show the total amounts spent on administration and management at around 6 per cent to 8 per cent since 2005. Total monies reported as distributed to charitable work operated by the PAOC (including the work of its missionaries) fluctuated from about 67 per cent to 89 per cent between 2005 and 2017. Clearly, the PAOC demonstrated organizational growth in all areas since 1919, with some slowing of growth and financial challenges in the 1990s. The past decade appears to show some return to stability but without the growth once experienced in its history.

However, a decade into the twenty-first century, with signs of slowing growth, the PAOC reported the closure of eighty-one congregations between 2008 and 2012, while 104 new congregations or ministries had begun, most of them associated with recent immigrants. For the PAOC, this slowing down caused some concern, so the General Executive initiated a new vision to roughly coincide with its

Table 1.2
Pentecostals, Charismatics, and Independent Charismatics in Canada, 2000–2015

	2000	*2015*
Pentecostals	334,000	390,023
Charismatics	1,765,000	1,907,408
Independent Charismatics	214,000	305,374
Total	2,313,000	2,602,805

Source: Todd M. Johnson and Gina A. Zurlo, eds., *World Christian Database* (Leiden, Netherlands: Brill).

Table 1.3
Adherents, Congregations, and Clergy, PAOC, 1920–2017

Year	*Adherents*	*Congregations*	*Clergy*
1920	3,101	27	39
1930	8,055	170	385
1940	37,122	350	732
1950	62,600	506	1,179
1960	82,153	664	1,546
1970	91,894	743	1,933
1980	117,362	805	2,510
1990	194,972	994	3,507
2000	228,003	1,103	3,431
2010	236,557	1,077	3,555
2017	247,042	1,060	3,685

Sources: PAOC Archives; PAOC Vital Statistics.

Table 1.4
Total Receipts as Reported by PAOC, 1919–1990

Year	*Total Revenue ($)*
1919–20	2,241
1929–30	73,441
1939–40	135,322
1949–50	474,662
1959–60	1,241,200
1969–70	2,201,889
1979–80	8,638,347
1990	20,402,843

Source: PAOC General Conference Reports, PAOC Archives.

Table 1.5
Selected PAOC Finances as Reported by Canada Revenue Agency, 2000–2017

Year	*Total Revenue ($)*	*Management and Administrative Expenses ($)*	*Management and Administrative Expenses (%)*	*Charitable Giving ($)*	*Charitable Giving (%)*
2000	17,600,771	1,879,003	11	14,443,107	81
2001	17,682,898	1,947,529	11	14,914,144	84
2002	18,123,104	2,457,100	13	14,826,669	81
2003	16,507,082	2,326,694	14	14,836,835	89
2004	17,729,036	1,830,739	11	15,902,813	89
2005	20,769,964	1,772,476	8	17,178,158	82
2006	15,976,975	1,457,658	8	11,007,672	69
2007	18,873,136	1,446,132	7	12,652,471	67
2008	20,681,610	1,500,371	7	16,500,926	80
2009	20,307,993	1,455,626	6	18,194,841	89
2010	24,178,880	1,630,262	7	18,835,357	86
2011	21,978,152	1,490,763	6	20,819,808	88
2012	21,783,671	1,611,321	8	17,714,623	86
2013	24,525,534	1,438,042	7	18,725,948	87
2014	23,103,692	1,501,129	7	19,799,388	88
2015	24,198,875	1,551,982	6	21,368,619	87
2016	25,110,205	1,670,035	7	20,829,265	85
2017	25,270,371	1,656,149	7	21,725,186	86

Source: Derived from Canada Revenue Agency.

100th anniversary. The PAOC leadership consulted with local pastors and college professors, lay people, and district leaders to ask how they might revitalize the denomination.[5]

The consultation became known as the "2020 Initiative" and was launched in November 2013 to fulfil its mission: "To glorify God by making disciples everywhere by proclaiming and practising the gospel of Jesus Christ in the power of the Holy Spirit." The PAOC said, "This initiative, which we are calling the 2020 Initiative, is rooted in both a healthy dissatisfaction regarding the current state of our discipleship and church/ministry planting. It is also an acknowledgement and an expression of appreciation for the missional impulse we do see in many of our churches and people."[6] The specific details of this initiative revolve around a vision of seeing 1 per cent of all Canadians, or approximately 350,000 Christians, actively participating in 1,500 congregations by 2020. This is an immensely ambitious plan considering that in 2017 the PAOC had 1,060 active congregations, eighty-two satellite sites, twenty church plants, and seventeen new initiatives, totalling 1,179 places of ministry (see table 1.2 above). The total number of people being served by the PAOC, whether members or adherents, was reported to be 247,042 people. Realizing the challenge of the 2020 Initiative before them, the PAOC hired a full-time person in 2017 to lead the Initiative and to close the gap.

The 2020 Initiative illustrates one of the major challenges for congregations in Canada that desire to grow but are attempting to do so in a cultural context that is not overly receptive to organized religion. While the PAOC talks about Canada as a mission field and has an internal culture shaped by a theology of evangelism and missionary work, the subculture is at odds with the changing landscape of Canada, which is increasingly diverse and changing. As such, evangelism, conversion, church growth, and discipleship are cultural tools from an available Pentecostal repertoire, devices used for telling one's story that serve to inspire, motivate, and call followers to action. Internally, such activities are inspirational and give focus for members. However, external to the subculture, activities like evangelism and conversion are frowned upon, spoken of pejoratively as proselytization, and generally not welcomed in Canadian society.

The development of Pentecostalism in Canada also coincides with the modernization of the country over the past 150 years. Modernization is characterized by social change, including the development of a range of specialized social institutions that orient Canadians around a set of ideals about work, health, education, family, government, and religion. The key religious groups in Canada that had a significant impact on shaping the cultural views about the emerging social order were most notably the Roman Catholics in Quebec and the Methodists, Anglicans, Presbyterians, and Congregationalists in English-speaking Canada. Generally, Canadians were well churched in the nineteenth and early twentieth centuries, with many congregations to serve the growing population of European settlers. Christian churches played a particular role working alongside the state to offer education, health, and social services. Mainline Protestant churches created stronger alliances and a mission of serving the population. However, among Methodists there were those aligned with the Holiness movement who believed they were losing something by seeking social acceptance. By the turn of the century, a growing number of radical evangelicals broke away from the Methodists and became the new face of a different type of evangelicalism in the twentieth century, including upstarts like the Missionary Alliance Church, the Salvation Army Church, the Church of the Nazarene, and the Pentecostal Assemblies of Canada. All these churches had their roots in the dissenting Methodist congregations, specifically the Holiness movement, and while they were organizing and establishing new religious organizations, the Methodists, Presbyterians, and Congregationalists would form the United Church of Canada in 1925 with a different vision of Canada, hoping to play the role of a national church. While the United Church of Canada and the Roman Catholic Church intersected with broader social institutions like health care and education, so too did the Pentecostals, albeit with a particular cultural view that is not well understood. How might we begin to interpret these statistical data, historically and sociologically? How did Pentecostals themselves understand their own history? What sociological explanations did they incorporate into their role in Canadian society?

PENTECOSTAL HISTORIOGRAPHY

Published histories of Pentecostalism in Canada can be divided into two categories: the popular denominationally sponsored histories and academic history. As the PAOC marks their 100th anniversary, five books published between 1958 and 2018 have recorded their history. An analysis of those works reveals that popular history serves a variety of purposes for its readers, most of whom are insiders to the movement, including celebration, exhortation, and strategy.

First, authors writing for the PAOC celebrated their movement's progress and looked for ways to explain the Pentecostal movement's growth. The most common way they could explain the phenomenal growth of Canadian Pentecostalism in the twentieth century was to point to God's direct intervention. Gloria Kulbeck's 1958 book is a prime example of a triumphalist and providential history, aptly titled *What God Hath Wrought: A History of the Pentecostal Assemblies of Canada.*[7] Kulbeck worked on the book under the direction of PAOC General Superintendent W.E. McAlister, who initiated the project by asking for submissions from long-serving Pentecostal leaders across the country. The rate of growth, with Canadian Pentecostalism expanding from just over 500 followers to more than 95,000 in just forty years, seemed miraculous indeed. Therefore, it is not surprising that Kulbeck's text cites divine intervention in human history, which is offered as the most plausible explanation of events.

At the same time, Kulbeck's book does credit human agency as a factor in the success of the PAOC. With celebratory portraits of individual Canadians, the book included profiles of the "founding fathers" of the movement who founded the PAOC by creating the institutional structures that helped to encourage and manage the denomination's growth. Indeed, the book's hagiographic tone is evident in the dedication: "To the memory of the faithful, consecrated and self-denying Canadian Pentecostal pioneers whose names are recorded in this book, and to their loyal co-workers and helpers, all of whose names are recorded in the Lamb's book of life, we dedicate this history of the Pentecostal Assemblies of Canada."[8] Like an official corporate history and typical of such publications from the 1950s, Kulbeck's book includes several pages of professional photographs of those male founders, whose images are reminiscent of bank executives or insurance agents. The intent was to reinforce the respectable and professional nature of the PAOC.

In the foreword to the work, A.G. Ward praised the commitment of early Pentecostals and traced how far they had progressed from their humble beginnings to a prosperous organization with sizable assets. He recalled that in the early days, "we met to worship in the most humble mission halls. We were few in number, under great reproach. Money was scarce – there was no organization – and almost everyone believed that at any moment the Lord would come."[9] He contrasted those early days of austerity and eschatological urgency with the mid-century comfort that Canadian Pentecostals enjoyed: "Today there are beautiful church buildings from coast to coast – tens of thousands of eager worshippers filling them from week to week – still worshipping God in Pentecostal fashion – a well-balanced and wisely-ordered organization with plenty of funds to carry on a world program which is having a telling impact upon all the peoples of the world. What God hath wrought!"[10] Significantly, Ward's context of postwar prosperity led him to cite real estate and furnishings as a sign of God's blessing. The providential approach to Pentecostal history, along with hagiographic tributes to the founders, were clearly in evidence.

Another volume of Canadian Pentecostal history appeared in 1962 when Gordon Atter published *The Third Force*.[11] Atter was clear in his criticism of Kulbeck's book, not for its providential approach but because he felt she had missed a significant part of the Canadian story by failing to emphasize the international scope of Pentecostalism and the important role that Canadians had played in missionary work. Atter was well placed to correct that oversight, as one author observed, being "the son of early Pentecostal missionary parents, [he] was an eyewitness of many events in the early years of the movement. He grew up surrounded by Pentecostals and writes with a great deal of authenticity about people and events."[12]

Atter explained in his preface to a later edition that by 1970 the term "the third force" was widely known as a reference to Pentecostalism and noted with a celebratory tone, "as this third edition goes to press, the Pentecostal Revival rolls on to ever greater victory."[13] Optimistically, Atter asserted that "the Revival still bears the characteristics of its early fervor." He offered evidence that the providential work of God was continuing to characterize Canadian Pentecostalism, asserting, "Its growth has been phenomenal, its leadership remarkable. Its doctrines are thoroughly scriptural. Its impact on the religious world of today is continually increasing."[14] Like Kulbeck's, Atter's book adopts the providential approach with a celebratory tone as he recounts with amazement the remarkable progress that the movement enjoyed worldwide, in part because of the sacrifices of Canadian leaders.

A second purpose that history served for the PAOC was to offer lessons and exhort readers in hopes of shaping their behaviour. By the 1990s, the PAOC had enjoyed a growing acceptance as part of the Canadian religious landscape over more than seven decades, and with that maturity, some expressed fears about the spiritual vitality of the movement, raising questions about whether societal acceptance for Pentecostalism had come at the cost of spiritual compromise. From that place of reflection, two volumes of denominational history were published: Thomas Miller's *Canadian Pentecostals: A History of the Pentecostal Assemblies of Canada*, published in 1994, and Douglas Rudd's *When the Spirit Came upon Them: Highlights from the Early Years of the Pentecostal Movement in Canada*, published in 2002. Both of these books took a turn away from the triumphalist providential model to inject some concern about how the movement was trending and what the future might hold if no course correction was taken. Here, the authors used history as a tool of exhortation.

Thomas Miller had impressive academic credentials,[15] and in writing a book to mark the seventy-fifth anniversary of the PAOC, he further justified the need for his book with reference to scholarship in the sociology of religion. Referencing the work of sociologist David O. Moberg from Marquette University, Miller sounded an alarm to the PAOC and its adherents.[16] Moberg had argued that "revivalist associations rarely have retained their primary religious emphases past the third or fourth generation,"[17] and Miller was convinced that the PAOC was on the verge of decline if action was not taken to restore the movement and recapture the deep spirituality of its founders. As he explained, "the PAOC has enjoyed eight decades of uninterrupted growth ... But the extraordinary accomplishments of the past 80 years have, in themselves, led some thoughtful observers to ask penetrating questions about the future. It remains to be seen whether the PAOC will follow the historical pattern from the origin to decline observed by Moberg, or be an exception."[18] Miller was quick to say that he hoped the latter would be true, and he saw "hopeful indications" in the fact that some members of the PAOC leadership understood "the critical stages of development" and were expressing "their determination to maintain the distinctive spiritual emphases."[19]

What sets Miller's approach apart from the earlier volumes is that although he shared an admiration for the early leaders of the movement, he urged the PAOC not to rest on its laurels (or even on God's providential moves) but to move from celebration of the past to sober thought about the future. General Superintendent James MacKnight reiterated the importance of Miller's emphasis on Spirit baptism and evangelism and expressed his hopes for the book, saying, "It is my fervent prayer that this volume will become a dynamic instrument to ignite another Pentecost."[20] Miller's academic concern with the demise of revivalist movements was useful rhetoric for PAOC leadership concerned about how the movement would fare in the coming decades with so many adherents who could not point to a family heritage as Pentecostals. The historian and the denominational leadership could agree that it was important to admonish PAOC members who were drifting into complacency and exhort them to return to Pentecostalism's distinctive foundations.

Douglas Rudd echoed that message with his 2002 book entitled *When the Spirit Came upon Them: Highlights from the Early Years of the Pentecostal Movement in Canada*. Emphasizing the vital spirituality of the movement's founders, Rudd cautioned, "Surveillance is vital."[21] Adopting the same tone of exhortation that characterized Miller's work, Rudd admitted that he was not attempting to write an objective, academic account. Confessing that he was deeply invested with the PAOC and making no apology for "being biased in favor of the Pentecostal way because of close association,"[22] Rudd argued that history should be written with a purpose. He cited a historical authority who claimed that "In the ancient world the idea of writing dispassionate, objective history merely to chronicle events, with no ideological purpose, was unheard of. Nobody wrote history if there wasn't a reason to learn from it."[23] What Rudd hoped his readers would learn was that Pentecostals shared distinctive practices that unlocked the source of spiritual power.

When the Spirit Came upon Them was limited to the events that had unfolded by 1925, and Rudd revealed that while he was doing research for the book he was "deeply moved by the great price paid by those early Pentecostal believers and their pastors."[24] Building on the way the pioneer stories had moved him personally, Rudd hoped that readers would be similarly moved and that the book would "inspire them today to exercise faith in the promises enjoyed by the pioneers, but most of all to re-ignite the passion for God and power He provides for evangelism at home and around the world."[25] Echoing Miller's concerns that the third and fourth generations of a movement typically move away from the fervour and fundamental practices of the founders, Rudd criticized the integrity of some PAOC congregational records when they measured growth largely based on members who transferred from other evangelical congregations. He also warned about the dangers of smug satisfaction that accompanied success when it was measured in worldly terms. Rudd warned PAOC members that they must not fall into the sin of pride "over numbers or material assets" because such measures were "Satan's most subtle snare."[26] Whereas material assets like property and healthy budgets had previously been regarded as a sign of providential blessing, Rudd warned that they could also be a trap.

But material temptations were only one of the troubling side effects of growth: if Pentecostal churches were expanding because of an influx of evangelical believers who did not share their convictions about Spirit baptism, then the growth was not progress. "It would be a fatal blow to the movement if the new believers who have swollen the ranks should compromise the distinctive truths and experiences which have been at the core. Failure is never further away than one negligent generation."[27] Similarly, if new converts joined the PAOC but were not immersed in the distinctive doctrines of Pentecostalism, then the growth was actually a setback and a liability.

Rudd ended his volume on a sobering note: "There is no easy route. The price of revival is still repentance, consecration, prayer, fasting, hard work, and faith in God. Our leadership is calling for renewal. Pastors and people must respond with one accord – that unity of faith and mission was present for the first church on the Day of Pentecost *when the Spirit came upon them*."[28] Rudd hoped that his readers would "pay the price," return to their roots, and experience a new visitation of the Spirit. Rudd, like Miller before him, used history as a tool to call believers back to the fundamentals.

A third way of using history is to make it a tool for shaping corporate strategizing about the future. In 2018, the PAOC published *Picture This!* a book that was designed to guide readers to consider the values, vision, faith, and tenacity of the pioneers. This anniversary book did not share the tone of unbridled celebration that was typical of the earliest PAOC histories, nor did it overtly exhort its readers to recapture the fervour of their forefathers. The PAOC could no longer claim that theirs was a story of uninterrupted progress and growth because their own statistics revealed that between 1991 and 2017, the total number of PAOC congregations had declined (see table 1.3). Given that statistical backdrop and the twenty-first century reality that church attendance among Canadians generally was declining, the PAOC looked to history to find a way forward. As Stacey McKenzie, PAOC publications manager, explained, "Anyone can see themselves in the picture mosaic [of *Picture This!*] and be inspired to find their part in the beautiful story that is the Pentecostal Assemblies of Canada."[29] The publication was an invitation to participate in the denomination's strategic planning for the future.

The General Superintendent, David Wells, urged readers to think of the legacy they were leaving "for the sake of our children, and grandchildren and next generations of Canadians."[30] When the book appeared, the PAOC was in the midst of revisiting and refreshing its Statement of Fundamental and Essential Truths, a process that Wells insisted "has never been a token exercise in denominational self-preservation" but rather "a passionate cry for God's Word, theology, and truth to be on the front burners of our lives. Pentecostal distinctives, and how we communicate them, matter. But the highest priority is our personal and corporate mission to be like Jesus and to help others to become disciplined followers of Him as well."[31]

The goal in publishing *Picture This!* was to take inspiration from the history. The book invites readers to dream about how the earlier histories of growth and expansion might inspire and ignite another period of revival and how their own spiritual practices might contribute to that renewal. Wells made clear that the challenge "for a Fellowship of churches approaching 100 years of age is to maintain vitality ... by keeping the main thing the main thing."[32] He was clear that the main thing was a call for "leaders to be models of prayerful, worshipful intimacy with God who teach and demonstrate a naturally supernatural spirit-empowered life marked by grace and truth."[33] In effect, *Picture This!* takes the tone of a strategic planning document, with the key strategy based on committed and consecrated individuals who are renewed leading to organizational renewal and growth.

In this brief overview of denominational publications, it is clear that the PAOC has invoked history for three different purposes: to celebrate, to exhort, and to strategize. In the earliest publications by Kulbeck and Atter, there was an eagerness to retell the story of the founders, in part to acknowledge their accomplishments but mainly to draw attention to what God had done through them. The tone of those early works is triumphalist and providential as the books encouraged readers to celebrate the founders and to marvel at "what God hath wrought." As the movement matured, history became a useful way for the PAOC to call its membership back to their roots in order to avoid the decline that some sociologists of religion predicted for revival movements in their third and fourth generations. Retelling the history of the PAOC became a cautionary tale to exhort readers to remain true to their denominational distinctives and focus on the spiritual encounters of the pioneers in hopes of recreating the circumstances where revival might break out again. One hundred years later, the focus was neither chiefly about celebrating providential acts nor exhorting the followers to defy the predicted demise of the movement. Instead, the PAOC used its centenary publication to invite readers into a shared experience of dreaming about the future, using the language of a corporate strategic planning exercise.

Unlike the writers of narrative history about particular denominations, academic historians strive to interpret the past by analyzing both what happened and how it was recounted. The *International Dictionary of Pentecostal Charismatic Movements* provides a very helpful historiographic essay about the ways that historians have approached American Pentecostalism.[34] Cerillo and Wacker identify four trends, including: the providential approach that traces God's hand in history; the genetic approach that studies Pentecostal origins; the multicultural approach focusing on ethnic and racial minorities in the United States and especially Latin American and African-American Pentecostals; and finally, the functional approach that traces how and why Pentecostalism worked for its adherents even in the face of opposition. Echoes of each of these approaches can be seen in histories of Canadian Pentecostalism as well; the earliest histories of the PAOC were clearly steeped in the providential approach, as we have seen. On the question of the "genetic" approach to Pentecostalism in Canada, there is no question that, like its American cousin, Canadian Pentecostalism was closely related to nineteenth-century Methodism and its offshoots, including influences from the Holiness movement like the Salvation Army, that emphasized evangelistic outreach and public roles for women in ministry.[35]

Along with the question of religious forerunners, in Canada a second aspect of the "genetic" origins of the movement is the debate about whether Pentecostalism in this country began as an American import, an entirely separate entity, or part of a larger global story. As early as the 1960s, in the *Third Force* Atter pointed to the complicated roots of Canadian Pentecostalism when he challenged the American version of events that privileged Azusa Street as the monogenetic origin point.[36] More recent scholarship from Europe and Asia continues to reinforce the idea of polygenetic origins, and most Canadian scholarship now takes the transnational nature of Pentecostalism as a starting point.[37] In particular, Canadian scholars have turned their attention to the Hebden Mission in Toronto to establish the fact that Pentecostalism was emerging there in 1906 simultaneously with (but separate from) the American Azusa Street Revival in Los Angeles. Thomas Miller's academic work acknowledges this, as does the more recent work of Adam Stewart, who calls the Hebden Mission "a Canadian Azusa," and William Sloos, who calls the Hebdens the "First Family of Pentecost in Canada."[38] However, the scholarship around the early origins of Canadian Pentecostalism is about more than simply establishing a nationalistic claim concerning who was first to the Pentecostal experience: Los Angeles or Toronto. As Stewart explains, the Hebden Mission in Canada adds to the complex story of global Pentecostalism, which is "best understood as a dynamic and multifaceted movement with multiple points of origin, which challenges the traditional and mythical monogenetic conceptualization of Pentecostal beginnings."[39]

A third historiographic approach to the academic history of American Pentecostalism is the "multicultural" approach, which centres on marginalized groups, most often with reference to race and ethnicity. The scholarship of Estrelda Alexander is a prime example as she points to the significance of African-American Pentecostalism and how that history has been contested and overlooked, especially in the case of Black women and their contributions.[40] A second significant theme for American historiography is the emerging scholarship on Latin American Pentecostalism, with studies such as Daniel Ramirez's *Migrating Faith: Pentecostalism in the United States and Mexico in the Twentieth Century* reminding readers that overlooking the story of Latin American Pentecostalism and those transnational migratory circuits renders the history of American Pentecostalism far from complete.[41] In Canadian scholarship, there is much work to do in exploring the history of marginalized groups in Pentecostalism, including First Nations groups and a whole variety of ethnicities in various regions of the country, particularly the largest urban centres where the majority of new Canadians settle. Néstor Medina[42] and Michael Wilkinson[43] offer assessments of Canadian Pentecostalism that incorporate multicultural assumptions as they relate to immigrant Pentecostals. Ongoing growth of Pentecostalism in various regions of the world also raises questions about the nature and definition of Pentecostalism. For example, the common categories of classical Pentecostal, Charismatic, and neo-Pentecostal are challenged with the establishment of new churches such as the Redeemed Christian Church of God that originated in Nigeria. We also address some of these issues in this book with discussions of the PAOC's mission efforts with Indigenous groups and the reality that ethnic congregations of new Canadians represent a significant proportion of Canadian Pentecostalism's growth and its transformation, particularly in the last decades of the twentieth century.

Fourth, there is the "functional" approach whereby scholarship explores how Pentecostalism has functioned for its adherents, why they are attracted to the movement, and what meaning they find through their involvement. This approach incorporates a great deal of scholarship from those who propose a deprivation thesis that argues Pentecostalism is particularly attractive to the most disadvantaged and marginalized in society. Adam Stewart challenges that notion for Canadian Pentecostalism on both empirical and theoretical grounds, arguing that it is both inaccurate and too deterministic to provide a satisfying answer to the question of why people join.[44] For one thing, Stewart points out that the assumption that Pentecostalism only attracts the least fortunate is simply not true. In the Canadian case, one need only look to the prosperous Argue family of Winnipeg to see that successful business people and their families have always been part of Pentecostalism from the earliest years. Our book reinforces this fact, especially as we consider the business acumen of the early Canadian leaders and the prosperity so typical of PAOC churches in the postwar years.

Grant Wacker's influential book, *Heaven Below: Early Pentecostals and American Culture*, explains, "the genius of the Pentecostal movement lay in its ability to hold two seemingly incompatible impulses in productive tension," impulses he identifies as "the primitive and the pragmatic."[45] While defining themselves as a movement that set out to restore Christian faith and practice modelled on the New Testament church at Pentecost, Pentecostals have never hesitated to embrace modern technologies to spread the gospel and have an uncanny ability to embrace aspects of American culture because of their conviction that God orchestrates everyday life and takes good pleasure in granting prosperity to those who follow. In short, Wacker asserts that for Pentecostals, "the otherworldly legitimates the thisworldly,"[46] and he points to the "creative tension" that Pentecostals maintain between the primitive and the pragmatic.[47] He marvels at how Pentecostals have an uncanny ability to live with a focus on "the life beyond in all its fullness, and the life at hand in all its richness."[48] We find Wacker's functional approach intriguing, although our focus is not on the lived reality of individual believers. Nor do we focus on the tension between the primitive and the pragmatic, the Spirit and organization, which can be interpreted as a dilemma for religion as it is organized. In this book, we focus instead on what we observe: how consistently Pentecostals draw upon both the Spirit and the organization for understanding how they experience the Spirit, develop an organizational identity, and establish subcultural boundaries while consciously and unconsciously negotiating their place in the changing context of Canadian society. We maintain that the PAOC's focus has always been on this world and the one to come.

SECULARIZATION, MODERNIZATION, AND RELIGIOUS MARKETS

Pentecostals in Canada are rooted in a particular historical context that revolves around the modernization and globalization of Canadian society over the past 100 years. Research among sociologists of religion has focused on a range of questions about the impact of modernization on religion, responses by religions to social change, the secularization of modern societies, and globalization. While recent debates among sociologists have questioned the assumptions of secularization, most notably from those working from a religious market model or rational choice theory, these theoretical debates still dominate the discipline. Not surprisingly, the sociology of Pentecostalism largely follows the theoretical developments in the sociology of religion, with important differences between European and American sociologists. While European sociologists of religion are more prone to interpret religion from a secularization perspective, American sociologists write about competitive free religious markets in the United States where the demand for religion is constant although the providers change. In this section, we review the key literature in sociology and show how the concerns of secularization and rational choice theory are used to interpret Pentecostalism.[49]

Secularization has a long history in the sociology of religion, and over time it has taken a number of forms. Key thinkers include Max Weber, Bryan Wilson, Peter Berger, David Martin, Karl Dobbelaere, and Steve Bruce. It is not possible to discuss all the theories and the criticisms, but what follows are the central arguments and how the logic of secularization shapes Pentecostal studies.

The key idea in the work of Max Weber is rationalization, a process which he believed was central to the modernization of European societies. Rationalization is characterized by a means–end orientation to social action and the development of modern social institutions. In *The Protestant Ethic and the Spirit of Capitalism*, Weber explored the process of rationalization on religion and economics, noting how Calvinism shaped the capitalist system around a range of views about God, vocation, and work.[50] However, as the economic sphere was further separated from the domain of religion and routinized, capitalism took on its own spirit of rationality, technique, and science that excluded religious justification. For Weber, the transformation of religion and the economic would lead to a disenchantment, a sense of loss in the modern world. To survive the modern world, some people practised magic as a form of religion or developed new religious movements that were sectarian in nature.[51] Those who gained special powers from these new religions were granted authority by followers, which Weber defined as charisma, a type of religious authority that characterized an individual with exceptional powers. As new religious movements emerged with charismatic leaders, they too in the modern world would go through a process of routinization whereby the authority of the charismatic leader is transferred to the authority of the institution.[52] The general assumptions of routinization, secularization, and modernization have shaped some important research on Pentecostalism, with the most sustained work by Margaret Poloma and David Martin.

The various problems of institutionalization were examined by sociologists, most notably Thomas O'Dea, who outlined a series of dilemmas for religions in the process of organizing.[53] The dilemmas included mixed motivation, how to keep the religious symbols alive, the tension of moving to an elaborate bureaucratic structure, how to translate the ethos of the movement into ethical principles, and the role of leadership. The key work in Pentecostal studies to utilize an institutional dilemma approach was Margaret Poloma and her work on the Assemblies of God and the Toronto Blessing. In her book *The Assemblies of God at the Crossroads*, Poloma examined the impact of institutionalization on Pentecostalism as it organized.[54] Poloma argued that the success and growth of the Assemblies of God was related to charisma along with glossolalia, healing, and prophesy. The success and further growth of the Assemblies of God also meant a move toward institutionalizing, which shifted the focus away from the charismatic and toward establishing a stable, bureaucratic, and hierarchical organization. This move, however, also brought into tension the organizational with the charismatic that contributed to a series of tensions and inconsistencies between beliefs and practices, adoption of conservative politics, ambivalence toward women in ministry, and a de-emphasis on spiritual gifts and experiences. Poloma was pessimistic about this process and saw the Assemblies of God at a crossroads. Her pessimism, however, was not found solely in the institutionalization of religion, but it is difficult to read her work without reading some sense of disenchantment with the routinization of religion in the modern world. Poloma then turned her focus to the Toronto Blessing in the 1990s to examine how Pentecostalism itself could be renewed, arguing that the events in Toronto were signs of the return of mysticism and charisma. In *Main Street Mystics*, Poloma saw the activities of the Toronto church as points in which the Spirit renewed institutionalized religion and offered hope for the dilemmas of modernity.[55]

David Martin is well known for his theoretical work on secularization and his book, *A General Theory of Secularization*, based on his Cadbury Lectures at the University of Birmingham, UK.[56] Martin worked out his theory empirically, with attention given to Pentecostalism in two important books, *Tongues of Fire: The Explosion of Protestantism in Latin America* and *Pentecostalism: The World Their Parish*.[57] Martin observed Pentecostalism as an example of how religion is transformed in the modern world and how religion adapts and innovates. He questioned the general assumption that secularization means inevitable decline for all religions and developed a series of historical case studies to examine the impact of rationalization, privatization, differentiation, pluralism, religious monopoly, and religious volunteerism on Pentecostalism. His argument is that Pentecostalism facilitates the transition from pre-modern to post-industrial societies in a similar way that Methodism did during the Industrial Revolution in England. Pentecostalism contained a set of ideas that contributed to a Pentecostal ethic that allowed them to engage the world with pragmatic flexibility. To be clear, Martin does not refute secularization or routinization as a social process but offers an assessment for religions like Pentecostalism that observes how followers are enabled to become modern, and quite successful too, in the modern world.

In *Canadian Pentecostalism: Transition and Transformation*, Michael Wilkinson organized the book to reflect a range of issues raised about the institutionalization of religion.[58] Wilkinson and the various contributors write about the charismatic impulse that characterized the emerging Pentecostal movement. There is also an assumption that as Pentecostalism is organized, something is lost. This is discussed at length, especially in the chapters by David Reed[59] on the Anglican charismatic renewal and by Donald Swenson on the Roman Catholic renewal[60] where charisma serves to reinvigorate a church that has become routinized. However, the volume does depart from the modernization and secularization debate with a focus on globalization, especially as it relates to cultural diversity. Although not the main feature of the volume, Peter Beyer shows how globalization can raise the kinds of questions about Canadian Pentecostals different from those generated around the secularization and modernization debates.[61]

While the work of Poloma, Martin, and Wilkinson reflected the assumptions of routinization, secularization, and modernization, a growing number of sociologists were critiquing secularization.

Borrowing from exchange theory, economic and game theory models, and rational choice theory, sociologists Rodney Stark and Roger Finke applied the insights from these theories to understand religion. In *The Churching of America* and *Acts of Faith*, Finke and Stark articulated the assumptions of a religious market model.[62] The argument included a modified view of secularization that stated that secularization is not the end of religion but only the end of specific providers. The demand for religion will always be high, but during periods of social change, some providers are not able to meet the demand, and they become the losers whereas the winners are those that grow. Some scholars, like Peter Berger, attempted to refine secularization theory, arguing that the process is not inevitable or linear and that some religions like Pentecostalism illustrate a process of desecularization or resacralization to account for what appears to be religious resurgence around the world.[63] Stark and Finke, however, questioned the modified view of secularization they initially proposed and in *Acts of Faith* argued that the theory of secularization no longer made sense and was not empirically supported. Steve Bruce, however, maintained that secularization was a valid theory and questioned the arguments of the religious market model, especially its assumptions about religious demand and innovation.[64]

Religious market models have shaped the analyses of Pentecostalism among some sociologists. Arguing that the demand for religion is always high but the providers change, Pentecostalism is presented as a new religious provider that simply outworked its competition as it grew to become the latest winner in the religious market. Donald Miller and Tetsunao Yamamori, for example, argued that worldwide Pentecostalism represented a type of religion that was characterized as progressive Pentecostalism: a holistic faith meeting not only the spiritual needs of its participants but also the physical, social, and economic needs of entire neighbourhoods.[65] Miller and Yamamori not only provided an in-depth picture of progressive Pentecostalism, with empirical work from hundreds of ministries and congregations around the world, they also argued that Pentecostalism is proof that secularization is a myth. Worldwide, religion is not in decline but growing, and those groups that are growing are replacing those that have failed to meet the demand. Progressive Pentecostalism, stated the authors, represents a contemporary example of how a new religion that opted for the poor has come to replace earlier versions found in the Social Gospel movement and Liberation Theology. As the authors stated: "In our view, the emergence of Progressive Pentecostals is simply one more nail in the coffin of secularization theory."[66]

A CULTURAL ANALYSIS

A cultural analysis of Pentecostalism is partly related to our shared dissatisfaction with the theories and assumptions of secularization and religious market models, but not solely. Adopting a cultural analysis offers us a way to consider the social processes that led to the organization of the PAOC, the development of its subculture, and the boundaries it constructed as it interacted with broader social and cultural patterns in Canada. Cultural analyses of religion, argues Penny Edgell, have a long history among scholars, and the questions from her work shape the theoretical assumptions for our study on the PAOC.[67] Edgell argues that cultural analyses in the study of religion are as old as Émile Durkheim's observation about the nature of the sacred and the shared symbols of groups and societies that serve to hold them together as a moral order. Scholars like Mary Douglas, Peter Berger, Pierre Bourdieu, and Robert Wuthnow have made significant contributions to our understanding of religion that address questions about its relation to culture, including the role of religion and civil society, religion and identity, religious subcultures and social engagement, the voluntarist nature of religion, and religious authority.[68] We build on the foundations laid by that scholarship and the specific observations Edgell makes from that literature with her new questions for further research.

Edgell summarizes the literature for the study of religion and culture around three areas, which include: studies of religion as a) an institutional field, b) lived religion, and c) symbolic boundaries and cultural tools. Religion as an institutional field focuses on how religion is organized and includes attention given to the role of religious elites, organizational forms, structures, tasks, how broader cultural practices like business models are embedded in religious organizations, the discourse that is used for analyzing official doctrine especially when it is contested, and the relationship of the religious organization to other institutions – namely, the scientific, political, economic, educational, family, and health care. Attention is given to local congregations and the role various religious leaders play in the engagement of core tasks like worship, religious education, and outreach programs that require some kind of mobilization.[69] Scholars who have taken an institutional approach have focused on religion as a form of social capital and the importance of the religious field for generating civic engagement. Some research focuses on questions about the role of religion for immigrant congregations and ethnic identity. The value of a cultural analysis for understanding the institutional aspects of religion, according to Edgell, is the ability to assess religious and social change without appealing to secularization as a master narrative.[70] Our book is in step with that trend.

The second area for cultural analyses of religion is lived religion, which gives attention to the everyday practices and experiences across social life for religious persons. Scholars taking a lived religion approach focus less on official doctrine and beliefs, often the primary focus of secularization and market models, and explore the embodied and emotional practices of religious people that attempt to sacralise the everyday and give meaning for participants.[71] Some research on lived religion examines the intersection of the everyday experiences of religion with other institutions, while other research examines conversion as an everyday process that is embodied and embedded within social life. Conversion is an important aspect of a cultural analysis and raises questions about conversion narratives, stories, or testimonies that illustrate how religion, and in this case Pentecostalism, is embedded in the everyday life of Pentecostals. We incorporate some of that focus as we note how the PAOC leaders were situated in their particular contexts.

A third area, according to Edgell, are those studies that examine the symbolic boundaries and cultural tools that serve to justify or legitimate boundaries, especially those that define what it means to be inside or outside the religion. This is where our work on the PAOC is most closely aligned with Edgell's observations. Cultural tools may include religious ideas, symbols, and metaphors that act as boundary markers. Boundaries create both a sense of belonging as well as dissonance. They define what it means, in this case to be Pentecostal, around notions of orthodoxy (beliefs), orthopraxy (practices), and orthopathy (sentiments). Boundaries also define the relationship of Pentecostalism to other Christians, whether they be evangelicals, mainline Protestants, or Roman Catholics. Boundaries also define the relationship between Pentecostals and other social institutions like the family and politics, illustrating the fluidity of these relationships where there may be agreement or conflict over time. Boundaries raise questions about religious authority and the authority of religion in other social institutions, which can have the effect of challenging institutional authority in other spheres of society. Boundaries can be defined around language, ethnicity, and indigeneity and raise questions about inclusion and exclusion. Boundaries can reinforce religious identities and the broader understanding of the country, or boundaries may challenge questions about changes in society like the role of the family, sexuality, and multiculturalism. According to Edgell, focusing on symbolic boundaries and cultural tools allows researchers to see "religion as a source of cultural power" and, second, how religious identity "can intersect with other identities" that are contextual.[72] This attention to context is central to our work on the PAOC.

Edgell outlines the main assumptions of a cultural analysis of religion as follows: (a) the importance of identifying the institutional fields that foster religious and spiritual expression in any given historical context; (b) a practice-oriented and contextual approach to religious identity and experience that recognizes their social embeddedness; and (c) a focus on how religious repertoires shape social relations of power and inequality through the provision of discourses and symbols, which may be employed strategically, and cultural models and metaphors, which shape automatic forms of cognition.[73] Edgell then proposes a research agenda that revolves around two key questions: "What organized fields of activity foster religious and spiritual expression in any given social context?" and "what kinds of coherence do religious fields, religious leaders, and religious culture provide for the larger society?"[74] We contend that for the PAOC, negotiating its place in relation to Canadian society has been of central concern ever since the early days of Pentecostal revival.

A cultural analysis, as proposed by Edgell, shifts our attention away from secularization and the problems of institutionalizing charisma. It also shifts our attention away from the competitive qualities of Pentecostalism that lead it to outperform other religious organizations to a series of questions about Pentecostalism as a subculture that is situated in a broader Canadian social context. A cultural analysis allows us to focus on the religious and spiritual expression of Pentecostalism, how it becomes organized with a set of practices that are oriented to the sacred but also to the everyday. A cultural analysis also points our attention to the institutional embeddedness of organizations like the PAOC and how leadership, organizational polity, finances, departments, and doctrinal statements are part of a cultural repertoire that connects the Spirit with the organization while shaping social boundaries for Pentecostals. A Pentecostal cultural repertoire is defined by a specific discourse around who they are, the world they live in, and the Spirit that directs and animates their personal lives, congregations, and national denomination. A cultural analysis also heightens our attention to the contested nature of the authority of religious organizations as they attempt to offer cultural coherence to followers in Canadian society. Coherence, however, is not reducible to a set of beliefs, or for Pentecostals in the PAOC, the Statement of Fundamental and Essential Truths. Rather, coherence focuses on the socially and historically situated processes among the PAOC that served to create and sustain a form of religious authority. Related to religious authority is identity, which is always fluid and varies over time as Pentecostals negotiate who they are and what they do in relation to the broader society. For Pentecostals, those processes of establishing authority, reinforcing identity, and negotiating their place in Canadian society have been continuous. We adopt a cultural analysis to examine how, after the revival and for more than a century now, Pentecostals engaged in the making of the PAOC, a Canadian church.

2

The Culture of Pentecostalism

INTRODUCTION

The stories of those individuals who were among the first in twentieth-century Canada to experience the baptism of the Holy Spirit offer a glimpse into the culture of Pentecostalism. All of those Pentecostal encounters happened within five years, from Ellen Hebden's experience of speaking in tongues in Toronto in November 1906 to Mrs Baker's healing in Ottawa in 1911. These stories, while they include some of the most well-known characters of early Canadian Pentecostalism, represent only a small sample of the hundreds who shared similar experiences in this period. The 1911 census of Canada records that 515 people declared themselves to be Pentecostal, and a century later, in 2011, that number was approaching half a million people. This chapter explains how the culture of Canadian Pentecostalism evolved from a set of stories about seemingly random, individual spiritual experiences to an organized group with international ties and the status of a recognized religious entity with a charter from the Canadian government. The early years of the movement were quite chaotic, and even after organizational structures were introduced, conflicts continued to surface between those who favoured organization and those who longed for the fluidity of the early movement. Those disagreements among early Pentecostals in Canada centred on questions of authority, and the solutions they eventually found illustrate how the PAOC engaged in boundary-making as part of its cultural repertoire.

THE PENTECOSTAL CENTURY

In 1904, just two years before the first Pentecostals emerged in Canada, Wilfrid Laurier boldly declared that "the twentieth century belongs to Canada."[1] The prime minister had every reason to express confidence in the young country. The dream of building a transcontinental railway had been realized in 1885 when the last spike was driven. Under Laurier's watch, two new provinces (Saskatchewan and Alberta) would be created in 1905. An aggressive campaign to attract immigrants to the west was in full swing, and as eastern Europeans and Americans poured in to take up the offer of free land, First Nations peoples were marginalized and removed to reserve lands provided under the numbered treaties. Politicians and white settlers perceived the land as empty and free for the taking,[2] and as problematic as that view is in hindsight, it gave way to an optimistic frontier spirit that settlers shared as they spread across the country. The population of Canada increased by 43 per cent in the ten years from 1901 to 1911 to just over 7.2 million people. Canadian industries were thriving, and the young dominion seemed poised to prosper. Indeed, historians have described the period from 1900 to 1913 as "the great boom" because while the Canadian economy produced manufactures totalling $550 million in 1900, by 1913 that number had almost tripled to $1,410 million.[3] Of the immigrants arriving in this period, "while many of the newcomers settled on farms, fully 70% joined the labour force in industry and transportation."[4] These industrial labourers lived in the rapidly expanding cities, of which Winnipeg is a prime example. Winnipeg's population grew very rapidly because of the railway, from 7,900 in 1881 to more than 179,000 in 1921.[5]

That population explosion had a variety of consequences. Rapid urbanization without time or thought for careful planning meant that the conditions in working-class neighbourhoods were deplorable during this period, and reform efforts among social gospellers like J.S. Woodsworth were undertaken because they were convinced that "the old methods of Christian charity work and a focus on individual salvation needed to be replaced with a collective approach that emphasized building the kingdom of God through new forms of social reform based on more scientific principles."[6] The slum-like conditions that existed in overcrowded and underserviced neighbourhoods drew the attention of middle-class Christian social reform efforts, but the emphasis on a collective salvation, or social gospel, was alarming to more conservative believers, who saw the turn from individual salvation as a turn away from orthodoxy.[7] The growing attention toward social reform gave revivalists like the Pentecostals additional motivation to double down on their message of personal salvation and the need for individual conversions. While social reformers hoped to get to the systemic and societal roots of poverty and alcohol abuse, revivalists with Holiness roots (including Pentecostals) remained convinced that the problem lay in individual hearts in need of spiritual transformation through new birth.[8]

Key figures in early Canadian Pentecostalism were participating in that boom. In the Winnipeg real estate boom, A.H. Argue and his family were poised to make sizable profits during the period. James and Margaret McAlister were raising a large family of thirteen children in the Ottawa Valley, and the economic opportunities drew several of their children to migrate west. John and Alice (Ritchie) McAlister lived in Winnipeg and were active in the Winnipeg Assembly with the Argues. John McAlister left Winnipeg in 1911 to move further west to Camrose and then Edmonton, Alberta. R.E. McAlister and his first wife, Eliza Jane ("Lizzy"), also spent time in Winnipeg after visiting Azusa Street. According to Walter McAlister, John's son, both his father and his uncle R.E. were employed at the Western Saddle Company in Winnipeg, a wholesale equipment supplier that was rapidly expanding because of the economic boom and expanding population in western Canada. The Winnipeg business is quite likely where the McAlisters gained important business skills, rendering the myth of them being dirt farmers from Renfrew County a little bit misleading. It is not clear exactly how long R.E. and Lizzy lived in Winnipeg, but Walter McAlister (born 1897) had fond memories of the music lessons his Aunt Lizzy gave him in Winnipeg when he was approximately ten years old. They made visits to Ontario, including in June 1908 when they returned home for James McAlister's funeral (R.E.'s father) and perhaps again in February 1909 for his mother Margaret's funeral. In the summer of 1908, R.E. took the opportunity to hold tent meetings in the Ottawa Valley and began to organize Pentecostal congregations associated with his name at Kinburn and Ottawa. It seems that the couple divided their time between Ontario and Winnipeg because when Lizzy died in May 1910, she was buried in the Elmwood cemetery in Winnipeg.

This rapid development in the west promised seemingly unlimited opportunity to build wealth for those with business interests in the area. Among Canadian Pentecostals, the most well-known name was the Argue family from Winnipeg. Prior to his personal Pentecost, A.H. Argue was in real estate. While the extent of his personal and family wealth is not known, the timing of his arrival in western Canada's fastest growing city meant that it was highly likely the Argues had done very well in the Winnipeg real estate market before he left the family business to travel full-time with his children as an evangelistic team.

The frontier spirit meant that religious seekers were open to new expressions of Christianity and not only in the western region of the country. News from other parts of the world meant that Canadian horizons were broadening in the realm of ideas and movements too. The Welsh Revival of 1904–05 is one example of revivalist activity that caught the attention of Canadians, perhaps because of family ties to Britain. Ready to make a fresh start in Canada, many new arrivals both from Europe and from the US were open to new expressions of religion and hungry for a sense of community. John McAlister followed the boom and moved from Winnipeg to Edmonton in 1911 to work for the Edmonton office of the Western Saddle Company. While he was there, he began to hold Pentecostal meetings in northern Alberta among Swedish farmers who eventually established permanent Pentecostal congregations.[9]

CONTROVERSY

David Reed astutely observes that "New movements are characteristically born in the crucible of controversy. The modern Pentecostal movement is no exception."[10] In the early years of the Pentecostal movement, the resolution of a range of issues proved to be painful because of the divisions they caused among co-workers and family members. Pentecostals in Canada were mostly from the Methodist-Holiness tradition, but many came from a variety of Protestant backgrounds, and coming to an agreement on many questions about the nature of Pentecostalism, the role of experience, doctrinal statements, and organizational relationships was no small task.

The first hurdle that Pentecostals faced was sorting out the question of whether or not these supernatural manifestations of the Spirit were biblical, a challenge they faced not only within their traditions, like the Methodist-Holiness groups that had debated the question of Spirit baptism for some time, but also from other traditions. For the many Canadian Protestants at the beginning of the twentieth century, the idea that manifestations of the Spirit, such as speaking in tongues, were biblical was unsettling and most likely unorthodox. A prominent view was that while the early church had experienced extraordinary demonstrations of the Spirit, including glossolalia and instantaneous healings, that was for a particular purpose to establish the church. Once the church was established, such charismatic demonstrations were not needed. The experiences of the first Christians were not to be replicated centuries later because the operation of those extraordinary gifts had ceased. Most respectable Christians agreed that one should not expect or encourage paranormal spiritual manifestations. Baptists were particularly strong on this position, but they were not alone. Among those from the Holiness tradition, including Methodists, there were rumours of such things still occurring, but the more gentrified believers were no longer open to courting such experiences. Not the least of the objections was the impression that giving way to such ecstatic experiences would lead to uncontrolled outbursts and unorthodox bodily demonstrations were deemed dangerous and best avoided. Ironically, some of the earliest Canadian Pentecostals originally came from those churches that opposed the use of spiritual gifts in worship settings and, particularly, the view of glossolalia as evidence of Spirit baptism that empowered Christians for missionary work.[11]

To reduce Pentecostalism to "speaking in tongues" is problematic and contributes to a caricature of the movement. Pentecostals, like the Methodist-Holiness family they primarily came from, were nineteenth-century evangelicals who believed that evangelism and missionary work were very important. Theologically, Pentecostals did not differ on key points that evangelical Protestants maintained about God, the Trinity, the Bible, salvation, sanctification, and evangelism. However, what many evangelical Protestants were concerned with at the end of the nineteenth century was the worldwide missionary enterprise along with the growing sense that Jesus was coming soon. This urgency to preach the good news of Jesus to the whole world required a supernatural means to address the global linguistic and geographical challenges of communication and travel. Speaking in tongues was believed to be one means by which Christians could miraculously preach in an unknown language without having to spend months learning a second language. This gift, which was believed to be biblical according to interpretations of passages in Acts 1 and 2, was referred to as the baptism in the Holy Spirit and would empower Christians or give them the ability to complete the missionary task.

The early Pentecostals often engaged in preaching that was two-fold, addressing the need for conversion but also calling Christians to recommit to the missionary task while seeking a fresh in-filling of the Holy Spirit to live an empowered Christian life. Pentecostals saw no need for a doctrinal statement or creed, and for the PAOC, none was officially adopted until 1926 (see Appendix).[12] Rather, Pentecostals operated with a theological and cultural framework known as the "full gospel" that shaped their activities. The full gospel hermeneutic was Christo-centric and focused on the following points: (1) salvation, (2) sanctification, (3) baptism of the Holy Spirit, (4) divine healing, and (5) the soon-coming kingdom of God.[13] Preaching by many early Pentecostals often focused on Jesus as saviour, sanctifier, baptizer, healer, and soon-coming King. The baptism in the Holy Spirit with the biblical sign of tongues was one aspect of a Pentecostal theology that addressed the urgent need for worldwide evangelism.

The ways in which individual leaders experienced their "personal Pentecost" varied. Some received the experience in spite of their own objections, as was the case with Ellen Hebden, who was not seeking the experience of speaking in tongues. On the contrary, Hebden objected to the idea and protested against the suggestion while she was praying. In prayer, Hebden heard the voice of God suggesting to her that she would find strength and be equipped for ministry in new ways through the experience of speaking in tongues. She recounted that "a very quiet yet distinct voice said, 'Tongues.' I said, 'No Lord, not Tongues.' Then followed a moment of deathlike stillness, when the voice again uttered the word 'Tongues.' This time I felt afraid of grieving the Lord and I said, 'Tongues or anything else that will please Thee and bring glory to Thy name.' One unknown word was repeated several times and I thought that must be Tongues."[14] The timing of Hebden's experience in the fall of 1906 makes her the earliest Canadian to speak in tongues, and although her experience was later reported in the publication from Azusa Street, she had not had contact with the Los Angeles group prior to her own ecstatic experience.

News about the unusual experiences occurring at the Hebden mission aroused concern among nearby churches, who were convinced that the Pentecostal experience was outside the boundaries of orthodoxy and orthopraxy. One neighbouring clergyman who expressed concern was George A. Chambers, a pastor of a nearby Mennonite Brethren in Christ congregation on Parliament Street in Toronto. According to historian Douglas Rudd, Chambers was eager to see revival come to Toronto and especially in his congregation. Rudd recounts that while Chambers and his wife were convinced that what was happening with the Hebden mission was "just too much to accept," Chambers had exclaimed in prayer, "O Lord, we want revival but not that fanatical stuff."[15] In 1908 at a meeting in Kitchener, Chambers was finally convinced that what he had called "fanaticism" was actually a genuine move of God, and he experienced it for himself. Chambers then took the step of going to Ellen Hebden to apologize for his previous accusations of "fanaticism."

Unlike the reluctant Hebden and Chambers, others spent considerable time and resources to travel and tarry in locations where the movement was underway. A.H. Argue's time in Chicago is a prime example, as is R.E. McAlister's trip to Azusa Street in Los Angeles. Evidently, both were eager seekers of this new phenomenon, which they saw as continuous with their Methodist and Holiness beliefs and practices.

R.E. McAlister, known as the "father of Canadian Pentecostalism," was born in 1880 to a Presbyterian farming family in the Ottawa Valley. McAlister had a conversion experience in the Holiness Movement church in Cobden, Ontario, under the ministry of Ralph C. Horner, described as "a fiery Methodist evangelist," who was expelled from the Methodist denomination in 1895. Shortly after his conversion, McAlister briefly attended Bible school in Cincinnati, Ohio, but returned home during his second year because of poor health. He married his wife Eliza Jane (Lizzy) in 1904, and when he heard about the miracles occurring in Los Angeles at Azusa Street, he went there in December 1906 and received the baptism of the Holy Spirit. It is not clear if Lizzy went with him to Azusa Street, but she was certainly with him during other travels to the west.

From these stories of early Pentecostal believers, one can see that some, like Hebden and Chambers, resisted the Pentecostal message out of concern for the fanatical tendencies that it represented. Others, including Argue and McAlister, spared no expense to seek out the experience. Some resisters had to overcome their previous convictions that the manifestations of the Spirit were only for the apostolic age and not for the present. Others were sorting out the relationship between the baptism of the Holy Spirit and sanctification and whether it was a second work of grace or what Pentecostals in some sectors referred to as a third work of grace, with speaking in tongues as a sign. The main view among Pentecostals was that Spirit baptism empowered Christians to fulfill the great commandment of world evangelism.[16]

When reports of Spirit baptism, especially speaking in tongues, began to circulate, persecution inevitably arose from those who could not accept these new expressions of spirituality. R.E. McAlister's Pentecostal magazine, *The Good Report*, defended the miraculous developments that were happening, asserting that "the day of healing and miracles is not past and were not confined to the Apostles, as some people suppose."[17] Yet readers were reminded that they would likely face persecution about their experiences and beliefs, especially from church people, because "with most people, the signs and gifts are attributed to the devil."[18] In another article entitled, "Called to Suffer for Jesus," McAlister wrote that "the Word of God abounds with examples of great sacrifice and suffering in the path of obedience. Take for example, Joseph who was sold through jealous hatred, misrepresented, falsely accused, cast into a dungeon to suffer for twelve years. True, he had enjoyment in the end, but his enjoyment was born through great suffering."[19] As in the biblical example of Joseph, sometimes Pentecostal believers discovered that their worst tormentors were "brothers." McAlister did not mince words when he told his readers that they could expect "opposers of the truth" to make false accusations "by seeking to lead the Christian public to believe that … [we] are latter day heretics."[20]

Persecution from outsiders was one thing, but Pentecostals also faced disagreements among themselves. Two key doctrinal disagreements arose: the so-called "finished work" controversy and the nature of the Trinity. Questions about the "finished work" centred on whether salvation and sanctification were separate stages in the life of a believer or whether both were accomplished simultaneously at conversion. Believers who came from a Wesleyan-Holiness background subscribed to the first view, that sanctification was a later stage of Christian development, and because God could not fill an "unclean vessel," then baptism in the Holy Spirit was a third stage in the life of a believer, only possible after sanctification had been attained. Durham and others from reformed theological traditions denounced that view and insisted that it was not possible for "a man to be born again and yet left with a heart still unclean and full of enmity with God."[21] The logic was that if God had changed the very nature of the convert, there was no need for a "second work of grace," and converts could readily expect that after conversion, they were ready to receive baptism in the Spirit with speaking in tongues. Durham observed that this was in fact happening in his mission, where receiving the Spirit and speaking in tongues was common, not just for those who were further along in the faith but also for the recently converted; in some cases, it all happened on the very same day.[22]

This controversy was not mere semantics because it went to the very heart of the Wesleyan-Holiness tradition. In the words of David Reed, for those who held to Wesleyan-Holiness doctrines about a second work of grace, Durham's new message was "a frontal attack."[23] For Pentecostals coming from that background, the idea challenged part of their core belief system and was no small thing. R.E. McAlister recognized that many Pentecostals had these Wesleyan roots, and in 1912 he published an article written by his friend Frank Ewart, arguing for the finished work position, saying, "Why centralize this discussion on whether John Wesley did or did not teach dogmatically that sanctification was a definite, second work of grace?" Ewart argued that Charles H. Spurgeon and George Whitfield "are surely worthy of as much credence as John Wesley" and "their teachings abundantly prove that they stood firm for the truths taught by those who advocate the 'Finished Work of Calvary.'"[24] With this logic, McAlister's *Good Report* publication was tying the Pentecostal movement to a broader history of Christian revivalism and insisting that those committed to particular traditions (in this case Wesleyans) must be careful to follow God rather than commit to human systems of belief. "When God performs a great work contrary to the opinions of men they will immediately endeavor to defend their tottering standards. Brethren, the truth is indestructible ... By defending heresies we imperil the truth and oppose GOD."[25]

Calling the Wesleyan-Holiness belief about sanctification "a heresy" was strong language indeed, but the fact that McAlister published this piece without nuancing that language is typical of his clear communication. He has been described as a "persuasive debater and inspiring expositor" who was able to "frame resolutions in such clear-cut language as to end all debate."[26] When McAlister held a personal conviction, he communicated it clearly and without apology. In a short statement entitled "Error Persecutes Truth" published in the same 1912 issue of *The Good Report*, McAlister claimed that "error requires to be bolstered by human arguments," and he explained his own change of heart on the matter, saying, "This was one of the strong points that made me consider the glorious truth of 'The Finished Work of Calvary,' and caused me to search the Word of God. I was standing for the second work of grace but became ashamed of the childish inconsistencies and persecutions inflicted on those who were standing for the one work, whom I had every reason to believe were true children of God, although at that time I considered them mistaken in their belief, but later was convinced that they were right even against my will."[27]

Although this controversy over the finished work arose before any formal organization in Canada was achieved, debates about it dominated the early years of Pentecostalism across North America. By the time the PAOC charter was developed, it was clear that the consensus of the majority was to side with the "finished work" idea, making baptism in the spirit a second, not a third, phase in the life of a believer. That two-stage view was adopted by the PAOC in 1919, and as Miller points out, "this doctrine has remained virtually unchanged in all subsequent editions of the PAOC Statement of Fundamental and Essential Truths." On this point, the Holiness camp conceded, persuaded by R.E. McAlister and their own experiences and observations of what was happening in the movement.

Another controversy circulating before (and continuing after) the PAOC's official beginning is variously known as "the New Issue," "Jesus Only," or "One Name." This view caused considerable debate and resulted in formal splits among Pentecostals, not just in Canada but worldwide. This controversy centred around the question of the Trinity and water baptism. Those who identify as "Oneness Pentecostals" perform baptisms in the name of Jesus only, not in the name of the Father, the Son, and the Holy Ghost. The issue caused considerable debate beginning in 1913 at the worldwide Pentecostal Camp Meeting near Los Angeles with thousands of Pentecostals in attendance. On that occasion, R.E. McAlister preached on baptism, pointing to the book of Acts in which believers were baptized in the name of the Lord Jesus Christ, not the trinitarian formula from the gospels. As the camp meeting went on, some became convinced that this represented a new revelation from God.[28] Debate over the issue continued to deepen, and when the Assemblies of God (AG) organized in 1914, the matter was a question of considerable debate. In the early days of Pentecostal organization, doctrinal formulations were in flux, and because of the division this was causing, the American group concluded that a definite position should be taken. In creating their statement of beliefs, the AG arrived in 1916 at a position that "became unacceptable to those who had embraced the One Name doctrine."[29] Those who could not accept the AG position joined another group called the Pentecostal Assemblies of the World with headquarters in Indianapolis.

Canadian Pentecostals had not yet codified their beliefs when the AG was working out its official doctrinal statement, but Canadians were watching with interest because the same divisions were present among them. R.E. McAlister held to a Oneness view until well after the 1919 charter was signed, and he was not alone. The list of Canadian leaders who initially subscribed to the Oneness view but later changed their minds includes A.E. Adams, C.E. Baker, G.A. Chambers, W.L. Draffin, and R.E. McAlister.[30] When it became clear that the PAOC would support the traditional orthodox view of the Trinity, Frank Small, one of the original signatories of the charter, left the PAOC and gave leadership to the Apostolic Church of Pentecost (ACOP), a oneness denomination that received its Canadian charter in 1921.[31] R.E. McAlister went to print explaining his change of heart on this question in an article entitled "Confessedly, Great is the Mystery of Godliness."[32] As R.E.'s nephew Walter McAlister asserted, going public with their change of position was "a painful thing for his uncle and others to do, for they had thought that the New Issue was a divine revelation."[33]

On these changes of doctrinal position, R.E. McAlister emerged as the major voice for Canadian Pentecostals in the PAOC. It was a role he would continue to play for decades. Even before he changed his position on the Oneness issue, McAlister recognized that the divisions caused by these differences were dangerous for believers because they jeopardized unity. In a statement called "The Basis of Unity," McAlister asserted that there was "a difference between the unity of the Spirit and the unity of the Faith." By this he meant that "we can love the truth of God and uncompromisingly stand for it, and yet deal in love and patience with those who do not see eye to eye with ourselves."[34] McAlister concluded his piece with an oft-quoted assertion: "In essentials there should be unity, in non-essentials there should be liberty, and in ALL things there should be charity." The problem, of course, came in determining which issues were essentials and which were non-essentials. For many Pentecostals on both sides, the question of the Trinity was non-negotiable because it was definitely an essential. The rift over the Oneness debate continues to the present, and the divide seems very deep indeed. And while his quote about unity and charity makes McAlister sound like a very good compromiser, in fact after he had settled his own views on these matters, he was also very clear about these matters. It is no coincidence, then, that when the PAOC constructed its doctrinal statement, they called it the "Statement of Fundamental and Essential Truths." These were not matters on which to find compromise. The statement also served to define the nature of Pentecostal culture and to create symbolic boundaries around which Pentecostal authority operated.

While Pentecostals had several points of disagreement to work out among themselves, there was one thing they all agreed about: missionary work was their number one priority, and the gospel was to be preached in every possible place by every possible means. That missionary impulse was driven by the conviction that Pentecostals were living in the end times, as evidenced by the outpouring of the Spirit in fulfillment of the prophecies in Joel and Acts; the need to preach the gospel was urgent. What the early believers disagreed about was how they should manage and administer missionary affairs. Canada's first Pentecostal missionaries were Charles W. Chawner and his wife Emma, who served in Africa for more than forty years after he left from the Hebden mission in February 1908.[35] As Chawner's own testimony makes clear, his Pentecostal experience of Spirit baptism precipitated his call to missions: "The dear Lord baptized me in His Holy Spirit in the beginning of Feb., 1907, and at that time gave me a very definite call to be His witness in a far off land. From time to time as I could bear it He made plain that I should leave all and follow Him to Zululand."[36]

The Hebden mission reported that by October 1909, they had sent out seventeen missionaries to Africa, China, Japan, and India.[37] In March 1910, the Hebdens revealed details about financing these efforts: "The missionary offering last week and on Sunday was $753. The total amount of missionary money given to date is $3,104.64, all of which, except the amount just now given – yea, every cent – has gone to the missionaries in the field, as need required, and although our missionaries are many and in widely distant lands, none have ever been in distress."[38] On the next page of that same issue of *The Promise*, this information about funding was reported: "Missionary income since our last issue has been $529.99; expenditure $570.65."[39] Transparency about the use of mission funds and accountability in their financial affairs would eventually contribute to the demise of the

Hebdens, but meanwhile, the question of how to manage missionary financial and personnel matters took centre stage. Just as disputes about doctrine were contentious, so was the whole question of whether or not to organize and if to organize, what kind of structure to create. The Hebden Mission in Toronto was indisputably the hub of Canadian Pentecostal activity, especially missionary activity. And yet the Hebdens were opposed to the idea of creating any kind of organization to manage the growth that was occurring.

EARLY ATTEMPTS AT ORGANIZING

Several important gatherings of Canadian Pentecostals took place from very early on, where ties were reinforced and talk of organizing was in the air. In 1908, the first Pentecostal Workers' Convention was held in Toronto for those associated with Pentecostal missions. They gathered at a hall on Concord Avenue, and although the Hebdens did not host it, there is no doubt that they were regarded as the leaders of Pentecostal work in Toronto.[40] The following year, during the Canadian National Exhibition in late summer, Pentecostal workers once again gathered, this time at the Hebdens' East End Mission, in a series of meetings that Ellen Hebden simply called "Thirteen Days with God." As she described it, "those were holy days, when many of God's people left their homes, their business life and cares and came apart to rest a while."[41] The gathering was clearly a time of renewal for all, as Hebden recounted, "We shall never forget those blessed days. At times our hearts were rejoicing until the cup of joy was so full it ran over, at other times many wept in the Spirit before the Lord." Hebden reported with amazement that "In one meeting the Spirit fell upon me, and took such control of my hands that I played the organ under the power of the Spirit."[42] The meeting was such a success that they planned to meet again that November on the anniversary of Mrs Hebden's initial baptism in the Spirit.

However, that meeting, which the Hebdens hosted in August 1909, was not the only gathering of Canadian Pentecostals that summer. A few months earlier, in June 1909, at a rural property in Markham, Ontario,[43] Pentecostals gathered in a large tent that A.G. Ward had purchased in Owen Sound.[44] The guest speaker on that occasion was Pastor Alexander A. Boddy, a vicar in the Church of England.[45] The main outcome of that meeting was the decision to create a simple organization to administer the missionary activity of Canadian

Pentecostals. Ward had previous experience with missionary organizations both in the Methodist and Christian and Missionary Alliance churches, and he understood the wisdom of having some structures and protocols in place to manage finances, logistics, and personnel.[46] Similar organizations already existed in both the United States and Britain, and based on those models, likely at Boddy's suggestion, the name "Pentecostal Missionary Union" (PMU) was proposed.

However, what seemed like a positive step forward was quickly denounced by those who had not attended, namely James and Ellen Hebden. In the next issue of *The Promise*, following the 1909 Markham camp meeting, Mrs Hebden was pleased to publish a report noting that most of the congregations that the East End Mission had spawned were standing by her in their opposition to organization. "Just before going to press our attention has been called to the fact that of the fourteen Pentecostal Missions in Canada, there are only about two which are yet in P.M.U. We are glad to say that reports are reaching us frequently now from missions and individuals that they are 'out of it.'"[47] In the following issue, the Hebdens made their position even more clear: "We desire to state most emphatically that in the Lord's work at 651 Queen St. and 191 George St., Toronto, we have no connection whatever with any general organization of the Pentecostal people in Canada. As a 'missionary church' we stand alone in God's divine order, and extend the right hand of fellowship to every member of the body of Christ and to every church or assembly gathered in His name and to the Lord Jesus, according to scripture, and we decline absolutely all responsibility for any so-called representatives of the Pentecostal work in Canada."[48] According to Thomas Miller, when A.G. Ward saw that the creation of the PMU was causing division among the believers and because he "wished to avoid controversy among the first assemblies [he] allowed his Pentecostal Missionary Union to die."[49]

Convinced that the issue of organization was behind them, Mrs Hebden expressed unbridled optimism in early 1910 about the progress of the work. Her positive outlook sprang from the fact that they had just hosted a series of very encouraging meetings. What she called a "God Appointed Convention" had been held at the Queen Street mission in February 1910. The list of those in attendance reads like a veritable "Who's Who" of early Canadian Pentecostalism. Anticipating the visit of Brother William Durham of Chicago, meetings began as Hebden and her congregation waited for him to finish the meetings he was having in London, Ontario, where "a great wave of baptismal power had swept." While the Toronto believers waited, they were graced with a visit from another well-known Canadian Pentecostal whose meetings set the tone for what was to come. Hebden's report verily gushed with praise: "Bro. McAlister, from Winnipeg, just opened his mouth, out of which his inner being flowed rivers indeed of living water till the vessels of the household of God were filled again and again with the bread and wine of the kingdom of God. It was just the pure Word of God administered in season to many, accompanied by the Holy Ghost, and under His power, as though Jesus had said, Come unto Me and drink."[50] Hebden mused, "We loved those brethren in the Lord. How could we help it?"[51] It was a significant admission and an honest question, since these were the very same brethren with whom she disagreed so vehemently about organizing.

The next pair in the lineup of leaders was none other than Robert and Aimee Semple, who came from the Durham meetings in London, Ontario, and brought great encouragement to the meetings. "Bro. Semple was so led of the Spirit that he always spoke to edification; we loved to hear him; and Sister Semple's gift of interpretation was such a blessing in giving to us the very words in given tongues, that it made the presence of God very manifest to all."[52] Hebden gushed with news of what happened when Durham finally arrived at the meetings: "Bro. Durham can only be fully appreciated to be seen and heard … When the Spirit of God came upon him everyone could easily see it and realize it in his ministry. He often spoke in tongues and frequently interpreted what was said."[53] At other times, it was Aimee Semple who interpreted during Durham's meetings, and according to the report, many were baptized and healed. While these meetings were still underway, Robert and Aimee Semple left for China "with the prayers of God's people for their success in the Lord's work."[54]

But the euphoria of the 1910 meetings would not last. Tragedy and trouble struck several of the leaders who had graced the platform. R.E. McAlister, who had spoken so powerfully at the meeting, buried his wife, Eliza Jane, in Winnipeg, just two months later, when she died in May 1910. He returned to the Ottawa Valley perhaps to cope with his grief and also to answer the call of God for the Pentecostal work that was spreading there. The Semples, who had ministered so powerfully in those meetings, soon faced unimaginable tragedy. Just six months after leaving Toronto to go out as missionaries to China, Robert Semple was dead. He died from malaria in August 1910 in

Hong Kong, while his young bride, newly widowed, gave birth to their first child (a daughter) that September. Overcome with grief, Aimee Semple contacted her mother in Ontario who wired the money for her daughter and newborn granddaughter to return to North America. Also at the 1910 meeting, James Hebden had felt called of God to go on a mission trip to Algiers, and by the time he returned to Toronto in April 1911, Ellen had sold the Queen Street property, made plans to build a new church, and taken an extended trip to visit family back in England. When the Hebdens returned to Toronto early in 1911, they found their congregation somewhat adrift. Within a year, there was a tragic turn of events for the keynote speaker at those 1910 meetings too: William Durham died of pneumonia in the summer of 1912 while embroiled in controversy over teaching the finished work doctrine.

Putting Hebden's triumphalist report of 1910 into the context of the troubles that unfolded immediately afterwards brings perspective to the question of why it took several years for a Canadian organization to emerge. Recognizing the personal troubles that beset so many early Pentecostal leaders helps to explain in part why the path to organization was not smooth or straight. Disagreements about whether or not to organize and about key doctrines were only part of the story. Ironically, while reports of healing were typical of Pentecostal meetings, many of those leaders were dogged with tragic personal losses.[55] Add to that the emergence of World War I, during which Pentecostals often faced severe persecution for their objection to war,[56] and it starts to make sense why the early efforts to organize, beginning with the Markham camp meeting in 1909, took ten more years to come to fruition as the PAOC.

Beyond the wartime context and the great distances that separated them, there were other factors that made the process of organizing slow. The vocal objections of the Hebdens were no small factor. Given that the Hebdens had been the driving force behind the hub of Pentecostalism in eastern Canada, it is somewhat surprising that talks about incorporation were held without them. But as we have seen, the Hebdens were not there because their authority had diminished, and given their "vigorous opposition to any form of organization,"[57] there was no future for them once the majority of Pentecostal leaders decided that organization was the best way to build a future for the movement. Despite the Hebdens' network of fourteen churches they had either established or influenced, their impact ended abruptly when they refused to condone the idea of a central organization. For them, and others who had come from the traditional churches, the idea of becoming an institutionalized entity was absolutely the wrong direction to take. While they held doggedly to that position, other prominent leaders, including Chambers, changed course and accepted that organization was inevitable and indeed a good and necessary idea.

But in addition to that larger context, some very specific elements led to the demise of the Hebdens themselves. Where once they had occupied a position of prominence as the first to experience Spirit baptism and the hosts of a strategically located mission in Toronto, the Hebdens faded into obscurity in the story of Canadian Pentecostalism. In 1986, Thomas Miller called the Hebden Mission "the Canadian 'Azusa,'"[58] but in his later work he offered an explanation about why they fell from that influential position. Miller revealed that the Hebdens were tied to the unorthodox teachings and practices associated with the "Latter Rain" movement, and like others who took that teaching to an extreme, there was a reluctance to submit to human leadership. As the PAOC historian explained, Latter Rain prophets preferred to privilege their individual authority based on direct encounters with the Holy Spirit and clung to the conviction that they heard directly from God. Obviously, individuals like that would have trouble compromising that unmediated relationship with God to come under the direction of other people, especially when those people asked for obedience to a more limited or conservative, or "safe," agenda. Moreover, according to Miller, Mrs Hebden apparently was prone to excess in her prophetic ministry. He explains: "One other factor contributed to the demise of their work: a steadily increasing emphasis on a 'prophetic' ministry by Mrs. Hebden. Eventually, it appears, she directed people to specific fields of ministry by this method. When most of the early Pentecostal leaders recognized the threat to orthodox Christianity, Ellen Hebden lost her preeminence in the movement. Though services at her mission continued at least until 1914, the moral and legislative leadership passed to those men who united in 1919 to form the Pentecostal Assemblies of Canada."[59] Miller's interpretation is part of the triumphalist story of PAOC historiography. Those people who stood in the way of organization are not shown in a positive light, and with Hebden, this includes the view that she overemphasized her own spiritual authority.

THE DEMISE OF THE HEBDEN MISSION

More recent studies complicate the picture. Writing in 2010, William Sloos described the Hebdens as "the first family of Canadian Pentecost" and takes up the question of why they lost their influence.[60] Sloos points to the fact that after they made it clear they would not be part of any formal organization of Pentecostals in Canada, the flagship work of James and Ellen Hebden quickly met its demise. Both James and Ellen made the ill-advised decision to absent themselves from Toronto for extended periods, even as their ministry was in the midst of a relocation and building program. James felt called of God to go to Algiers in 1910 to assist a missionary colleague, and later that same year, Ellen made a trip to England to visit friends and family. By the time they both returned, James in February 1911 and Ellen in April 1911, it became clear that there were money problems associated with the East End Mission, including a very public legal dispute in 1912. These affairs received press coverage in the *Toronto Daily Star*, and as Sloos observed, "Ironically, the same paper that brought them added exposure to the revival fires five years earlier was now contributing to their frustration and embarrassment."[61] All of this trouble eventually led to a church split, giving the Hebdens the dubious distinction of being "the first known Pentecostal pastors to suffer a congregational dispute that resulted in a church schism."[62]

The leadership group that formed the PAOC overrode the Hebdens' objections and pushed forward with the task of organizing. Just as the doctrinal differences had caused division, the question of whether or not to organize was painfully divisive, especially for those who opted out. While Ellen Hebden had refused to compromise on her position and while she made the stinging accusation that some leaders favoured organization "with the prospect of receiving honors from men," she refused to see all of those who disagreed with her as selfish individuals. On the contrary, she assumed that "the great majority are no doubt endeavoring earnestly to promote the cause so dear to their hearts."[63] Moreover, she felt that the urge to take sides was a sign of immaturity in the faith: "Many who innocently take sides in the conflict of opinions are not yet grounded in the Word of God regarding [organization], and thus innocently promote division."[64] And while she was not willing to change her own position on the matter, Hebden recognized that the unrest and conflict that were arising were not pleasing to God. "In this condition of unrest we should all unitedly bow to the Word of God and seek to keep the unity of the Spirit in the bond of peace, remembering our Savior's prayer that they all may be one that the world may believe."[65]

Chambers explained his own change of heart on the subject, saying that initially, "we took the position that God was forever through with organization" and therefore, for a number of years early Pentecostals operated on the principle that "every man was sort of [a] law unto himself."[66] Chambers admitted that it was less than ideal because there was no financial security and no accountability. "After years of battling along, each man for himself (some calling it the faith life), seeing and doing some quite foolish things, we finally woke up to the fact that some order and system was needed and right."[67] Whereas the initial decision not to organize was taken as a step of obedience to God on the assumption that "God was forever through with organization," as the movement grew in scope and complexity the men at the helm became convinced that "order and system" would provide financial stability (as opposed to "living by faith") and it would protect the churches from "foolish things."

Foolish things were a real threat. A.G. Ward became convinced that there was wisdom in organization because it would provide a way to distance the movement from those "itinerant teachers, preachers, and evangelists criss-crossing the country, [who] had been proven to be unsatisfactory in theology or conduct."[68] Having an organization would allow authorities to confirm or deny association with questionable characters. Moreover, organization would protect against "con men" who falsely posed as Pentecostals in need of funds for overseas missions ventures. That scenario had presented itself when Arthur Atter was preparing to leave for China in 1908–09. A man had visited Atter, "claiming to be collecting funds for a leper colony in Shanghai," and although Atter was leery about the request, it was only after he arrived in China that he could confirm that the fundraiser was a fraud, wanted by American authorities.[69] Without any formal organization, Canadian Pentecostals were liable to be duped into supporting individuals who sounded earnest but were not genuine. That cautionary tale convinced many of the leading figures that surely there was wisdom in systematic organization to provide support for those who were genuinely called to serve overseas and to protect believers who had resources to support the venture. Logic dictated that perhaps God was not "through with organization" after all. Now, it seemed, the Spirit would endorse the wisdom of it.

Indeed, leaders eventually began to make the argument that "God Himself is the author of system and organization."[70] Addressing objections from those who did not agree that organization was of God, John McAlister offered this logic:

> Some say that the church is an organism, and that you cannot organize an organism. But we are not trying to organize the organism, but the human members, for we have found that if you do not have some way of governing the unruly members that the unruly members soon govern the body, and this is just what we found in the early days of this Pentecostal movement. We thought, as a number think today, that we would have no organization of any kind, but let everyone just do as the Spirit moved. This might possibly have worked if everyone had been perfect, and had the perfect guidance of the Spirit. But we found to our sorrow that all were not perfect, that many came in who as Paul said brought in damnable heresy.[71]

Echoing other leaders of like mind about the need to organize, McAlister also made the argument that organizing was necessary to create a system for a responsible way of administering funds for missionaries because "we found in our unorganized state that our missionaries were sadly neglected. While some were receiving scarcely any support, at the same time others were receiving far more than they needed. We had no way of knowing or of regulating it if we had known. And even yet [more than five years later] we are struggling with some of the results of our foolishness at the time."[72]

By the time World War I was underway, the Hebdens had definitely faded from the scene, and their objection to organization was no longer something to be managed or navigated.[73] In the spring of 1917, a group of Canadian Pentecostals met in Montreal to make plans toward a formal organization. One significant factor influencing this decision to proceed was no doubt the fact that the AG had organized in 1914. Canadian leaders were very familiar with what was happening in the US, since they were regularly travelling to fellowship and speaking at gatherings across the country and across the border. Canadians would have been well aware that two years after their initial organization, the AG took a stand on doctrine in which they accepted the finished work doctrine and rejected Oneness. Canadians were not completely in step with those positions. While they agreed on the finished work question, they were divided over Oneness. Generally, those who accepted Oneness were in eastern Canada, including R.E. McAlister and Chambers, while those who rejected it were in the west, led by Argue.

Those who were present at the May 1917 organization meeting in Montreal were R.E. McAlister, G.A. Chambers, R.E. Sternall, Frank Small, A.M. Pattison, Harvey McAlister, and W.L. Draffin.[74] It is very interesting to note that one individual who helped the Canadian group to create their organization was Howard Goss, a well-known American Pentecostal who rose to leadership among Oneness Pentecostals. Also notable is the absence of A.H. Argue. The first 1917 meeting led to further discussion that summer at a camp near Ottawa. The following year, in November 1918 as World War I was ending, the men who were crafting the organization met again in Milles Roches and then one more time in Montreal in the winter of 1919. Out of their discussion, they resolved to apply for a charter of incorporation from the national government that would grant their organization the same status as other churches in Canada. As William Griffin points out, a newly simplified process for incorporation had recently been introduced through an act of parliament known as the Companies Act 1917. This new procedure meant that a not-for-profit organization could receive a charter directly from the Secretary of State without going through the cumbersome process of presenting a private member's bill to be voted upon in the House of Commons. Griffin wryly comments, "It hardly needs to be said, but Pentecostal 'holy rollers' were not that popular and might have had some difficulty getting a majority vote in Parliament."[75]

While the churches in eastern Canada agreed to join together under the banner of the Pentecostal Assemblies of Canada, those in the west opted instead to join the American Assemblies of God, to be recognized in December 1919 as the Western Canada District Council of the Assemblies of God. The reason for that division might seem at first to be simply a logical decision dictated by geography, since the AG headquarters was located in Springfield, Missouri. But in fact, that move to reject the new organization in eastern Canada reflected some unresolved doctrinal differences. While many of those in the east clung to the Oneness doctrine, the prominent voices in the west, specifically A.H. Argue, found the rejection of the Trinity to be outside of orthodoxy.

That doctrinal stalemate had to be overcome if the PAOC was ever to become a truly national body. In November 1919, R.E. McAlister took steps that he had hoped would convince the west to come on board with the fledgling PAOC. At a meeting of the General Assembly of the PAOC, he addressed the issue head on, saying: "Whereas much contention and confusion has been caused over the issue of One God and Trinitarian views, also the baptismal formula, be it resolved, that we as a body go on record as disapproving not only the above issue, but the other issues that divide and confuse God's people to no profit, and that aggressive evangelism be our motto."[76] McAlister's proposal went on to make clear that "we recognize the three-fold relationship of Father, Son and Holy Ghost being clearly taught in the New Testament," and he proposed that the group pass a resolution expressing its agreement with that interpretation but leaving the baptismal formula up to the individual.[77] While it was a good gesture, it was too late to convince the group in the west that their position was truly changed. A month later, western Canadian Pentecostals joined the AG.

Griffin presents McAlister as a strategic mastermind behind a grand plan to win back the west and unite the Canadian Pentecostals within the PAOC structure. McAlister took out credentials with the AG, a move that showed his personal convictions were trinitarian, since he would not have been approved by the AG credentialing body if he still held his previous Oneness views. The following year, the PAOC General Conference was held in Montreal at the same time that Aimee Semple McPherson (an AG minister at the time) was holding a series of highly successful meetings. Relying on oral history from Walter McAlister, Griffin paints the picture of a highly contentious meeting where the two groups from east and west both agreed to join the American AG as District Council of the Assemblies of God yet without surrendering their name or the charter they had recently attained from the Canadian government. Griffin quotes from the minutes of that meeting that "several of the brethren spoke their convictions" as "polite code for a passionate no-holds-barred debate that lasted all afternoon." Moreover, while the ballot count from that vote does not exist in the records, Griffin posits that the motion to join the American trinitarian-based Assemblies of God "was won by a narrow margin."[78]

The new "united" Pentecostal groups of east and west had to work out some differences in the coming years about where their meetings would be held, what business could be conducted by each regional grouping, and how many representatives of the east and west would comprise the national executives, but they managed to work out those differences. At the 1925 General Assembly held in Winnipeg, the final step toward true national unity and independence was taken when the PAOC made the decision to officially separate from the AG in a move that Griffin characterizes as a "coming of age for the PAOC."[79]

Having settled the dilemma of "to organize or not to organize," the question remained: which governance model should they adopt? The answer to that question would reflect years of discussion and diplomatic negotiation because with Pentecostals coming from a variety of backgrounds, there were options. Those who came from a Methodist, Congregational, or Mennonite background were adamant that control needed to rest with local congregations. But those who came from more hierarchical churches, including Presbyterian and Anglican systems, recognized the value of having a central body, both to streamline and maximize the financial systems and to make decisions that could bring a degree of consistency and unity among the local bodies.[80] William Griffin sums up the story of the early years of organizing this way: "The road to a suitable and acceptable organizational structure for the PAOC, something that could provide stability and curb excesses while allowing for freedom and individual initiative, proved to be longer and more torturous than our founding fathers probably expected."[81] In the end, a hybrid Presbyterian/Congregational model was adopted with a view of a "fellowship" of autonomous congregations organized around geographical districts with superintendents and presbyters giving leadership to the new denomination.

What this convoluted and contentious history shows is that the path to organization for Canadian Pentecostals in the PAOC was neither straight nor smooth. In the tale of rapid growth, theological disagreements, and personal conflicts, one observes the uneven social process of organization and the difficulty of securing cultural cohesion that characterized the emergence of the PAOC. While the group eventually landed with a workable organizational structure as an entirely Canadian, incorporated body that held to orthodox trinitarian views, that outcome was never guaranteed. Those who wished to situate the story within the subculture would recount how the Spirit led the revered leaders through a series of compromises to move toward this model of organization.

Scholars of organization theories remind us that there is "the existence of continuous processes of convergence and divergence, stability and instability, evolution and revolution in every organization."[82] In the early years, Canadian Pentecostalism displayed those tendencies toward organizing with various debates about the specifics of the organization and a culture that served to animate the PAOC. From different parties expressing different ideas, power, and authority, first coalescing around the Hebden Mission and then eventually transferring to the men who obtained the PAOC's government charter, the culture of the organization was emerging and developing. From what appears to be a series of seemingly random, individualized spiritual encounters, the movement experienced phenomenal growth, strong personalities, and several roadblocks when the principal parties could not agree on the question of whether or not to organize and on competing interpretations of experience. In the end, those calling for order and system won the day, and the PAOC rose out of its seemingly chaotic origins, stumbled in its attempt to become truly national, and then eventually stood united, firm in its conviction that a model of system and accountability was indeed from the Spirit. The story of the emergence of Pentecostalism and how it was organized illustrates how religious coherence revolves around the development of a culture that is partially about belief but also about experience and the creation of boundaries by individuals and the organization that serve to define what Pentecostalism is and how the organization will operate. The way forward for the PAOC would be done "decently and in order."[83]

3

Building a Church

INTRODUCTION

After the 1919 charter was drafted and accepted by the federal government, the Pentecostal Assemblies of Canada (PAOC) was an officially recognized religious body in Canada. Gloria Kulbeck asserted that "almost from the beginning it was evident that a form of permanent church government would be necessary, if the best features of the revival were to be conserved."[1] The urge to preserve the "best features" of the revival was a real concern, especially given the context of the so-called "roaring twenties" in Canada. Popular culture in the decade following the Great War was filled with all manner of "worldly" temptations, and the trappings of modernity threatened to entice believers, both young and old. From commercial entertainment in dance halls and movie theatres to the spread of automobile culture and the ubiquity of radio broadcasting, there were assorted reasons to worry about preserving the culture of revival in the PAOC and battling against the sins on offer to pleasure-seekers.[2]

But many Canadians experienced a different reality from the carefree existence depicted on the big screen and promoted by advertisers of cosmetics, fashion, and cigarettes. In the aftermath of war, Canadians were trying to make sense of the sacrifices that had been made and collectively reeling from the staggering loss of life and the disabilities that surviving veterans lived with, including the mental breakdowns suffered by at least 15,000 Canadian soldiers and countless more "unseen injuries" that plagued survivors.[3] Added to that tragedy, Canada was hard hit by the Spanish flu epidemic of 1918–19, which claimed 50,000 lives and led to the creation of the federal

Department of Health in 1919, followed by provincial departments being formed soon after.[4] In addition to the pandemic, other health problems plagued Canadians through the 1920s as child and maternal mortality rates soared to levels rivalling those of less developed parts of the world. That concern prompted officials to implement the advice of Dr Helen MacMurchy, whose government-sponsored study recommended the creation of "Well Baby Clinics," medical inspection of schoolchildren, and other public health measures, based on the shared conviction that "nations are built of babies."[5] Against that backdrop of cultural change and social distress, Canadian Pentecostals knew that their message of healing and hope could have wide appeal if only they could find a way to make the revival into something more permanent, something as enduring as the more established churches.

Yet how to build a church (or whether they should even attempt to do so) was not evident to everyone, and in the decades following the charter, the organization was put to the test. As the PAOC took its first steps to develop systems, departments, and the necessary bureaucracy to manage its burgeoning growth, some Pentecostals challenged the organization, claiming an allegiance to the earlier days of the revival when the untamed Spirit moved where it willed, breaking free from the limitations of denominational structures. Those who pushed to create an organization, like their secular counterparts battling the public health crisis, did so from the thoroughly modern conviction that order and system held the best promise for a strong future. The rapid growth that Pentecostalism experienced provided one of the strongest arguments among Pentecostals that formal organization was necessary.

If the leaders were going to build a Canadian church, growth had to be managed, and beliefs had to be reinforced. For these purposes, the PAOC created a national office and appointed key leaders to provide leadership for the expanding number of congregations and the growing finances. The answer, it seemed, was to turn to practices that had proved effective for the business community, borrowing from the economic realm a model that became institutionally embedded while reinforcing the organization's identity and place within Canadian society.

With the charter in hand, the PAOC set out to create and reinforce its culture and identity as a Pentecostal organization. By adopting particular organizational structures and proven business methods, the early PAOC leaders moved continuously toward a conformity among their flocks. Insisting that they were creating a "fellowship," not a denomination, the founders went to great lengths to find a workable model of organization. However, given the diversity of religious backgrounds from which Pentecostals came, that would prove to be no small feat. Those who hailed from Methodist backgrounds favoured a congregational model of governance, while those from other churches were convinced that a hierarchical model would be most effective. In the end, the governance model that PAOC adopted was a hybrid, what Thomas Miller called "Presbygational."[6] There was a strong central executive providing structures and direction, while at the same time a congregational philosophy of local church governance prevailed, meaning "the independence of each congregation should be carefully guarded."[7] While that model seemed like a brilliant compromise, maintaining the balance between the authority of the central office of the organization and local congregations meant that PAOC governance structures would be tested.

Sociologist of religion Penny Edgell asserts that as people adopt a particular religious identity, they may align with a movement or denomination.[8] And as a cultural analysis of religion reminds us, the process of identity formation is a fluid one. Religious organizations adopt creeds and particular institutional cultures in order to solidify boundaries for inclusion and exclusion and cultural cohesion. The decades following the 1919 charter provide an example of that process of boundary-making, which culminated in a serious challenge to the organizational culture of the PAOC in the late 1940s when Pentecostals in Saskatchewan challenged its authority with the activities that became known as the Latter Rain movement. The Latter Rain movement illustrates how religious organizations negotiate differences at the level of beliefs and practices and how boundaries serve to warrant the authority of the PAOC over and against competing groups. In the conflict that ensued, and its resolution, one sees a classic example of boundary-making, reinforcement, and maintenance, and several scholars of Pentecostalism have concluded that what happened in Saskatchewan in the late 1940s was, in fact, a resistance to the bureaucracy that had come to dominate Canadian Pentecostalism.[9]

ADOPTING A MODERN BUSINESS MODEL

When one is walking through the halls of the PAOC national office, the parallels with a corporate headquarters are striking, from the central reception desk, to the multiple department offices, to the walls lined with portraits of revered male leaders. PAOC historians have attributed this legendary status to their national leaders, in one case calling them the "architects" of Canadian Pentecostalism and in another, the "founding fathers of Pentecostalism."[10] The ambiance at the PAOC national office makes it very clear that these men built the foundation for the denomination and their work continues today. Several official histories of the PAOC have been written, and each one features prominently the professional portraits of the men who founded and guided the PAOC over the decades. Business-minded Pentecostal men found agreement around the idea that structures should be created to make more efficient use of resources, not only for missionary efforts abroad but also for domestic expansion. After the 1919 charter that gave the PAOC official recognition, the business culture that the PAOC created was established and ready to expand. The main functions of the national executive were to organize and oversee the missionary efforts and to receive and disperse the funds that flowed in from local churches and districts. When the PAOC organized in 1919, the annual budget was approximately $2,000, but that amount quickly increased so that within ten years, the office was administering more than $73,000.[11]

Creating a central national office was the first critical step in running the PAOC operations efficiently, and as one PAOC historian explained, "Since Rev. R.E. McAlister was the key to much of the business life of the denomination in the early days, the national office of the Pentecostal Assemblies was located where he was pastoring: first in Ottawa, Ontario; then in London, Ontario."[12] McAlister held the role of secretary-treasurer for the PAOC until 1937, and in that same year the national office relocated to Toronto. In 1920, McAlister was paid approximately $1,000 for this work in addition to the salary he earned as a full-time pastor. Within five years of its establishment, the executive took the decision that every PAOC worker should contribute at least part of their tithe to support the work of the national office. Expenses were mounting, especially with the travel commitments as the organization grew and consolidated across the country. The 1920s were fondly referred to as "the roaring twenties," and the pace of expansion for PAOC business was right in step with the times.

In addition to overseeing the funds to support missionaries, both foreign and domestic, PAOC executive members performed various functions for the fellowship, and within five years a series of committees had been established including: Roster Committee, Resolutions

Committee, Adjustment Committee, Missionary Committee, and Ordination Committee. What began as a very simple administrative structure quickly became complex, reflecting the growth of the organization and the kinds of issues that came before the national executive. Sometimes those were issues of discipline for pastors or congregations that were not in line with PAOC policies and practices.

By 1927 a Statement of Fundamental and Essential Truths (SOFET) had been developed and adopted, despite the resolve in 1919 that such a statement would not be necessary or desirable.[13] This statement of codified beliefs would make it easier to establish insiders and outsiders, and it proved to be a key cultural tool in developing and maintaining the PAOC's organizational identity. The minutes of the 1927 meeting make clear the purpose of the statement: "Be it further resolved that a copy [of the doctrinal statement] be presented to every worker, licensed or ordained, which each worker shall be expected to use as a constitutional order of practice in all Canadian Assemblies."[14] Conformity to the statement was one measure of Pentecostal orthodoxy, and it provided one guideline to establish when disciplinary measures might be necessary for credential holders who departed from it. While the minutes are cryptic about the nature of rogue Pentecostal leaders, there are several references to the need for ensuring that workers who wished to be ordained should first prove themselves to be reputable and in line with PAOC beliefs and practices. Sometimes this meant deferring requests for ordination for at least one or two years.

The PAOC was growing at an impressive rate, and by 1940 its 37,000 members were being served by 732 Canadian missionaries, ministers, and licensed workers serving approximately 350 congregations across the country.[15] That growth, and the need to manage it, explains why the national executive was so busy in the first decades after 1919. While the PAOC's official historians have explained that growth as the blessing of God, there are cultural and organizational explanations that help to add context about where the new adherents and leaders were coming from. One major source of membership was from the traditional churches as congregants rejected the move toward more liberal theology and the embrace of modernism. Pentecostalism presented exactly that kind of alternative to believers who found their traditional church experiences less than satisfying. Historian Kevin Flatt asserts that in the United Church of Canada (UCC), for example, leaders were well aware of "the stiff competition of these non-mainline evangelical networks, with their proliferating Bible schools, radio stations, and summer conferences, presented to mainline churches."[16] UCC leadership "worried that the teaching of the United Church, seemingly lukewarm by comparison, was driving people to 'places where an outlet for their emotions is provided, and where the words from the pulpit and platform are more definite, and therefore more assuring.'"[17] Pentecostalism is a prime example of a religious subculture that provided both the experience that believers seemed to crave and a definite set of non-negotiable beliefs that provided assurances about truth rather than intellectual conundrums. There is no question that the PAOC benefitted from the exodus of believers who were unwilling and unable to embrace liberal theology and modernism.

RESISTING MODERNISM

Pentecostals claimed that modern churches were abandoning spiritual concerns in an effort to conform to society and attract congregants, often relaxing moral standards in the process. This kind of moral panic was a common critique of the "roaring twenties," sometimes called the "jazz era," because commercial entertainment establishments, including dance halls and movie theatres, were becoming ubiquitous in Canadian society. Pentecostals accused mainline churches of unabashedly endorsing the dance floor and the cinema, judged sinful in Pentecostal circles. It is, of course, quite ironic that the Pentecostals reproved so-called "modernist" churches for their adoption of worldly methods of attracting people when they were doing precisely the same thing themselves, incorporating radio broadcasts, new musical styles, and dramatic presentations into their meetings.

Modern theology was anathema to Pentecostals, who deemed it "the work of the devil"[18] and an "anti-Christian abomination."[19] "Modernism," according to *The Pentecostal Testimony*, was a system of theology adopted by some mainstream Protestant denominations that denied several core Christian tenets, including the fall of humanity, God's final judgment, the existence of heaven and hell, the infallibility of the Scriptures, and the divinity, virgin birth, and resurrection of Christ. One writer succinctly described modernism as "that man-made system of theology which still wishes to be called 'Christian' after it has denied practically every Christian fundamental; it is the great apostasy which is insidiously coming into pulpits which are still classed as 'orthodox.'"[20] Modernism, because it deceivingly portrayed itself as Christian, was very dangerous – "worse than paganism,"[21] as one Pentecostal evangelist inveighed.

Taking their stand against liberal theology and the traditional denominations from which many Pentecostals had come, the national executive of the PAOC was clear about the dangers of modernism in all its forms. One of the means for communicating that message about the dangers of modernism was through the special evangelistic and healing meetings that were headlined by well-known Pentecostal celebrity preachers, including Canada's own Aimee Semple McPherson and one of her converts to Pentecostalism, Charles S. Price. With a very high profile in North American media, Sister Aimee came home to Canada on several occasions to preach at meetings in several Canadian cities, including Winnipeg, Lethbridge, and Montreal, to name but three. Invariably, these meetings were widely publicized by secular media as well as by the host churches themselves. Reports of miraculous healings and other dramatic signs and wonders never failed to draw crowds. In addition to her gospel message and prayers for healing, Sister Aimee took the occasion to condemn modernism in the strongest possible terms. She spoke against evolution, liberalism, and the follies of higher learning. While she adopted many of the so-called worldly technologies, including radio broadcasting and musical drama productions, as part of her sermons she made clear that the evils of the jazz era and commercial entertainment establishments were demonic in origin and places from which the saints should steer clear.

PRINT MEDIA AND PENTECOSTAL CULTURE

One of the cultural tools that helped to bind the PAOC together as an organization was print media. This was not a new strategy for Pentecostals because there had already been a plethora of magazines and newsletters created by numerous Pentecostal leaders, including the Hebdens and R.E. McAlister, to name but two early Canadian examples. Soon after the 1919 charter was attained, a new official publication of the PAOC, *The Pentecostal Testimony* (PT) was soon launched, with its first issue appearing in December 1920. Historian Brian Hogan asserts that religious newspapers, magazines, and journals serve an important purpose for organizational culture because as readers consume the content of these publications, they "provide the factual and interpretive glue that binds and guides the committed into communities."[22] That was certainly the case for *PT*, according to Thomas Miller, who praised the publication for its contribution "to the unifying and the growth of the young Fellowship [that] cannot be adequately calculated."[23]

When the PAOC launched a campaign to increase the readership of *PT* and encourage readers to buy a subscription, they invoked the rhetoric of joining a "family" of readers, a clear indication that the publishers were consciously trying to create the sense of culture and community that Hogan referenced. Robyn Sneath has analyzed the Mennonite publication *Mennonitische Post*, using Benedict Anderson's concept of "imagined community" to argue that for believers who were widely scattered over vast geographic distances, the paper "brought them together in an imagined community"[24] as readers were "drawn together by common language and shared ways of speaking and writing."[25] Sneath argues that through this publication, Mennonites created a shared "cultural script" and created "dense networks" among subscribers for whom "maintenance of that community is contingent upon communication."[26] Pentecostals were doing exactly the same thing as their *PT* provided the communication that would draw readers together in a sense of shared community with reports of crusades, healing meetings, new congregations, and reports from the various departments of the national office.

By the 1930s, the PAOC's adoption of business techniques was obvious, and one example of it was a full-fledged advertising campaign underway to attract subscribers to *PT*. Pentecostal publications in the first two decades of the twentieth century relied upon a system of financing based on free will offerings. As the PAOC became more business-like, they abandoned the model of voluntary donations and the unpredictable income it generated for the publication and turned instead to a subscription-based income model. In the October 1937 issue, this full-page advertisement appeared:

> Our circle of subscribers is every-growing [*sic*]. The mail man now delivers personally each month hundreds of individual TESTIMONIES into the homes across the Dominion. This month we again invite YOU to join this family. And in doing so we should like to make it as pleasant a bit of business as possible. So we offer for your one dollar (1) the following: (1) THE TESTIMONY – to be delivered to your door each month for the next seventeen months, anywhere in the world. (2) Your choice

> of any one of the four premium books shown above. You may have one book for each new subscription or renewal which is forwarded to our office as is indicated at the bottom of the page. Use the coupon below.[27]

Analyzing the rhetoric of that ad reveals three significant things about Pentecostal publishing in general and the central role of marketing techniques in particular. First, a business model is clearly in operation here, complete with a persuasive ad campaign, a mail-in coupon, and a book incentive. From a business perspective, the PT was a marketing tool adopting techniques that were common among revivalists from decades before. Indeed, the obvious attempts to promote their movement are reminiscent of the kind of marketing techniques that historian Kevin Kee identified in his book *Revivalists: Marketing the Gospel in English Canada, 1884–1957*.[28] Printing handbills, publishing news of upcoming meetings, and reporting back to stakeholders about results are common business practices, and the PAOC adopted them all. But this scheme to persuade readers to pay for a subscription was something new.

Second, the idea that buying a subscription was equivalent to "joining the family" reinforces the idea that consuming the PT was an important way for the PAOC to create a sense of identity among its readers. Separated by great distances across the country, subscribers would feel connected to meetings that featured speakers whom they had heard, and they could rejoice over the establishment of new congregations and new church buildings, even from a distance. The PT featured regular financial reports as well so that readers could see which congregations, Sunday schools, and individuals were contributing to the missionary fund. Scanning those reports for the mention of one's own name or congregation served to reinforce the notion of participating in something much bigger than oneself or one's own hometown.

Third, given Pentecostalism's commitment to giving women prominent roles in ministry, it is significant that all four of the books on offer as incentives to subscribe were written by a woman, Zelma Argue.[29] Argue, the eldest daughter of A.H. Argue of Winnipeg, was making significant contributions to the spread of Pentecostalism, not only as a travelling evangelist and a regular contributor to the magazine but also with her books. Argue's writings were proving so popular that the editors of PT proclaimed, "Miss Argue's books sell themselves.

They are a devotional series with readings for everyday in the month. In this way their value never wears out … May we again remind you that it is a good time to subscribe now and thus take advantage of receiving one of Miss Argue's books ABSOLUTELY FREE."[30] Zelma Argue was one of North America's most widely travelled Pentecostal speakers, particularly during the early years of the movement, and one of the most widely published as well.[31] By the end of her fifty-year public ministry, she had authored five books and almost 250 articles in Canadian and American Pentecostal publications.

It was not uncommon for women writers to be published in religious periodicals, and in her reflections on the history of women and publishing in Canada, Carole Gerson asserts that "publications emanating from women's religious organizations" were one of the most common forms of women's publications during the twentieth century.[32] Zelma Argue was particularly well placed to write about Pentecostalism in Canada because of her close relationships with men who were leading the movement, including her famous father A.H. Argue, her brother Watson Argue, and her brother-in-law, C.B. Smith,[33] and in her writing she made it clear that she had her finger on the very pulse of the Pentecostal movement.[34] Argue sometimes wrote for American Pentecostal publications too, and in one she featured a church camp in southern Ontario, encouraging Americans to attend the meetings there, describing in detail the amenities, accommodations, and driving directions.[35] With this promotional role Argue encouraged her readers to visit each other's sites whenever the opportunity arose, thereby reinforcing the ties between members of the Pentecostal "family." Using her books to encourage regular readers to pay for their subscriptions is a prime example of how the PAOC executive adopted a business model. Asking readers to pay for the publication would provide a predictable revenue stream so that those who enjoyed reading about and celebrating the organization's growth could be called upon to contribute to its financial stability. Leveraging the well-known Argue family name was a sound business practice. *PT* played an important role in the development of the subculture and cultural cohesion within the organization.

BIBLE COLLEGES

For those who could not claim their authority through a close association with one of the "founding families" of Canadian Pentecostalism as Zelma Argue could, there was another way to qualify for leadership in the PAOC: training at one of its Bible colleges. Establishing a series of Bible schools across the country served the PAOC in several important ways by once again reinforcing the networks of the fellowship, expanding the pool of ministry leaders, and standardizing their training. Gloria Kulbeck explained in her history of the PAOC that the need for education facilities for PAOC leaders became apparent when "Pentecostal pioneers in Canada discovered the importance of theology and formal training for the Christian ministry, if Pentecostal truth was to be perpetuated beyond the lifetime of those who had been present in the Pentecostal revival of 1906." In keeping with the triumphalist tone of her work, Kulbeck celebrated the fact that "between 1924 and 1947 at least six Pentecostal Bible schools were to spring up, across the land."[36] Kulbeck depicted it as a spontaneous development resulting from "the normal result of a deepening spiritual awareness and hunger for God in Pentecostal believers."[37] However, the establishment of Bible schools can also be read as a sign of organizational development that served to socialize future PAOC clergy in the subculture.

The first school was established in Winnipeg in 1925, and by the Second World War six other regional schools had been created in Saskatoon, Toronto (later moving to Peterborough), Halifax (from 1944 to 1947 only), Edmonton, Victoria (later moving to Vancouver and then Abbotsford), and Montreal.[38] The fact that most of these schools emerged in the same period is no coincidence. The explanation has been offered that this growth was a sign of God's blessing on the organization or that the PAOC was simply being pragmatic in their attempt to expand the training of clergy. However, we offer a cultural explanation for the rapid expansion of the PAOC Bible school network. Bible schools were created as a defence against modernism, designed to establish social and moral cohesion within the subculture and shaping students into leaders in the organization. In short, these schools were central to socializing clergy while constructing a PAOC identity. Kulbeck herself admitted that the schools were arising "at a time when Pentecostal youth needed to be fortified against modernism, false cults and fanaticism."[39] *PT* also reproached modernists for their perceived immoral conduct, which was seen as fundamentally linked to their heterodox beliefs. That modernism had permeated a number of large denominations and many institutions of higher learning meant it was even more threatening to early Canadian Pentecostals. All the more reason that they needed to create their own schools.

For the PAOC, organizing their own Bible colleges was a key strategy to counter the powerful influence of modernism by teaching Pentecostal doctrine to young adults and ultimately training the next generation of pastors to protect their congregations from modernist heresies. In the context of fear about the proliferation of worldly influences in the surrounding culture, Bible colleges were more than just a pragmatic strategy to train more clergy; they were established as a response to social and cultural change. The schools received a further boost in enrolment as World War II drew to a close because returning veterans were offered tuition exemption as a reward for their service and Bible college education was included in the range of options available to them. This provision in the Veterans Charter was a significant factor in shoring up recruitment and retention for Bible school enrolments. Moreover, the veterans benefit also had a significant effect on the gender balance of enrolments. While women continued to attend Bible schools, they no longer dominated the numbers, nor did they enter into the programs of ministry that were clearly designed to attract men to the ministry and the postwar cultural move that encouraged women to "return to the kitchen" after their non-traditional war work roles. The assumption among Bible college attendees was that women went to these schools to get the "Mrs" degree. However, that characterization is not a fair assessment of the significant contributions and participation that women held in PAOC schools, and it is an example of how the PAOC was in step with the culture around them. Without intending to, Pentecostals were compromising on their egalitarian position that had welcomed women to their pulpits in the early years.

The principal of the Winnipeg school was the Rev. James Eustace Purdie, a somewhat surprising choice of leader. Purdie was a committed Anglican, though theologically conservative and thoroughly evangelical, having graduated from Wycliffe College in Toronto. After his own experience of "spirit baptism" in 1919,[40] he became associated with Pentecostalism, and in 1925 he was seconded by the PAOC to lead the new Bible training school in Winnipeg. Although Purdie was outspoken and clear about his encounter with the Spirit and the evangelical, charismatic orientation that resulted, he never completely cut his ties with the Anglican Church. Indeed, he continued to wear his clerical collar that symbolized what some Pentecostal "come-outers" were reacting to when they left mainline churches to join new Pentecostal congregations. However, the adage "never judge a book by its cover" applies to Purdie, about whom one might say, "never judge a clergyman by his collar," because for all his commitment to his Anglican roots, the Pentecostals had little to worry about when it came to Purdie's devotion to the PAOC. Despite his traditional-looking collar, it is clear that Purdie had been thoroughly shaped by the evangelical culture at Wycliffe and that his collar absolutely did not represent any commitment to liberal theology or the modernist impulses discussed earlier in this chapter. Quite the contrary. Yet Purdie used the collar to establish his authority as one who was a product of the world of theological higher education. From there, he leveraged that identity to position himself as one who was uniquely qualified to explain the follies of modernist thinking to Pentecostal students.

Scholars of Canadian Pentecostalism have noted that Purdie's greatest contribution to the fledgling PAOC was the theological training and systematic statements of faith that he brought to hundreds of Bible college students.[41] Purdie solidified PAOC beliefs by codifying them in the curriculum he developed. His efforts were undeniably important given his anti-modern impulse and his stance in countering liberal theology. Purdie's correspondence makes it clear that he thought of the program he created at Winnipeg as an antidote to those modernist trends, and he popularized those more conservative views when he imparted them to his students. His teaching was the uncontested core of the PAOC curriculum for students who would become the pastors and lay volunteers in Pentecostal churches across Canada. But his influence reached beyond the students who sat in his Winnipeg classrooms because his course notes and curriculum became the foundation for all of the other PAOC Bible schools across the country.

Purdie's time at Wycliffe not only meant that he had been thoroughly trained in evangelical, anti-modern ideals, but he also was very supportive of women in ministry, and he welcomed women into the world of theological higher education. Purdie's first wife, Frances Emma Morrison, was an Anglican deaconess whom he met during their student days in Toronto. Frances Purdie's role in the Western Bible College has largely gone unnoted in the existing literature, but archival sources make it clear that her role as a partner in ministry to James was indispensable. Her involvement in the college revolved around their family situation: she was less involved when their children were young, but after the children were grown, her involvement with the college grew to full-time, salaried faculty member. Frances was a capable administrator, and her roles at the school spanned from student recruitment to classroom teaching to alumni relations. Indeed, the newsletters she compiled for former students now comprise a significant archive of materials that hold many clues about the gender history of the school, its staff, and students. Frances Purdie invoked the metaphor of a family to describe the relationships that existed between alumni members and their former instructors. In that Bible school family, there was no doubt that Mrs Purdie was perceived to be the mother of them all.

The Purdies had a shared commitment to the role of women in ministry, and the PAOC's pragmatic eschatological urgency that the gospel should be preached by any and every means available meant that the Western Bible School was very welcoming to women as students and as members of faculty. One faculty member was Ethel Bingeman, a returned missionary who had served in Liberia for almost twenty years, beginning in 1915. When Bingeman first became a missionary, her travelling companion and co-worker was Miss Laura Arnold, who later married R.E. McAlister. Bingeman joined the faculty of the college as a middle-aged woman whose "exotic" experiences overseas certainly contributed to her reputation as an intrepid woman, equal to any challenge. The Purdies were delighted to welcome her to the faculty of the college as an example to the students but particularly as a role model who could inspire students to take on the adventure of ministry and to embrace it fully. Bingeman's teaching included courses in practical nursing because she had trained as a nurse before she left for the mission field, and she brought the pragmatic and vocational side of this Bible school training to life. Given her mature age and her marital status as a single woman when she joined the faculty, it is not surprising that Bingeman was recruited to serve as dean of women. This "deanship" was not an academic position but rather like a residence advisor to the female students, one who was expected to inspire the women but also to discipline them and exercise surveillance over their life in the dormitories.

Another woman who joined the faculty at Winnipeg had a very different profile: Gladys Lemmon, who had been the class valedictorian in the charter class of 1928, was recruited to teach part-time while she was still a student at Winnipeg. Lemmon joined the faculty on a full-time basis immediately after graduating and remained on staff until the school closed in 1950. Over the years, Lemmon rose to play a central role at the college, eventually replacing Bingeman as dean of women and becoming a respected colleague and decision-maker on issues about faculty hiring, student discipline, and curriculum development.

Minutes of faculty council meetings reveal that Lemmon's salary level was higher than that of many others, including some of the men on faculty. This reflected her full-time status but was also evidence of the fact that her roles as secretary to the faculty council and dean of women were highly valued in the life of the college.

In 1950, as part of the twenty-fifth anniversary celebrations of the Bible school, Frances Purdie compiled a list of 328 alumni members, including their ministry involvements. From that source, one can begin to build a prosopography of the graduates and look for gender patterns. Alumni records show that many of the women took up "modern" roles as independent single women either at home or overseas serving as pastors and missionaries. Having trained alongside the men for ministry, many of the female graduates did marry, of course, and yet surprisingly, marital status did not seem to impact these ministry choices, since many married women reported that they were co-pastors with their husbands in church work as opposed to describing themselves as "pastors' wives."

Yet the gendered nature of the student experience definitely changed over time, as illustrated by the photographs of graduating classes over the years. In the school's very first graduating class (1927–28), for example, there were eleven women and six men. Yet by 1950, in a class of seven graduates, six were men, and only one was a woman. Clearly, something had changed over the two and a half decades of the school's operation. In the 1920s, women who graduated from the college were quite likely to assume ministry roles that called for an adventurous "new woman" outlook, but by the time the school closed, its female graduates were fewer in number and more likely to assume a traditional subordinate role to their ministering husbands. That pattern is in keeping with theorists who have argued that as a movement becomes more institutionalized, women are often marginalized.[42] The PAOC, with its expanding organizational structures and reinforcing cultural patterns, seems to be a case in point.

WAR SERVICE AND RELATING TO THE STATE

When it came to the male students, one question that illustrates the social process of boundary-making and cultural cohesion that the PAOC had to sort through was the position it would take on war service. This is yet another example of the cultural process of boundary-making and identity formation that the PAOC was undertaking. The war years were a critical period in the history of Canadian

Pentecostalism as well because they reveal a range of issues about the interaction between the PAOC and other spheres of society. In the first war, prior to the PAOC's establishment, some Pentecostals faced intense persecution for their stance as conscientious objectors.[43] Meanwhile, those who had joined the movement from mainline churches were likely to regard war service as their "reasonable sacrifice" and a means of demonstrating their loyalty to the empire and their commitment to citizenship responsibilities. Still others regarded the war as a distraction from their main mission of preaching the gospel before Christ's imminent return to earth.

A survey of *PT* reinforces the fact that Pentecostal views about war varied because in its pages, leaders of the movement expressed a wide range of opinions in the years leading up to World War II. For example, in the early 1920s Pentecostal evangelists like Zelma Argue took a decidedly apocalyptic view, expressing the idea that while war was inevitable, it was not an issue that should distract Pentecostals because the second coming of Christ was imminent. Argue and others like her believed that "wars and rumours of wars" were only further proof that the prophecies predicting Christ's return were about to be fulfilled and true believers should be busy preaching the gospel, not becoming entangled in worldly affairs.[44]

In 1935–36, George A. Chambers, who had served as the first general superintendent of the PAOC from 1919 to 1934, published a four-part series of articles in answer to the question "Should Christians Go to War?" Chambers' emphatic answer was "no." His was a classic expression of conscientious objection to war, arguing that "there is no such thing as a holy war," that Jesus forbade his disciples to use violence as a means of defending him in the Garden of Gethsemane, and that there were no references to the Church in the Book of Acts ever "taking up arms or returning evil for evil." Moreover, Chambers maintained that while the Apostle Paul taught believers to be "good soldiers of Jesus Christ," he also told them that a Christian should not "entangle himself in the affairs of this world."[45] Chambers's position was no surprise, given that he came into the Pentecostal movement from his background as a minister in the Mennonite Brethren in Christ Church.[46] His views were also in step with the PAOC, which had adopted an official pacifist position in the original Statement of Fundamental and Essential Truths, though it was later removed.[47]

Despite those objections during the interwar years, by the 1940s articles in support of going to war were appearing regularly in *PT*. PAOC historian Thomas Miller observed that as the war progressed, the publication began to regularly "feature articles of special interest to military men and women," and examples of that kind of writing abound.[48] In September 1941, Rev. D.N. Buntain, the PAOC general superintendent from 1937 to 1944, wrote an article entitled "If I Were Caught in the Draft." Buntain, who was ordained as a Methodist minister in 1918 and had become a Pentecostal in 1925,[49] addressed the tricky question of what stance Pentecostals should take on conscription. While Buntain did acknowledge that some Pentecostals were conscientious objectors, his main argument was that military service would present Pentecostals with a unique opportunity for making converts among their comrades. Subtitled "Words of Encouragement to Our Young Men Who Are Answering the Call to the Army," Buntain pointed to a model recruit who was serving as a petty officer in the Royal Canadian Navy, saying that this young Pentecostal "sings, testifies, and prays before and with the men with a holy joy and finds many opportunities to lift up Christ where there is no one else to do so."[50] Buntain told readers that "if I were caught in the draft, I would put myself afresh into the hands of God and say, 'Lord, thy will be done. Keep me true, that in and through the experiences that lie ahead, I may like Joseph and Daniel rise to a place of useful service in thy kingdom.'"[51]

Not all Pentecostal leaders were convinced that such willing compliance was the best course of action. While Purdie was principal of the Western Bible College in Winnipeg, he went to great lengths to help his students avoid serving when they were called up to enlist. Yet by his own admission, Purdie clearly was not a pacifist. A loyal supporter of the British Empire, Purdie declared in 1944, "This College and the members of the Faculty are 100% behind the Allied Cause to fight the demon of Hitlerism."[52] As mandatory enlistment came into force, having established that he and his college were firmly behind the war effort, Purdie argued that given the high calling on the lives of theological students to serve the country as clergy, all Bible college students (not just Pentecostals) should be exempt from war service.

Some students wrote directly to Purdie asking for his advice about how they should respond to the call for military service. One such student from small-town Manitoba wrote to say that he had complied with the required medical examination and he had assumed that given a previous injury, he would not have to serve. Yet it turned out that he was called up in the summer of 1942, and he wrote to ask Purdie whether or not he should also tell the authorities that he was a student at the Bible college because he wondered if that would help his case or "would it be best to leave all as it is?"[53] Principal Purdie did write to authorities, arguing that the student's theological training and future clergy status was a higher priority than his recruitment.[54] Another case involved a young farmer from northwestern Ontario who wrote to Purdie in the summer of 1942 to explain that when he appeared before the army officials in Port Arthur, Ontario, he had been given a choice to declare himself a conscientious objector or be "'frozen' to the farm for eight months of each year." As he explained to Purdie, "I chose the farm."[55] Purdie responded to assure the student that he had made a wise choice because this would still allow him to spend his free months off the farm at school continuing his training for the ministry.[56] The examples above were quite standard grounds for exemption (medical limitations, clergy status, and essential farm work), but in other cases Purdie tried to push the authorities further by making a case that Pentecostals should no longer be regarded as a group on the margins of Canadian society but rather as loyal Canadians who, like other Christians, were central to the public life of the country.

When Purdie sought exemptions from war service for his students, he challenged the liberal order of Canadian society by making an argument about a fundamental Canadian value: inclusiveness. Suggesting that Pentecostals deserved the same considerations that were given to other Christian churches who could either claim exemption for their seminarians and clergy or else have them posted to serve as military chaplains, Purdie implied that the Canadian state was not being fair to Pentecostals. This marked one of the earliest instances of PAOC engagement with the Canadian state making claims about Pentecostals as citizens with rights that needed to be respected and voices that needed to be heard. Yet while Purdie made this case on behalf of a handful of his Bible college students, Pentecostal men and women enlisted to serve their country in the war effort. Still others resisted the call to service, claiming that their pacifist convictions required them to obey their consciences and refuse to serve.

In the end, one of Purdie's students who did serve in the armed forces did so only for a few months because Purdie arranged for him to receive an early ordination and placement as co-pastor in a local church near the Bible college. Although the student had not completed his college training, he was granted a release from service under a clergy exemption.[57] For Purdie and the Pentecostals associated with

Western Bible College, efforts to resist military service were a complex mix of pragmatism and apocalyptic convictions, together with self-preservation and social justice. Separating the moral or theological reasons from the material is not always straightforward. Purdie wanted his students exempted from serving because he wanted to "save them for the church," and he was also motivated by an eschatological urgency to spread the gospel message before the imminent return of Christ took place. When he realized that he could not successfully prevent the conscription of his students, Purdie lobbied instead for them to serve as military chaplains, even though it was clear that their numbers did not warrant such appointments under the established system. In spite of their small numbers, Purdie invoked the rhetoric of social justice by arguing that failing to treat Pentecostals the same way that the older mainline churches were treated amounted to discrimination. Purdie's shifting arguments demonstrate that it is impossible to arrive at a simple answer to the question of Pentecostals' position on war resistance in Canada.

TESTING PAOC AUTHORITY – THE LATTER RAIN CRISIS

In his sympathetic history of the PAOC, Thomas Miller laid out the tremendous progress and growth that the organization had enjoyed, but when he introduced the Latter Rain controversy he sounded a somber note: "The history of the PAOC, however, was not one of trouble-free development and continuous growth." Miller continued, "In the late-40s and early-50s, the Fellowship faced a doctrinal threat so serious that its very existence was in question. That threat consisted of the so-called 'New Order of the Latter Rain.' The theological controversy had its origins [at a PAOC Bible school] in Saskatchewan but spread its influence over much of North America."[58] In keeping with its organizational development, in 1931 the PAOC's General Executive had created the National Committee of Bible Schools. The rationale for that committee was that it would help with "avoiding the perils" associated with seeing the next generation of Pentecostal leaders being "trained by haphazard methods." According to Purdie, "the goal of the committee was not to force all schools into the same mold. However, it was realized that a unity of policy and teaching in all Canadian Pentecostal Bible schools was essential."[59] That unity was severely tested with the Latter Rain controversy.

In 1947, when General Superintendent C.B. Smith first spoke out about the problem that was unfolding around the Bethel Bible Institute, the PAOC Bible college in Saskatchewan, he was clear that unethical behaviour and mishandling of resources were woven into the problem. As the crisis unfolded during 1949, it became clear that this was a complex battle over several things, including faulty scriptural interpretation, the use and abuse of spiritual gifts, and "immature leadership" that was out of step with the maturity and sound judgment offered by the steady hand of the PAOC. These accusations and defences grew to become personal and divisive, challenging the authority of the General Executive and all of the structures that had been put in place over two decades of administration. It was also about the real and potential loss of organizational resources as the Latter Rain represented a challenge to the authority of the PAOC.

General Superintendent C.B. Smith spoke very forthrightly about the situation in a *PT* article entitled "An Explanation Concerning Bethel Bible Institute," although he prefaced it by saying that he had hesitated to go public with the details at all: "It was not our desire to give any publicity to recent difficulties encountered in the leadership of this Institution, but due to enquiries by interested parties, an explanation of recent developments seems to be imperative."[60]

The Bethel Bible Institute, in Saskatoon, Saskatchewan, opened in 1935 in Star City, thanks to the leadership and investments of the Rev. George R. Hawtin and the Rev. P.G. Hunt. Smith acknowledged both men in his remarks, stating that they had been "instrumental in the establishment and development of this school." However, by the fall of 1947, he gave the update to *PT* readers that "both have withdrawn from The Pentecostal Assemblies of Canada and established another Bible School at North Battleford, Sask." More to the point, he reported, "Their actions have caused us sorrow," not just for their actions and decisions but "because of the division it has brought among members of our Fellowship."

Outlining the series of disagreements that had led to the departure, Smith recounted that the PAOC had been eager to establish "a good school in Western Canada," but the vision of what form that would take led to significant differences and conflicts. The supporters of this idea had envisioned a school with "suitable buildings and equipment, and one which would be staffed with qualified teachers." Disappointingly, "Brother Hawtin opened Bethel Bible Institute in defiance of their wishes." However, rather than block the school's opening, the PAOC decided to proceed with recognizing the institution as one of their growing network of Bible school facilities. As part of that negotiation, real estate transactions involved Hawtin and Hunt turning the property over to the PAOC, and Smith revealed in his statement that the deal involved a series of payments to be made by the PAOC to Hawtin and Hunt over a ten-year period. However, the usual terms of operation for a PAOC school were not established, and when the two founders failed to seek and submit to the authority of the PAOC district leaders, the trouble began. Smith explained that Hawtin and Hunt recruited PAOC students but were not willing to follow PAOC procedures, contending that "this School drew the students from the churches affiliated with the Pentecostal Assemblies of Canada, and was financed through the co-operation of these churches yet no elected representative of the District had any real voice in the management of the School for several years." Although the appropriate committees were established to oversee both the "management of the school and its matters of finance, policy and expansion" and "the more routine business of the School," it seems that these committees never really became operational, and difficulties arose when Hawtin and Hunt continued to act outside of the established structures of committees and the denominational bodies. As Smith explained, no one wished to minimize the important role that the two had played in establishing the school, but there was objection to the fact that they refused to comply with existing lines of authority. Smith noted, "there has been a desire on the part of the District Executive as well as the National Bible School Committee to have the standard conform to that which was decided upon by the Pentecostal Assemblies of Canada." What is of interest is the PAOC's appeal to organizational authority and not to the charismatic authority that was associated with the early movement and now the basis of disagreement with Hawtin and Hunt.

The situation escalated when Hawtin and Hunt proceeded with their plans for expanded facilities at Bethel, including a five-bedroom house for the school's principal and another structure, a six-storey building intended to serve as a residential high school facility. The objection from the PAOC was not only that these grandiose plans were proceeding very quickly but that the existing projects were never properly finished. For example, "the roof of the school building had never been finished and it leaked; no trim had been put on the windows and water ran down the inside and spoiled what plastering had been done under the windows. Only sub floors had been laid in much of the building. Radiators leaked, and the whole place needed paint. The outside wall was in need of stucco." That level of detail about the shortfalls of the property belied the fact that General Superintendent Smith had married into a Winnipeg family of real estate businessmen, the Argues.

Smith went on to describe how Hawtin and Hunt had colluded to avoid coming under the authority of the district executives and that as they withdrew from the PAOC by offering their resignations, they aired the whole matter before students and they took $6,000 from the school funds because that was the amount owing to them from the PAOC. Adding that Hawtin was not really highly educated enough to run a school, Smith claimed that "I do not wish to touch upon other things which might appear as mud-slinging." However, he did add that "stories are circulated to the effect that these brethren were so spiritual the Executive became jealous and other fabrications too ridiculous to relate." Then, as though he could not resist, Smith also revealed that Hawtin and Hunt had "referred to the General Executive as 'big shots' who made certain decisions, but boldly stated their opposition in the presence of students." In a parting shot, Smith conceded, "No doubt there is still room for them to work in God's great vineyard. We would have preferred to have them labour in co-operation with us, but since they have chosen otherwise we do trust that they will extend the same courtesies to us that we are prepared to show them. We have no thought to interfering with their work and trust that they will treat us in the same manner."[61]

Of course, there is always more than one side to every story, and to Hawtin and Hunt's loyal students and followers, the PAOC executive members were overstepping their authority and, more seriously perhaps, quenching a move of the Spirit. Hawtin was convinced that he was operating in the gifts of the Spirit and that was the source of his authority. What was unfolding in Saskatchewan, however, had troubling tendencies, including the excessive use of authority by Hawtin and others who were self-declared leaders of the new movement as well as a direct challenge to the PAOC and its work. While they refused to submit to the PAOC leadership, ironically they demanded strict obedience from their own followers. The excesses they imposed included particular teachings about the ways in which gifts were imparted (at their own hand) and the forms that prophecies took (very detailed, personal messages, from the mouth of the prophet himself). Those strange modes of operation, the PAOC leadership argued, were not biblical, since gifts were imparted by God and not mediated through people. Moreover, the delivery of prophetic messages should not be by means of individuals called out of the audience with specific messages, including, at times, whom they should marry. That level of interference in personal matters was dangerous, the PAOC leadership argued, because it was autocratic and led to abuses. The way the leaders of Bethel Bible Institute operated in the gifts was outside of the orthodox and more restrained manifestations of the Spirit that had come to mark the organizational culture of the PAOC in the 1930s and 1940s. The controversy clearly illustrates the relationship between organizational culture, boundary-making, and organizational authority, with various theological arguments used to justify competing administrative orders.

Several Pentecostal authorities waded in with criticisms of Hawtin and his colleagues, including leaders from the Assemblies of God in the US, Donald Gee in the UK, and several of the PAOC's own leaders, including Bible college professors. Sometimes the criticisms were direct, and other times they were veiled as "teaching articles" published in *PT*.[62] What is clear from all of these publications is that the PAOC felt the need to reinforce its basic teachings and stance on the operation of spiritual gifts among the readership of *PT*. This matter was so widespread that it could not be left to be debated in classrooms and church boardrooms. The PAOC took the aggressive step of publishing continually on the issue. R.E. McAlister, though he had retired from the PAOC's national executive by this time, became a main spokesperson on the follies of the Latter Rain movement. He interrogated Hawtin's publications and critiqued them almost line by line. McAlister published a series of articles in *PT* that appeared through 1949–50 in a column entitled "Questions and Answers," refuting what he and the PAOC regarded as false teaching. Later these columns were collected into a book format.[63]

Of course, there was more going on among the Saskatchewan believers than a willful disobedience to PAOC authority. Those who followed Hawtin genuinely believed they were hearing directly from God through him. As historian Edith Blumhofer assesses it, these believers dreaded the idea of "missing God" if they failed to follow where the wind was blowing and the latter rain was falling.[64] Historian Joshua Ziefle builds on that scholarship, suggesting that the intent behind the Latter Rain movement was to "re-Pentecostalize Pentecostalism." However, what we cannot do is simply reduce the Latter Rain to theological differences about the meaning of Pentecostalism. The organizational challenge to the PAOC by the Latter Rain was also about a loss of capital, including people, congregations, a college, and money to support PAOC efforts. The leadership of the PAOC had been working hard to gain and maintain a reputation for being a well-run organization with sound business practices. As a result, they doubled down on the enthusiasm of rogue leadership who claimed special authority from the Spirit.

Smith was well aware that his critics were accusing the PAOC leadership of stifling the Spirit, and he did not back down, editorializing that "the divisive nature of this teaching is harmful. It is often given out as the revival of the last days, and those who do not accept it as such are branded as being unwilling to move forward with God." Moreover, he defended the reputation and judgment of himself and his colleagues at the national office, asserting that "The General Executive is composed of a group of matured workers. The editor knows of no member who is opposed to the manifestations of the Spirit, but is pleased to state that they are willing to accept only that which can be supported by God's Eternal Word."[65] With this statement, Smith defended the PAOC position on spiritual gifts and insisted that their judgments were mature and with an unwavering commitment to Scripture. By inference, Smith levelled implicit criticisms at the Latter Rain leaders, implying that they were immature and that they mishandled the Bible.

Divisions are never pleasant, and it becomes clear, even from reading one side of the story as presented in *PT*, that the controversy with the Latter Rain movement was multi-faceted. It was a dispute over leadership style and structures, property matters, and money, and it was a dispute about how the gifts of the Spirit operated among believers. The dissenters found the PAOC too hierarchical, with too little emphasis on missionary efforts and spiritual gifts. The building of a church with its rapid growth had caused unintended consequences, including questions about the organization's structure and whether or not there was room in it for those with differing beliefs and practices.[66] The boundaries marking who was in and who was out were quickly emerging, and there was no obvious way for the PAOC executive to change course, even with an appeal to the simplicity of the early days of the movement. It seemed inevitable that the rapid growth and development of the PAOC meant that those Pentecostals who challenged its authority could not, even with an appeal to early Pentecostalism, change its direction.

Sociologist Penny Edgell reminds us that religious group "identity is always inherently fluid and intersectional, with boundaries that are actively made and defended (or blurred and changed)" and that "the relative boundedness of religious identities can vary across and with contexts, and the boundary-making process is a locus for simultaneous inclusion and exclusion."[67] Boundary-making was the central issue in the case of the Latter Rain movement in Saskatchewan in the late 1940s because lines were drawn about who was acting in acceptable ways according to the PAOC leadership and who was not. At the same time, from the perspective of those on the other side of the controversy, including students and laity who were loyal to dynamic spiritual leaders like Hawtin and Hunt, there was an eagerness to participate in a new move of the Spirit. The emphasis on the part of denominational authorities was to provide oversight, ensure consistency across the country in their Bible schools, and provide the organizational structures to guide the growth and development of Canadian Pentecostalism. In short, they were making and reinforcing boundaries. The PAOC reinforced a cultural identity around the view that the expressions and experiences of the Spirit could be ordered and organized in respectable ways, based on sound organizational principles. On the other hand, those whose identity was tied to another expression of the Spirit wanted to pursue spiritual experiences and organizational patterns that reflected their own aspirations. When it came to living within the terms of the PAOC's organizational structure, regional figures were expected to submit to national authority figures. This was clearly a case of testing the boundaries of authority, with the PAOC defining and imposing normative subcultural definitions and practices around religious beliefs and experiences, including those of the Holy Spirit, for the intended purpose of establishing organizational cohesion.

4

Postwar Consolidation

INTRODUCTION

As World War II came to an end, Canadian society defied the postwar planners' dire predictions about economic downturn and entered one of the country's most prosperous periods ever. Optimism about the future manifested in the population explosion known as the baby boom.[1] Canadian postwar society prioritized the nuclear family, creating programs to support families and expanding its capacity to absorb the burgeoning population into the education system, from elementary through post-secondary levels, with resources including more bureaucratic structure, new buildings and facilities, and more teachers. The idealized nuclear family, including women as homemakers and men as breadwinners, was reinforced in popular culture, urban planning, and a seemingly insatiable housing market that gave rise to the suburbs.

The PAOC echoed this social trend with remarkable growth: in 1941, 57,742 Canadians identified as Pentecostal, and by 1951 that number was 95,131, with 62,600 naming their denominational affiliation as PAOC. By 1971, the number had mushroomed to 222,390 Canadian Pentecostals, and about 40 per cent (91,894) of them were PAOC members and affiliates. Canadian society had experienced a housing boom with the creation of suburbs, and PAOC church building projects echoed that larger trend. Some of Canadian society's most dominant postwar questions and ideals characterized the PAOC as well: What to do with the women who had made such heroic efforts on the home front during the war? How to encourage postwar men to thrive as family men, breadwinners, and homeowners? With marriage and birthrates rising, what kinds of programs and structures would meet the needs of children and youth?

WOMEN'S MINISTRIES

For the culture at large, the woman question was managed with an exaggerated emphasis on the so-called "return to normal" that emphasized separate gender roles whereby men would provide income as the breadwinners and women would nurture families as household managers. The PAOC mirrored this pattern as men occupied roles as preachers, lay leaders, and board members of churches, while women were channelled into more domestic roles with the creation in 1944 of a separate division known as the "Women's Missionary Council" (WMC), later shortened to WM for "Women's Ministries." The creation of a women's ministry department within the PAOC served to recognize the gifts of women, and yet it also confined them to culturally acceptable roles within a highly gendered church subculture. Created as a body to serve the overseas missions efforts, the PAOC's women's program bore deep resemblance to the women's auxiliaries that had typified mainline churchwomen's work in the nineteenth century. But in the postwar years, this emphasis on turning attention overseas was seen as thoroughly modern because it was in step with Canadian society inasmuch as it echoed secular bodies that originated in this same period with their spirit of internationalism, such as the United Nations, UNESCO, and UNICEF.

While the "world" was striving to bring pragmatic help to disadvantaged nations around the world, the PAOC was busy with its own parallel efforts.[2] PAOC mission work in this period focused on bringing practical aid to the mission field in the form of health care, education, and infrastructure. These were the very things that the fledgling Canadian social welfare system was concentrating upon both at home and in its international aid programs. In attempting to negotiate its way in the Canadian postwar world, the PAOC had taken two pages from Canadian society's playbook: get the women "back" into suitably domestic roles and provide opportunities to extend that domestic work by provisioning and praying for missionaries. It was an opportunity for Pentecostal households to contribute to international projects by sharing the wealth that was derived from postwar prosperity.

Ethel Bingeman was the national director of WMC from 1944 to 1956, followed by Gladys Lemmon, who served from 1956 to 1965, when Marion Parkinson became the third national director. The three women all had long and successful careers with the PAOC as they helped to train ministry personnel by serving as missionaries, Bible college professors, and mentors to the next generation of leaders and ministers. To understand why a division of women's ministries was created and what it served to accomplish in the PAOC, it is useful to analyze *The Pentecostal Testimony* (*PT*) and reflect on the language that was used to describe women's work in the church. Those reports, illustrating the implicit cultural understandings of gender roles that underpinned PAOC's programs for women, help to illustrate both the intended and unintended outcomes that arose from this new gender-specific ministry and its role in the organization.

The creation of a separate division of women's ministries rested on a particular rhetoric about gender construction that was in step with postwar Canadian culture but, ironically, was out of step with the gender-blind roots of the early Pentecostal movement. When Pentecostalism was launched almost four decades earlier, the emphasis was on spirit-empowered service for men and women, fulfilling the biblical prophecy about "sons and daughters prophesying." When WMC was launched at mid-century, the descriptions of women's work in the organization's magazine did not sound much like those early days, but it did sound very similar to the roles that the broader society was suggesting women should appropriately occupy in the postwar era. Unintentionally, by letting that secular ideology inform its own practices, the church pushed women to the sideline of ministry leadership and discouraged them from exercising roles that were deemed more appropriate for men. While the civil authorities strategized about how to ease the transition from wartime to a peacetime economy by devising ways to welcome returning service personnel to mainstream society, the PAOC had strategies of its own.

Photographic evidence from yearbooks demonstrates that while women had equalled or outnumbered men in training for ministry during the first two decades of Pentecostal Bible colleges, the picture was different after the war. Partly because of government programs providing tuition relief to veterans, male Bible college graduates outnumbered female graduates in larger numbers than ever as the organization made way for an increasing number of men to enter pastoral ministry and denominational administration roles after World War II. This development was closely in step with broader trends in Canadian society, and as government bureaucracy set about creating a variety of incentives, the central piece was the Veterans' Charter to make way for a peacetime society that was highly gendered according to structuralist thinking about "normal" gender roles. Jennifer Stephen has written at length about the measures taken and specifically the rhetoric that was used to convince women to leave the paid work force and subscribe instead to the ideals of the "good life," which rested on the pillars of glorified domesticity and male-headed households.[3]

When the PAOC created a separate women's division, just one year before the war ended, many highly gifted women in PAOC leadership turned their attention to work that would see them minister solely to women and no longer to mixed groups as they had been doing in their earlier careers as missionaries and Bible college professors. There was no shortage of gifted women who rose to prominence in the WMC organization at both the national and regional levels. While many women took up active ministry roles prior to the Second World War and were held up as the very fulfillment of Joel's prophecy about "sons and daughters" prophesying "in the last days," women's roles in the postwar years were a marked contrast. After the war, the PAOC was steeped in the same highly patriarchal model of gender relations that dominated the broader culture. Those postwar ideals glorified domesticity and reinforced separate spheres for women and men.

Three samples of the rhetoric about women found in the pages of *PT* in the postwar years illustrate the kind of messaging that was shaping postwar women's experience within the subculture of the PAOC. The first example is a 1948 restatement from the founding director of WMC, Ethel Bingeman,[4] about why a separate women's ministry was necessary. In October 1948, *PT* published highlights from the General Conference about the WMC. The report recounted that in 1944 a recommendation had been passed "that a women's department be set up in the Pentecostal Assemblies of Canada, to be known as the Home and Foreign Missions Women's Auxiliary"[5] and that it would have a variety of purposes, including to encourage prayer, encourage education among the youth, provide clothing and supplies for missionaries, prepare the "out-going supplies" for missionary outfits, and assist "in any co-operative work which may have the endorsation [*sic*] of the Movement [*sic*] from time to time."[6] That emphasis on prayer and material aid, together with educating young people about missions, was clear and enduring. Throughout the postwar years, the organization continued to call its members back to these purposes.

The rhetoric that followed that statement about why the WMC was created is surprising. Ethel Bingeman, a missionary to Liberia for eighteen years and the first national director of the women's organization, offered a further rationale for why the group had been created. Four years after the WMC was founded, she wrote that "all this had started many years before," and indeed, other reports pointed to very early work of this sort originating in Winnipeg in the home of Mrs A.H. Argue, who hosted gatherings of women to pray and sew for missionaries who were leaving the country for a variety of international locations. Bingeman herself had benefitted from Mrs Argue's practical help when she was leaving for the mission field in Liberia in 1915.

But Bingeman was not referring to her Winnipeg supporters when she made her 1948 report. When she stated that the work had begun "many years before," what she meant was that it had really all started "when God created Eve as an help-meet for Adam. Wherever man has a task to do, God has ordained a part for the woman as well. The New Testament contains many references to the woman's share in sending the Gospel into all the world."[7]

The complementarian thinking is surprising for several reasons. First, when Bingeman herself left for the foreign mission field in 1915, she did not go in the company of a husband, father, or male co-worker. She was single, a registered nurse, and her co-worker was another young woman, Laura Arnold. So Bingeman was clearly familiar with the model of women in frontline ministry as she herself had been for many years. She had professional nurses' training, and upon her return she worked for many years at the Western Bible College as a professor. It was only when she left that work and moved to Toronto that she took up the leadership of the newly formed women's division of PAOC. Bingeman was by experience and association well acquainted with women who did ministry work outside the role of a mere "helpmate" to a man.

The second reason why this description of women's ministries seems surprising coming from Bingeman is that her association in Winnipeg with the Argue family meant that she was also very familiar with women like Zelma and Beulah Argue, who had done important work as single women, and it was their mother, Mrs A.H. Argue, who set up home prayer meetings and sewing circles to prepare materials for women like Bingeman when they first ventured out on the mission field. While Bingeman was familiar with the work that women in PAOC churches did, it seems odd for her to invoke the language of "help-meet" rather than the prophetic fulfillment language of the Joel–Acts texts that mention sons and daughters prophesying together and exercising equal giftings of the Spirit. Indeed, it was only when Bingeman herself "retired" from her work as a nurse, a missionary, and then a professor that she took up a more traditional "maternal" role as the matron of the Bethel Missionary Rest Home in Toronto. In that role, while she was still single, she acted as a house mother and host – the closest she would come to the role of homemaker until she married later in life and returned to a mission field as a bride, although by then she was elderly.

To find in the PAOC's own publication this complementarian rhetoric about women as "help-mates" to the men whom God had given work to do is a surprising departure from earlier Pentecostal thought about women and men as equal partners, exercising spiritual gifts that were not gender-specific. Yet in 1948 Canada, that kind of "separate spheres" ideology was very common in the culture at large. Here, it seems that PAOC women were encouraged to embrace the socially constructed gender roles that created a hierarchy in which men had work to do for God and women alongside them to assist.

Another example illustrates the postwar mindset that PAOC women were encouraged to adopt as they did their unpaid work at home and in the church. This example, taken from an issue of the magazine published twelve years later, was clear that women should be careful to check their motives for serving. By the 1960s, WMC groups had firmly fixed their attention on reaching the girls and young women in their own families and congregations with groups known as "Missionary Action Girls."[8] According to an article entitled "Why a Girl's Work?" published in the summer of 1960, Pentecostal women were waging a cosmic battle with the devil who was stealing the hearts, minds, and souls of their daughters. The statement of purpose by this time was "A WMC group in every church. Every woman a member. A Girls work in every church. Every girl a member."[9] In the June 1960 issue, the story is recounted of a little girl named "Jean" who observed that in running the household, her mother paid people who provided services to the family, such as delivery people and maintenance providers. In that spirit, the "little girl [who] did a great deal for her mother" resolved that she too should be paid. "She began to notice that others got paid for what they did for her – they sent in their bills. She thought she would do the same." And so she presented her mother with a bill for her childhood chores: washing dishes, making her bed, and practising piano: "At tea time [the mother] placed the bill on Jean's plate and on it $1.00. Then beside it was placed another bill. Jean owes Mother: For 10 years of a happy home .00; For food and clothing .00; For nursing through sickness .00; For just being good to her .00; Total .00. You can imagine how Jean felt when she read that."[10] Jean was expected to feel shame for asking to be rewarded for the simple domestic tasks that small girls were being socialized to take up in the postwar years when a re-emphasis on glorifying domesticity meant that they should dream of the day when they too would be homemakers. Yet the structuralist emphasis on separate spheres dictated that unpaid work was the "normal" gender role for girls and women. The lesson here for Jean was that she should learn to accept and even celebrate that future.

The article ends with this moral to the story: "What if God rendered a bill to us? But He never does. All He asks is that with heart, mind, soul, and strength we just LOVE HIM." There is much that could be said to unpack the many layers of this story. Most notable is that young girls were socialized to devalue their own work. Although delivery men and service providers rendered bills and collected cash from households, the work of women and girls was to remain outside that cash economy. Girls were taught to think of their unpaid work as "expressions of love." It would be difficult to imagine telling the milkman, the letter carrier, or district superintendents and lead pastors in the PAOC that they should work "as an act of love" without pay.

One is left to wonder whether Jean was still in the church or in an unpaid role as housewife ten, fifteen, or twenty years later. Was she, during the turbulent years of the second-wave women's movement, an unpaid homemaker like her mother? If Jean was a homemaker in the 1970s, she was likely also supplementing the household income with paid work outside the home. Jean would have become a young adult during the late 1960s and early 1970s when feminist initiatives such as "the double day" and "wages for housework" began to draw attention to the inequities associated with women's unpaid domestic work. If Jean grew up and as a thirty-year-old active in the WM attended the general conferences of the PAOC in the early and mid-1980s, she might have wondered why women pastors were still the subject of debate about waged work, gendered titles, and hierarchies of ministry credentials. Indeed, if she continued to be involved with her parents' denomination, in 2019 Jean would be a PAOC woman of approximately seventy years of age. Would she feel differently about how and why women's work is or should be valued in the twenty-first century? But in the 1960s, Jean was being taught to do her unpaid work in the home and the church without any thought of economic reward or consequence and that women do their work (and their ministry) not for money but for love.

One more example from *PT* illustrates how women were taught to step to the sidelines in the life of the church and shun visible leadership roles. This is clearly illustrated in an April 1965 article entitled "Step up to the Wall!" written by Ella Parmenter, who had addressed the "Ladies meeting" at the PAOC General Conference in Montreal in 1964, hoping to call women back to prayer, one of the original goals of the WMC.[11] Yet the message that was given to women was troubling because it assumed that even if a woman had spiritual gifts of leadership, wisdom, or discernment, she was not to exercise those gifts in a way that would challenge male authority figures in the church. The rationale for that instruction, based on an Old Testament story about a "wise woman," employs a hermeneutic that is clearly filtered through a postwar complementarian lens of appropriate gender roles.

Parmenter based her remarks on a text from II Samuel in which a "wise woman" perceived a way to de-escalate a military threat. The woman, who is never named, approached the male leaders, encouraging them to negotiate a solution to the impending attack on her fortified city. Her solution was that she would reason with the men in charge, meet the terms of their invaders' demands (gruesomely, in this case that meant presenting the head of the wanted man to the attackers by throwing the head over the wall), and thus prevent the breach of the fortified wall. In effect, the woman's wise counsel was to pay the lesser price and save the city. Her idea, to find compromise rather than insist on a "winner take all" military contest, actually saved the day. This story, which is not widely known or often preached, is the kind of narrative that makes a feminist heart leap. The moral of the story seems obvious: listen to wise women and minimize the damage.

Wise women make good strategists. But this is not the lesson that Parmenter communicated to PAOC women in 1964. Rather than use a plain text reading or even a literal interpretation of the text, Parmenter used the text to reinforce the PAOC postwar cultural norm of male leadership and superiority. At first, the speaker seemed to empower women when she exhorted her listeners, "I am persuaded that the women of the Pentecostal Assemblies of Canada can spearhead a great move for God in our midst, if we will dare, as this woman did, to take the initiative – put our concern into *action*, [italics in original] – and get an audience." That is what the wise woman in II Samuel did when she asked for and was granted an audience with the male decision-makers. However, that is not what the speaker instructed PAOC women to do. Instead, she recommended a covert strategy of female influence that was outside the all-male realm of strategy, leadership, or decision-making.

Parmenter continued, "get an audience, not with a great general, but with our Great Commander – Jesus Christ! Let us *step up to the wall*, pour out genuine concern for others before the One in Command, and see things happen for God!" This is a very intriguing hermeneutical maneuver because rather than ask women to literally follow the example of the wise woman and risk challenging the logic of male leadership strategies, she softened the moral of the story by calling PAOC women to a role as silent intercessors. Parmenter suggested that postwar PAOC women should not literally confront the men. Rather, she suggested that women should "go over the heads" of male leadership and act, not like an adult partner in resolving situations but rather like a schoolgirl who "tattles" to a higher authority when her brother takes an action with which she does not agree.

That covert action is not at all what the wise and strategic woman in II Samuel did; Parmenter suggested that for PAOC women, the more effective way would be to "step away" from leadership and decision-making and instead retreat to their prayer closets. The rhetoric here is that PAOC women were taught to read scripture by making the text align with the patriarchy of Canadian society rather than letting the text suggest that women might actually have better ideas about how to strategize or lead an organization.

In the postwar years, Canadian women were unlikely to assume leadership roles in the PAOC beyond Women's Ministries. Instead, they were taught and socialized into the church's subculture to adopt a complementarian view about how they could best "support" and play the role of "help mate" to the men. That assumption was the result of postwar instructions to women, such as those published in the pages of *PT* in the 1940s through the 1960s. The PAOC publication emphasized three things in the postwar years:

1 Women should embrace their roles as ancillary support workers to the more important leadership roles played by men.

2 Women should do their unpaid work in the home and the church motivated by love, not money.
3 Women should expect to participate in the organization covertly from their private prayer closets, not directly as strategists who challenge, counsel, or give advice to men.

It seems somewhat ironic, then, that the PAOC lamented in the 1980s that they could not find enough women who seemed to be of the same calibre as the early female leaders, evangelists, and preachers who had played such important roles in the movement's founding years. In an article in *PT*, it implored the "Next Generation of Women in Ministry [to] Please Stand Up!"[12] Considering the ways that the PAOC's own publications taught Pentecostal women about appropriate ways to exercise their roles and callings in the postwar era, it is hardly surprising that a few years later there was a shortage of women preachers, evangelists, and church planters.

MEN'S FELLOWSHIP

While the popularity and success of the WMC in the postwar years was undeniable for the sociability it produced among churchwomen and the impressive levels of support provided to missionary families, it caused concern among male leaders. There was a fear that the work of women in local congregations was displacing men in terms of providing local leadership and corporate efforts to support missionary efforts. As one denominational leader explained, "The splendid work done by the WOMEN'S MISSIONARY COUNCIL for many years have finally literally shamed the men to form a companion organization of men."[13] The solution was not to curb the efforts of women or for men and women to join forces in one group. Instead, the PAOC leadership proposed that laymen in their local churches would best be served by an all-male organization of their own, not modelled on what the women had accomplished but on civic service clubs. In step with postwar ideals about masculinity, the PAOC took a page from the playbook of secular men's organizations. One national leader in the PAOC observed that

> Service clubs like Rotary, Kiwanis, Kinsmen, Elks, etc., are thriving because they seem to satisfy a desire in the hearts of men. The

> organizations do not merely exist for the purpose of friendship and association, but they sponsor projects and enterprises to give an outlet for the energies, means, and abilities of their members. Their organizations are humanitarian and noble for the most part, but they are not geared to harness the potentialities in men for the glory of God and the advancement of His kingdom. This is the purpose of our Men's Fellowship organization.[14]

The answer was to create yet another division of church programming: men's ministry, a group where men could be men. They could bring their individual and collective talents to the work of the church's mission. Specifically, men could build and maintain church facilities as they brought their transferrable business skills to the work of the church. And, like other men's service clubs, the PAOC's Men's Fellowship required membership dues for participants so that there would be a budget to work with, and it was made clear that this amount should be over and above each man's regular offerings to the church.[15] In the realm of missions, men were encouraged to establish relationships with men on the mission field to mimic what women were doing for female missionaries: pray for them, befriend them, correspond with them, and provide them with what they needed to do their work. While women would tend to the missionaries' domestic needs with parcels of food and clothing, birthday greetings for children, and Christmas gifts to replicate the holiday back home, men were encouraged to discover and provide equipment that would ease the work of missionary men, especially in the realm of technology and transportation devices. In an article entitled "Keeping up with the Ladies," Harold Underhill offered the example of a men's group at Calvary Temple in Winnipeg to explain why a men's ministry group was needed, writing, "While our ladies have done a wonderful job in seeking to supply the needs of the missionaries and their families, yet there are certain articles which we men require at times which are difficult for the ladies to choose. For example, we may need a new universal joint for our jeep or a new condenser for our Public Address System or one of the other numerous gadgets which we use in our work."[16] Even as the PAOC supported overseas personnel, the gendered assumptions about men's particular aptitude for sourcing automotive parts and broadcasting systems further reinforced the gender divide. Both men and women were encouraged to pray, but practical help was highly gendered because women's expertise was tied to caring for families while men were assumed to be experts in mechanics and technology.

Men's groups were formally launched as a national effort in 1955,[17] and a notice published in *PT* explained that the General Executive had appointed the Rev. James Montgomery to lead the "National Department of Men's Fellowship" and coordinate the groups that were forming across the country. The notice encouraged readers to correspond with the PAOC head office in Toronto, declaring "Brother Montgomery will be very pleased to hear from you."[18] An inventory of men's groups compiled in the summer of 1960 listed fifty-four active Men's Fellowship groups, with representation from every region of the country. Within eight years of the national office commitment to coordinate the groups, the PAOC launched a separate publication for men in the clubs entitled *Real Living.*[19] The magazine typically featured biographies and testimonies of successful Pentecostal professionals and businessmen, urging members to deepen their spiritual lives and form relationships with their male co-workers for the purpose of personal evangelism. As the denominational magazine explained, "The official emblem for Men's Fellowship consists of the monogrammed letters 'MF' on a gold fishhook. With that emblem on our lapel, we tell all we meet that we are fishers of men. Some of us may draw in a net full of fish at times, but for the most part we are users of the fishhook. We may not minister from pulpits and influence large congregations, but we are soul winners. Our Lord has called us to be His fishermen and we will obey His summons."[20]

With this personal evangelism mandate, Pentecostal men's groups were clearly different from their secular counterparts, and yet the idea of networking with professional and business contacts was a common tactic in secular organizations as well. And this personal evangelism emphasis served to set Pentecostal men apart from women because it was assumed that women worked within their own homes, with their children, and did not have the same "fishing" opportunities as their husbands, whose worlds revolved around their paid work outside the home. Pentecostal women did not sport a similar lapel pin to tell the world they were evangelists. In true postwar fashion, Pentecostal men's and women's groups were based on shared assumptions about binary gender roles: men were breadwinners with outside connections because of their workplaces; women, by contrast, were assumed to be homemakers and mothers who nurtured the life of the family and the church.

CHILDREN AND YOUTH

At the same time that roles for women and men were clearly delineated in the subculture of the PAOC with the creation of women's and men's groups, the postwar focus on nuclear families meant that children and youth also were central to the church's programming. In step with the larger Canadian culture, the baby boom caused attention to turn toward catering to children, youth, and families, and while the Canadian state was busy creating a full-fledged social welfare system to cater to baby boomers' every need, the PAOC was doing the same thing in its church programs. Indeed, in the prosperous years of the postwar era, PAOC building projects echoed the housing boom that led to the spread of suburbs. New Pentecostal church buildings were built, and existing ones were renovated to serve families at every stage. Larger PAOC congregations built multi-purpose meeting spaces and gymnasiums, commonly called "fellowship halls." Sunday Schools, midweek children's programs, youth groups, and family "fellowship" nights expanded exponentially in the postwar years, mirroring the culture's attention to child-centred education and its concerns over curbing the (perceived) rising rates of juvenile delinquency. The PAOC organized such a complete menu of programming for its constituents that it became possible for committed members to operate entirely and exclusively within their own subculture.

The PAOC subculture was designed in no small part to shield their children and youth from the larger culture and create a comparable experience for them that represented a separation from the world and a commitment to the organization. Ironically, while mainline churches like the United Church of Canada sought to update their curriculum in the mid-1960s, the PAOC attempted to distinguish itself from liberal churches, with an emphasis on Christian "fundamentals" but doing so with programs that reflected the cultural views of gender and family. PAOC programs expanded in number but contracted in scope as they became more focused on serving their own growing church families. This was the height of the so-called "attractional" model of evangelism whereby the strategy was to draw people into the church with an "if you build it, they will come" approach rather than an outward focus on social justice or attempts to serve the marginalized in Canadian society.

The PAOC, like other evangelical denominations, concentrated its efforts on a proliferation of programs for children and youth from

1945 to 1970. For a picture of how extensive this programming was, it is useful once again to turn to the PAOC's monthly publication, *PT*, and collections at the PAOC national archives in Mississauga. Those sources make clear that programming initiatives for Pentecostal children were fuelled by fear of children being influenced by the world around them and premised on the need to withdraw from the surrounding culture in order to retain the next generation in the church. That is how the infrastructure the PAOC established supported growth: through retaining children and youth in a faith-nurturing program that was distinct from the broader culture but also in line with it.

The leader behind the PAOC's postwar programming for children and youth was James Montgomery (1903–1989), who rose from the ranks of the PAOC to join the National Executive of the PAOC in 1946. Montgomery played a crucial role for the next twenty-five years, giving direction and oversight to the development and management of programs for children, youth, women, and men during the critical postwar period at the height of the baby boom years. Montgomery retired in 1968 from his role as coordinator of Christian Education initiatives with the PAOC, briefly returning from retirement in 1972 to fill the role of national secretary-treasurer on the PAOC National Executive because of the untimely death of C.H. Stiller. Montgomery was committed to the role of the PAOC in providing an alternative to what he believed was the growing secularity of Canadian society. In 1966, he reiterated that conviction stating, "The greatest revival now in progress is that of pagan secularism. Though advancing as silently as death, its depths and influence are penetrating even our own church life and are shifting the moral foundations of our entire country. This has cut many from their spiritual moorings and caused them to suffer the attacks of unfettered human passions."[21] More than just the pessimism of a discouraged man ready for retirement, that sentiment about how dangerous Canadian society was for church families was widely shared in Pentecostal circles – and other evangelical circles – at the time. Indeed, much of the PAOC's postwar Christian Education programming was premised on the assumption that "Canada is not the cozy cot of a country it was early in the century," and while "the natural romanticism of childhood must be recognized," the PAOC's national leaders noted that Pentecostal children needed to be "carefully prepared for the bold reality of a desperately real and changing world."[22]

Montgomery was an Irish immigrant who arrived in "the cozy cot" of Canada in the 1920s after having experienced a very dramatic conversion in his youth and a traumatic estrangement from his family because of that Pentecostal experience. He was born in 1903 into the household of a successful businessman, and his testimony recounted that he "did not grow up in a Christian home" and that he "never heard [his] parents pray." As a youngster, Montgomery was an enthusiastic Sunday School scholar whose parents, although they never accompanied him to church, endorsed his attendance. Indeed, a member of the extended family saw young James's interest in religion and set aside money for him to be educated at Trinity College in Dublin with a view to becoming an Anglican priest. However, that plan for higher education never came to pass because James's religious experience took a Pentecostal twist.

Montgomery recounted that when he was a teenager, he and his peers at the Anglican church he attended had gone through a string of different Sunday School teachers who each left defeated because of their inability to control a group of rowdy boys. But when a man who had recently experienced the baptism of the Holy Spirit took over the class, Montgomery was intrigued, and shortly afterwards that teacher helped young James to pray through and receive the baptism of the Holy Spirit. When that Pentecostal experience was confirmed a few weeks later through the endorsement of the Welsh evangelist George Jeffreys, who is credited with founding the Elim Pentecostal Church in the UK, Montgomery's future was cast. Embarrassed by their son's newfound spiritual experiences and claiming it was bad for his father's reputation in the local business community, James Montgomery's parents gave him an ultimatum: either tone down his religious expression or leave their home. At the age of fifteen, James took his stand and found himself out on the street. That dramatic development was deeply formative, and given his personal experience, Montgomery remained committed to working with youth and children for the rest of his life.[23]

His own dramatic experience of baptism in the Holy Spirit was followed by an immediate acceptance into the ministry world of itinerant preaching and evangelism. A few years later, Montgomery sensed that God was telling him to emigrate from Ireland, and he found himself in Montreal where he quickly bonded with a group of like-minded believers from the Drummond Street mission. Soon after, Montgomery married the Irish woman who had been his partner in ministry back home. With his bride, Mabel Kelly Montgomery, by his side, James went into full-time ministry with the PAOC, serving as pastor in several different communities in Ontario, including Kitchener where he worked as assistant pastor with "Brother Chambers" from 1923 to 1925. From there, Montgomery worked in the Maritimes (where he also served as a district superintendent) before returning to Ontario, where he was recruited to the National Executive of the PAOC in 1946.[24]

In addition to having a Pentecostal experience and originating from the UK, Montgomery is noteworthy because his own unhappy youthful home life meant that he had an aversion to mainline churches. Indeed, he adamantly reinforced the notion that traditional state churches were not really "Christian" at all. And, for the purpose of tracing the development of Canadian Pentecostal work among children and youth, it is deeply significant that Montgomery's personal Pentecost occurred during his youth. Unlike many of the other names associated with early PAOC testimonies such as Chambers, McAlister, and Hebden, Montgomery was not an adult when he came into Pentecost. Because of his own testimony, Montgomery was unshakeably committed to the idea that children and youth were a vital part of the PAOC, and that personal experience framed his term in office, which corresponded with the baby boom, when Canadians were turning their attention toward catering to children, youth, and families. While the neighbours' children attended Scouts or Guides as a midweek activity, Pentecostal youngsters participated in parallel groups that Montgomery's department created and oversaw: "Christ's Ambassadors" for teenagers and young adult members and "Pentecostal Crusaders" for children.

The number of Crusader groups and Sunday Schools grew continuously during the years of Montgomery's leadership (see table 4.1).[25] When the Crusader program first launched in 1954, it got off to a slow start so that by 1956 there were only sixteen groups in 626 PAOC churches where it competed with Sunday Schools already in operation. Yet by the time of Montgomery's retirement in 1968, there were 320 Pentecostal Crusader groups organized across the country, representing half (52 per cent) of all the PAOC churches across Canada that operated Sunday Schools. As Montgomery took his retirement, he must have found it very satisfying to know that 10,000 children and youth were enrolled in the program he had created.

Still, even at its height, the number of Crusaders represented only one out of every eight children who were in Sunday School. And two years later, in 1970, Montgomery's successor reported that "the [Crusader] Units report that 70 per cent of all previous members are

Table 4.1
PAOC Sunday Schools and Crusader Groups, 1956–1970

Year	*Churches*	*PAOC Sunday Schools*			*Crusader Groups*	
		Number	*Enrolment*	*Attendance*	*Units*	*Members*
1956	635	626	63,437	50,020	16	N/A
1958	650	656	65,353	50,875	41	550
1960	664	650	75,288	68,178	85	1,800
1962	670	570	60,000	46,225	111	2,000
1964	685	562	62,000	48,000	149	3,200
1966	688	570	68,978	N/A	187	5,200
1968	745	616	70,262	N/A	270	5,500
1970	743	614	81,600	N/A	320	10,000

Source: Derived from PAOC Archives, PAOC General Conference Reports, 1956–70.

still serving the Lord." Yet with a 30 per cent attrition rate, those numbers do not seem particularly encouraging. Still, the new executive director of Christian Education put a positive spin on the trend, insisting that "This indicates the solid spiritual foundation which Crusading builds in the lives of its children and youth."[26]

Clearly, retaining youth in the church and grounding them in the Pentecostal faith was Montgomery's motivation for creating the Pentecostal Crusader groups. He often reiterated the maxim that "It is better to build a boy than mend a man!" and "How much wiser to grow a girl than years afterward to try to retake the citadel of a woman's soul for God."[27] In a report on the programs under Montgomery's department, the distinction between Pentecostal youth and those caught up in the 1960s culture of protest was described this way: "Not all modern young people are involved in rebellion, delinquency, rioting, demonstrating and drug trafficking. Some 18,000 young people in Canada feel responsible to God and to the laws of their country. These are Pentecostal Christ's Ambassadors."[28] This was intended to reassure PAOC members that not all Canadian youth were hopelessly caught up in the spirit of the age. And yet the attrition rate of Pentecostal youth leaving the faith and fears about youth, especially young men, "sowing their wild oats" was woven throughout *PT*, with parents forewarned that it was quite likely that they would have teenagers in their households during the "turbulent years" who challenged parental authority and questioned family rules around church life. In Montgomery's own writing and correspondence as he developed the

Crusader program through the late 1940s and into the 1950s, this falling away of young people was his main concern. As he expressed it, "The objective of Crusaders is not alone to save the souls of our youth. If that were the case, Crusaders would not be justified. We already have Sunday Schools and Christ's Ambassadors [programs] which cover the field well. The objective of Crusaders is to save lives, whole lives, with their complete span of years for the Master."[29]

The programming, expressed in language that sounds awkward to our twenty-first century Canadian ears, was deliberate. Montgomery wanted to invoke a militaristic tone, and he wanted to draw the lines between "right" and "wrong." Montgomery was convinced that children would enjoy the pageantry of Crusaders and that the symbolism of the "excursions" they performed to earn badges and the uniforms they wore to weekly meetings would be deeply meaningful. He explained to the readers of *PT*: "The term 'crusading' was chosen because it is indicative against the forces of wrong. Pentecostal Crusaders is based upon the theme of guarding against wrong and standing for the right. As far as possible the terminology has been chosen to interpret living for Christ as a Crusade."[30]

Indeed, a great deal of what Montgomery built into the program was to differentiate or distance it from other, parallel groups offered by secular agencies or mainline churches, especially Scouts. Sometime in the 1940s, Montgomery had first envisioned creating a program like the Crusaders, and from that point until it was officially endorsed at the PAOC General Conference in 1954, Montgomery did a great deal of research and corresponded with other youth organizations, including church-based, parachurch, and secular groups.[31] What Montgomery hoped to capture with Crusaders (originally only offered to boys but eventually extended to include girls as well) was "to build a boy into a man by means of free time activities."[32] Convinced that too much free time led to problems of delinquency, Montgomery built the Crusader program following advice he had received during his consultations, such as "The working plans of a youth group must be packed with Activity [emphasis in the original]. Keep the Saint busy for God, and he'll have no time to think about the flesh, the world, and the Devil."[33]

But Montgomery was convinced that mere busyness was not the answer because as he and his assistant, B.T. Parkinson, reasoned, even community-based groups could accomplish that with their attention on athletics and activities. "Traditional recreation and community activities offer a great service to youth who are drifting without anchor. But [church youth] need more … They need an undergirding of Christian principles and Pentecostal doctrine."[34] One of the ways that Crusaders would imbibe doctrine was tied to the uniforms they would wear. One particularly important element was the helmet. Crusaders were taught that historically, "The Crusader's Helmet was very important. He did not dare proceed into battle without it, for he would most certainly have been killed … We, today, also wear Helmets … Our helmets are made of cloth, and of course, do not protect us from the attack of Satan. But each time we put them on, they remind us of Paul's words, 'Be sure you have your minds protected against Satan with the Helmet of Salvation.'" It is indeed a creative hermeneutic that takes the scriptural metaphor of the "helmet of salvation" and concludes that Pentecostals should be worried about dangerous ideas or books that threatened their unprotected minds if they let their helmet of salvation slip. That is the application Pentecostal Crusaders were taught to make. Wear your helmets at these meetings, Crusaders were told, and when you venture out into the world, "Watch out for people and books which doubt the authority of the Bible; which teach evolution instead of creation; which say Jesus wasn't a real person and that He isn't coming back again; or which infer that salvation isn't necessary."[35]

Based on a survey that indicated some deep criticism of the fledgling program, Montgomery anticipated resistance from some skeptical pastors, parishioners, and parents when his department insisted that local churches should add one more program to their children's busy schedules. Starting a Crusader unit meant adopting the elaborate uniforms, studying the detailed manuals, and finding more volunteers and resources to commit to the venture. But Montgomery and B.T. Parkinson insisted that Pentecostals needed to adopt and adapt their own parallel to Scouting or Guiding programs. And they should be prepared to do so with an eye to the future: "Traditional manual techniques such as semaphore and knotting which are excellent for physical and mental coordination are still taught. While these are colorful and interesting, we remember we live in a world where these are being replaced. Youth today are interested in mechanization, radio communication, electricity and aviation."[36] That comment bears the marks of the pragmatism that informed so much of Pentecostalism's adoption of modernity yet bundled it with the traditional doctrine of holiness and sanctification. Pentecostal boys wanted to learn modern things.

But as Crusaders, they would learn those life skills and emerging technologies in a program bundling that new information with "Christian principles and Pentecostal doctrine." It bears repeating that Montgomery's personal testimony of conversion at age fifteen had been deeply formative, and clearly, he used that personal experience to imagine what boys and teenagers might enjoy as part of their church life.

But the context in which Montgomery formulated the Crusader program was about more than memories of his own youth. A two-part article that appeared in *PT* in 1961 entitled "Crusading in a Changing Canada: Canada Is Changing ... Swiftly Changing!" outlined why PAOC leaders felt they needed to redouble their efforts to reach and retain youth. Among the many challenges that postwar society posed, they listed the following: increasing rates of immigration, the declining age of marriage, the expanding reach of post-secondary education, the growing number of wives and mothers working outside the home, the increasing rates of juvenile delinquency, the damaging influence of media, especially crime comics and television, the alarming rate of rural depopulation and growth of suburbs, the dizzying speed of technological advances in the atomic age, and the rising preoccupation with materialism. In short, the postwar world was dangerous, and Pentecostals had to take steps to counter the threat. Armed with recent data from the 1961 census, Pentecostals were warned: "the teen group has increased 300% and ... will easily top another 100% more before we write 1970. The 15–19 year-olds have been increasing twice as fast as the total population."[37] The alarmist tone behind this message was a call to arms for Canadian Pentecostals: they must do something to capture the hearts and minds of the baby boom generation before it was permanently too late.

Obviously, PAOC leaders and parents could not stem the tide of all social, cultural, and demographic change, but they could work to protect their own children and youth from being swept up by the forces of the world with "Crusaders to the rescue!" As Parkinson explained in *PT*: "The idea of Crusading is a philosophy with a tremendous sense of righteousness and justice. It is pictured by a brave and gallant knight in shining armor and mounted on a spirited steed. But it is more than a myth. It has been born again, born in different surroundings, born in a fast-shifting panorama, but one that is not less hostile to the wrong."[38] To meet the challenges of the postwar years, the PAOC proposed a militant counterattack to the culture, expressed in this poem:

CRUSADERS
Bugles are calling
Banners are flying
Helmets and swords flash bright in the sun
Children and Youth are marching again
Gallant, their captains
Unfailing their cause
Brave is the song of hope that they sing
Christ the King is enlisting today.[39]

As an alternative to the "complicated and often wicked surroundings" in which Pentecostals found themselves from the 1940s to the 1960s, a Pentecostal's best offence was to retreat into their own subculture and attempt to shield and retain their youngsters from the threat of evil in the culture around them, even as they borrowed models from the broader culture.

During the postwar years, the PAOC mirrored Canadian culture in many ways, with its emphasis on the nuclear family as the cornerstone of society. Churches structured themselves in the same way, pouring resources into the creation and development of programs for women, men, and children. By placing the emphasis on distinct roles for the sexes, with men dominating leadership roles and women supporting those efforts, the PAOC was a mirror image of the larger society. This highly gendered structure meant that the church was accepted as mainstream and respectable, a perception that Pentecostals reasoned would make their efforts at community outreach more acceptable. Yet the tension of being "in the world but not of it" was pronounced for PAOC members. Stepping away from their own roots of gender equality based on the equitable distribution of spiritual gifts, the PAOC doubled down on the worldly idea that church leadership and governance was for men and nurturing was for women. These binary gender ideals would dominate PAOC subculture for decades to come, and with ministry models rigidly tied to the heteronormative ideals of nuclear family structures, the church would struggle to adapt to the changing realities of Canadian family life.

With elaborate children's programming, curriculum, and structures around Sunday School and midweek programs for children and youth, the PAOC mirrored the secular society with limits: alternative programs that paralleled those of the broader society but at the same time repudiated the secularity of the culture. The central focus on children was also in step with postwar Canadian society where schools and extracurricular activities for children dominated community development and government programs. Civic programs offered through the mainstream churches and parachurch organizations like the YMCA/YWCA emphasized civic engagement and citizenship, but for Pentecostal children and youth, the emphasis was on programs that warned against the dangers of the world while teaching them to resist cultural norms that were not in step with their church culture. Pentecostal programs emphasized that spiritual battles were to be anticipated in everyday life for Canadian children and that the world was a dangerous place in need of the church.

5

The Secular World and Social Concern

INTRODUCTION

In July 1969, Earl Kulbeck wrote an editorial in *The Pentecostal Testimony* about the Criminal Law Amendment Act and a series of bills that were before the Canadian Parliament, proposing to amend the law on a number of items, including lotteries, gun control, homosexuality, abortion, and drinking and driving. Kulbeck wrote:

> Someone has said that "Adanac" is Canada spelled backwards. A mere two years ago Canada celebrated its centennial with observances from sea to sea. Religious observances were prominent in the activities of that historic year.
>
> Now, two years later, Canada's lawmakers on the national scene have decided to disregard the divine Lawgiver. Some of the changes in the Criminal Code are certainly the most far-reaching in Canada's history and may bode ill for our nation's future. The so-called "Omnibus" bill has three features that are morally repugnant by any test of Holy Scripture: gross indecency, abortion and state operated lotteries. At the time this is being written, the debate is still going on in Parliament, but there is little doubt that the result will be that charted by the government majority. Certain members of parliament have made an outstanding contribution in the airing of these objectionable amendments. To give these worthy members credit might be interpreted as a partisan expression. However, concerned Christians should read Hansard covering the last two weeks of April, 1969, and carefully note how your local members spoke and then voted.

> We would further suggest that you write expressing your disapproval of his voting for the reprehensible amendments. Also write a letter of commendation to those who consistently worked and voted against the amendments, bearing witness to historic Christian values, even though the advocates to today's unlimited permissiveness carried the day in the House.[1]

The response by the Pentecostal Assemblies of Canada (PAOC) and its clergy to the Omnibus Bill of 1969 focused primarily on abortion with very little said about homosexuality. The main concern revolved around what the PAOC perceived as a threat to the institution of marriage.

However, the entrance of the PAOC into public debate was not simply about protecting its ideological or theological interests. The PAOC was also concerned about its material interests, which revolved around the declining role of religion among Canadians and the secular world that was emerging.[2] Together, the ideological and material round out our cultural analysis of the PAOC and its response to social change. By mid-century, the PAOC held significant assets in real estate and buildings, something that their own historians had noted as a sign of God's blessing on the organization. With the cultural shift that was occurring as Canadian society liberalized, the PAOC had reason to worry about declining attendance and potential loss of revenues. If they lost this cultural battle over shifting social mores, they could also potentially lose much more, including their substantial material assets. This was so much more than an ideological difference of opinion; it would give way to a moral panic.

The 1960s in Canada was a time of rapid social change. After much debate, the country got a new flag in 1965 as the iconic red and white maple leaf replaced the Union Jack. The country celebrated its centennial in 1967 as middle-class Canadians with the financial means and the paid vacation time escaped the suburbs to flock to Montreal for Expo 67. In the spring of 1968, the country was swept up in a wave of "Trudeaumania" as the new Liberal Party leader, Pierre Elliot Trudeau, ran a successful election campaign characterized by personal popularity, sex appeal, media frenzy, and youth involvement. Trudeau came to symbolize the major shifts that were underway in Canadian society as increasingly liberal views about sexuality, family life, and participatory democracy captured public attention. Those trends echoed larger social movements of youth protest, the sexual revolution, war protest, and hippie culture. By the end of the decade, a native rights movement had launched in reaction to the federal government's 1969 White Paper, women had successfully lobbied for a Royal Commission on the Status of Women, and Quebec's Quiet Revolution was leading to the 1970 October Crisis. The times were changing![3] Religion in Canada was not immune to these changes, with the collapse of Christendom ending the Protestant vision of Canada as "God's Dominion," Roman Catholics embracing the changes introduced by Vatican II, a secular narrative gaining traction, and among evangelical Protestants (including Pentecostals) the attempt to stem the tide of social change.

In this chapter we focus on how the PAOC responded to these sweeping societal changes, in particular the Criminal Law Amendment Act, 1968–1969 and its aftermath. First, we introduce the idea of moral panic to frame the response of the PAOC to social change. We elaborate on this idea in our analysis of the Omnibus Bill, with the PAOC developing a social awareness, then the mobilization and social activism through the newly formed Social Concerns Department and its demise, with a call for course correction by the general superintendent in the 1990s. The foray into public life, however, cannot simply be viewed through the official work of the Social Concerns Department. Bernice Gerard, a Pentecostal minister from Vancouver, offers insight into public engagement on a range of issues at a more local and grassroots level. With the closing of the Social Concerns Department, the PAOC relied more heavily upon organizations like the Evangelical Fellowship of Canada (EFC) for the articulation of position papers on issues, especially the debates about marriage equality. This shift supports the argument made by some scholars that the PAOC was becoming "evangelicalized."[4] We also discuss why the religious right and political mobilization among evangelicals in Canada was incapable of offering a public response that captured the imagination of evangelicals in general and Pentecostals in particular. Finally, we consider how Pentecostal notions of the body are shaped and contested as a site for the debates about LGBTQ issues.

MORAL PANIC

Historians Mark Hutchinson and John Wolffe write that with modernization and secularization in the middle of the twentieth century, a growing sense of unease was prevalent among evangelicals.[5] Social change, evangelicals believed, was creating problems for religion, especially with the view that secularism was winning and the churches were losing. Already marginalized from the mainline denominations, evangelicals attempted to enter public life, seeking to protect not only their ideological interests but also their material interests. Hutchinson and Wolffe offer a number of examples to show how evangelicals in the United States, Australia, and elsewhere attempted to enter the public arena and influence local politics. Hutchinson and Wolffe describe this period among evangelicals as characterized by "moral panic" but offer no conceptual definition or theoretical orientation to explain what is meant by the idea.

Erich Goode and Nachman Ben-Yehuda discuss "moral panic" conceptually and theoretically to explain specific historical cases that represent fear, concern, and threat in particular times and places.[6] In an attempt to address the question of why "moral panic" arises, the authors argue that in each case there are some consistent patterns, including specific agents, an assessment of the threat, and often an exaggerated or misplaced fear. Moral panic revolves around the political and social construction of specific social forces, typically understood as social problems. These social problems manifest in particular ways, including: (1) organized collective action in the form of a protest; (2) introduction of legal arguments to deal with the particular condition; (3) ranking of the problem in such a way as to convince the public that it is the most pressing issue; and (4) public discussion in the form of media such as magazines and newspapers. The authors ask: "How do groups, classes, or segments of the society struggle to establish their own definition of social problem? How is problemhood established? And by whom?"[7] More specifically, they argue that researchers need to pay attention to how social problems are defined, the range of solutions proposed, and the specific action taken.

Goode and Ben-Yehuda state that "moral panic" consists of five key elements or criteria that include: a heightened level of concern over the behaviour of a specific group; an increased level of hostility toward the group; some minimal measure of consensus or agreement in the society or subgroup that the threat is real or serious; a level of concern that is out of proportion to the nature of the threat; and the idea that moral panics can erupt suddenly, lie latent, disappear, and re-emerge. Moral panic can be observed from different perspectives depending on whether it is being led by elites, interest groups, or grassroots movements. Elites, like political leaders, can create panic among constituents, for example, about the threat of other countries or policies or leaders. In the case of the PAOC, we would consider the role of denominational leaders and pastors. Interest groups, like the EFC, are organizations that focus on informing denominations and constituents about specific issues in order to mobilize and take action either in the form of writing letters to government leaders or advocating certain positions and courses of action. Grassroots movements are those that appear to come from the local level and often represent sets of concerns very different from those of a small group of individuals who attempt to orient interest groups or leaders to take particular concerns seriously. As we shall see, Bernice Gerard is one such example, whose public voice worked closely with local grassroots groups.

There is a level of complexity that must be nuanced when assessing what role material interests or moral interests play in influencing the response. And it may be difficult to determine if one plays a more important role than the other. What is clear is that the PAOC was attempting to draw distinct boundaries between themselves and the larger society based on their conservative position on social issues. Furthermore, it is not always easy to separate what role leaders play from the role of organizations like a denomination or an interest group. What we do observe are interactions between the organization, leaders, and individuals in their efforts to establish and maintain boundaries. However, when we think about the relationship between individuals in PAOC congregations and the denomination in relation to proposed legislative changes, it is clear that the organization represents an insightful case of an interest group responding to social change. Interest Group Theory is, according to Goode and Ben-Yehuda, "the most widely used perspective on moral panics."[8] Interest groups, like religious groups, and more specifically in this chapter, the PAOC, play an important role in generating and sustaining moral panic through activism and mobilization of members. We also give attention to the role of Pentecostal clergy like Bernice Gerard who engaged local-level issues while working with grassroots groups, sometimes in tension with the official Social Concerns Department and the leaders of the PAOC.

THE DEVELOPMENT OF SOCIAL AWARENESS

In August 1968, in response to the Criminal Law Amendment Act of 1968–1969, the PAOC General Conference presented two resolutions contesting the government's proposal to decriminalize abortion and homosexuality.[9] A search of *Pentecostal Testimony* (PT) between 1969 and 1977 reveals forty-three documents (articles, editorials, news reports) and 317 instances of the word "abortion." For example, in August 1969 PT published a full-length article on the problem of abortion for Christians by Louis Tamminga, a Christian Reformed minister from Iowa and president of the Christian Action Foundation.[10] In February 1971, an article by David Mainse, a PAOC pastor (and later the host of the televised Christian television program "100 Huntley Street"), titled "More Prophesies Fulfilled – Revival Is a Must," discussed social problems like population explosion and abortion as eschatological signs of the end of the world.[11] Later, in August 1971, two more articles appeared, including "Therapeutic Abortion from the Medical Viewpoint" by C.R. Stiller and "Therapeutic Abortion from a Theological Viewpoint" by Virgil L. Gingrich.[12] These last two articles concede that abortion was justifiable, both theologically and medically, under specific circumstances.

The two articles by Stiller and Gingrich offer insight into the internal debate among Pentecostals. Stiller argued that a fetus was not viable under twenty weeks, and (even if one was to take the lower figure of twelve weeks) no one should be concerned about therapeutic abortion. Gingrich, a PAOC credentialed minister, reviewed a number of ethical cases to assess when an abortion would be justified. Gingrich offered a number of examples like rape or threat to a mother's life and argued that in these cases abortion was justifiable. He also entertained an economic argument. When a mother in relative poverty already had several children and was unable to afford another one, Gingrich asked if abortion could be justifiable. After reviewing the argument, the author claimed he was unable to decide if this case could ethically be open for therapeutic abortion. Gingrich critiqued several theological views by Roman Catholics, Calvinists, and biblical literalists and dismissed them for being inconsistent. In doing so, he advocated for what he called "abortion by prescription," arguing that most evangelicals, including Billy Graham, would allow for abortion in certain cases – for example, when a mother's life is in danger.[13]

If this is so, and abortion was sometimes considered justifiable among Pentecostals, then why were they unsettled by the changes in the law? The main issue, it appears, is not with abortion per se but with the regulations surrounding what might count as justifiable grounds for abortion and if regulations were removed, what potential problems might be created. Furthermore, Pentecostals were concerned that Canadians would use abortion as a form of birth control and easier access to abortion would lead to greater sexual promiscuity among unmarried people.

In response to the bill, the PAOC passed numerous motions on abortion at its General Conferences that highlight its views and potential responses to the issue. For example, at the 1968 General Conference, a motion was proposed calling upon the members to affirm "Biblical principles as the only basis for a successful national or personal life" [14] and reinforcing the perception that the proposed legal changes were a threat. PAOC clergy were asked to participate in a "gigantic nationwide write-in campaign, voicing their objections to the above-mentioned changes in the Criminal Code." Following the presentation of the resolution, there was considerable discussion from the floor followed by two insightful amendments that were supported by the PAOC. The first was the inclusion of the statement in the resolution that the PAOC ought to respond "to safeguard the Canadian people from the irresponsible use of the privilege of abortion for selfish pursuits." Second, the resolution was amended to state that "a Commission be appointed to arrive at a decision on abortion which may act as guidance for our ministry and people." The resolution was carried as amended. The addition of these last two points highlights the cultural view among Pentecostals that abortion was a "privilege." The point was that the practice needed to be regulated to assess and determine in each case if an abortion was justifiable. Ironically, such considerations were already at the heart of the state system through its creation of hospital therapeutic abortion committees whereby each case required close scrutiny by a team of medical personnel. Second, the amendments turned the focus toward the PAOC creating greater awareness of the issues among its constituency.

By the mid-1970s, views among Pentecostals about abortion were crystalizing, and increasingly, articles in *PT* and motions passed at the General Conference focused on the use of abortion as an unjustified act of birth control, usually associated with immoral licence for premarital sex and the erosion of biblical marriage. By the 1980s, activism among leaders in the PAOC resembled that among the religious right in the United States, with calls for stronger laws that would prohibit abortion completely. The PAOC pressed its clergy to ask politicians to change the law to prohibit abortion. That shift from privilege to prohibition marked a significant turn toward conservatism and resisting the liberalization of the law that the 1969 bill had first proposed.

POLITICAL ACTIVISM

The 1980s was the high point of political activism in the PAOC. The decade saw the development of a full-time director of Social Concerns, expansion of the denomination's offices, new budget allocations, a shift from informing PAOC members about social issues to opposing legislation, engaging governments, networking with like-minded activist groups, and passing a large number of resolutions at the General Conference garnering the support of local pastors and national leaders. The PAOC believed that the best strategy to counter the advancement of secularism in Canadian society was political activism. They were quite bullish about this work based on the strong belief that they could influence leadership in politics, law, and civil service. The main person who guided the PAOC's entrance into public life was Rev. Hudson T. Hilsden. In 1978, the PAOC adopted a motion to establish a "National Committee on Moral Standards." The terms of reference included:

1 To conduct ongoing research into trends on all social issues as related to the role of the church.
2 To ascertain positive courses of action, on appropriate levels, which members of The Pentecostal Assemblies of Canada may take in the face of increasing degeneracy within our society.
3 To keep the constituency informed.
4 To take leadership in positive social action that our voice may be heard in such a way as to achieve optimum effectiveness.
5 To share with the National Officers in committee their findings and proposals prior to action being taken.[15]

The 1980 General Conference approved a change to the committee name calling it "The National Committee on Ethics and Social Concern." The group was to have an expanded focus to "relate not only to the constituency of The Pentecostal Assemblies of Canada, but also to the nation."[16] As the committee developed, it also became integrated into the PAOC structure with office space and a budget for its operation. These developments marked the PAOC's most direct interventions into public life in its history, standing in contrast to the early postwar focus on their own congregational programming for families.

In 1983, Hudson T. Hilsden was appointed as the national coordinator for the PAOC's newly developed "Social Concerns and Public

Relations" department. Hilsden's article "Evangelism and Social Concerns in Partnership," published in *PT*, illustrates the denomination's strategy and articulates the basis for its activism.[17] One of the main points was an attempt to show that social activism is biblical and that responding to public issues shared importance with the PAOC's focus on evangelism. In Hilsden's view, social concern was not an equal priority to evangelism but an integral part of evangelism and discipleship. Hilsden argued that Pentecostals must act in such a way as to prepare their constituents to understand what the issues were and to respond through a number of means, most notably preparing young people to enter into public life. He stated that the PAOC must "speak out against the actions of those who have advanced to places of leadership in politics, law, education and civil service and who are rapidly turning our society to secular humanism and paganism. But we have a responsibility to prepare our young people to enter these influential professions in order to bring a Christian perspective to the public market place,"[18] suggesting such a foray was a continuation of the defensive tone that had typified the PAOC rhetoric around postwar children's programs whereby Crusaders were trained to defend themselves against books and ideas the PAOC found to be threatening (see chapter 4). The Crusaders from the 1950s and 1960s were now the leaders of the PAOC focused on abortion and homosexuality. These conservative concerns were shared with the broader evangelical world. Hilsden was silent on what some considered the pressing social issues of the time, including the environment, gender inequality, nuclear threat, the Cold War, and economic issues. The irony is that while the PAOC did not include these issues in its official statements, *PT* published numerous articles by its ministers and members on these topics. The response of the PAOC also reflected the cultural and theological support of a Pentecostal cultural repertoire. According to Hilsden, "It is understood that the positions and actions taken by the Pentecostal Assemblies of Canada in regard to social concerns will be influenced by our strong theological positions of the affirmation of the Bible as our all-sufficient source of faith and practice, our subscription to the historic creeds of the universal Church, our belief in the fall of man and the provision for our salvation through belief in Jesus Christ as Saviour, Healer and Coming King and the Baptism of the Holy Spirit, with speaking in tongues as the initial evidence to empower the believer to live and work for God."[19] Hilsden was clearly attempting to show that because of their distinctive beliefs (especially about healing and Spirit baptism), the PAOC stood apart from other evangelicals in what motivated them to take a stand on social issues. Such distinctions were undoubtedly lost on the general public.

Throughout the 1980s, the National Committee on Ethics and Social Concern wrote numerous position papers, published articles in *PT*, distributed briefs and information packets to PAOC clergy, and passed motions at General Conferences, mostly related to issues of sexuality, including opposition to abortion, homosexuality, and premarital sex. Hilsden also worked to form coalitions with other evangelical Protestants and Roman Catholics to publicly respond to social change. In 1986, he made a submission to the members of the Legislative Assembly of Ontario about an amendment to Bill 7 to include sexual orientation in the Ontario Human Rights Code. The submission was prepared by the Coalition for Family Values, of which Hilsden was the chair. The coalition included the EFC, the Canadian Organization of Small Business, the Ontario Catholic Conference of Bishops, the Fellowship of Evangelical Baptist Churches, the PAOC, Realwomen of Canada, the Free Methodist Church of Canada, Queensway Cathedral, the Baptist Convention of Ontario and Quebec, the Baptist Federation of Canada, and the National Citizens Coalition. Given who those partners were and what they believed, the PAOC's theological "distinctives" were secondary to finding a common voice with like-minded conservatives. The objective was to defend what were defined as "traditional family values" and to raise fear by requesting that the government "reconsider any legal measures to recognize and protect homosexuality in this province."[20] What the PAOC intended as a "defense of decency" was perceived by many citizens as entrenched homophobia. In 1989, Hilsden spoke at a Canada Day event at which Liberal Party politician Paul Martin, Jr, was present about a range of issues including radical socialism, hedonism, materialism, growing secularism, the decline in the role of Christianity, and the threat of New Age philosophy. In his address, Hilsden linked these problems to the 1969 Omnibus Bill, the 1982 Charter of Rights and Freedoms, and court decisions around abortion and Dr Henry Morgentaler, a well-known doctor who operated free-standing abortion clinics in defiance of government regulations designed to control access to abortion. Hilsden also referred to other issues like declining birth rates, increase in the number of women working outside the home, high divorce rates, pornography, drugs, and drunk driving. At the conclusion of his presentation, he offered seven points of action, which included prayer and fasting, revival, a national awakening, prophetic preaching, marketplace participation as lawyers and researchers, rebuking offenders, launching media campaigns, and maintaining a resolute moral standard.[21] However, by the end of the 1980s, PAOC leaders were questioning what they had gained through political activism.

COURSE CORRECTION

Sensing that they had lost many battles and wondering if they should change strategy, in 1988 General Superintendent James MacKnight called for a "course correction," with new statements about how the priority of PAOC congregations ought to be on evangelism and baptism of the Holy Spirit, not political issues. MacKnight's call for change was also an administrative one in that he would now require all statements about social concern to be authorized through his office. MacKnight also tried to make distinctions between social concerns and social issues, arguing that to be informed about an issue does not require a response and that the PAOC ought to be focused on evangelism, not social concern.[22] However, some highly vocal clergy in the PAOC questioned MacKnight's direction and what they believed to be an error in his distinction between concerns and issues and the separation of social justice or action from the work of the church. MacKnight's initiatives also included decentralizing responsibilities at the national office so that informing the constituency about social concerns would occur through grassroots groups or at local levels, not the national office. This change to the Social Concerns Department was also part of a larger issue at the National Office. The PAOC was experiencing a budget crisis caused in part by the expense of a move to a new national office in Mississauga. The costs associated with the new building led to the restructuring of the National Office and its departments. The Social Concerns Department lost its funding for a full-time director. While the PAOC considered options for staffing and plans to reshape the Social Concerns Department, Hilsden resigned. He was replaced by two part-time workers for the next decade. However, they were unable to sustain the momentum created by the Social Concerns Department, so the department closed. The PAOC took the view that they no longer needed to be directly active on public issues. Instead, they could rely on other groups like the EFC to voice their concerns and to facilitate and coordinate activities.

This is not surprising, because the PAOC and the EFC had a long history, and indeed the PAOC had played a role in the EFC's formation.[23] Beginning in the 1950s, Harry Fought, a PAOC pastor, began organizing meetings with like-minded Pentecostals and evangelicals to discuss the formation of a Canadian organization similar to the North American Association of Evangelicals in the United States. Fought was instrumental in the meeting that brought about the formation of the EFC in 1965 when he was also elected executive chair. In 1966, he became the EFC's second president. The role of PAOC leaders in the EFC, however, was not always welcomed, and in 1965–66, meetings to promote the EFC in Atlantic Canada were not held because some evangelicals would not attend a meeting where a Pentecostal would be speaking. Still, a number of PAOC leaders served the EFC in different roles from president to chair, including Rev. Charles Yates, Rev. Kenneth Birch, Rev. Brian Stiller, and Rev. David Wells, elected as the general superintendent of the PAOC in 2008. Given the long history between the EFC and the PAOC, it is not surprising that the PAOC relied substantially upon the EFC following its course correction in the 1990s. These types of transdenominational relationships, along with a generic evangelical theological framework, have served to facilitate cooperation, albeit not without some concern for the erosion of particular theological identities for some participants like the Pentecostals.[24]

BERNICE GERARD

While the denomination came to rely upon the EFC to voice its concerns nationally, some PAOC pastors took it upon themselves to act locally. The Rev. Bernice Gerard (1923–2008), a Vancouver pastor and university chaplain, was one such person. Gerard was deeply involved in social concerns in the City of Vancouver, and she took the unusual step of running for municipal office and serving as a city councillor from 1977 to 1980. In that role, Gerard spoke out frequently on a variety of issues and was caricatured in the Vancouver press as a right-wing crusader who set out to curb civil liberties and freedom of expression. Yet an analysis of her autobiography and archival materials, including her notes from speaking engagements and sermon series from the same period, reveal how she understood the actions she was taking and what motivated her. As a Pentecostal considering the question of social engagement, she concluded, "when it comes to those things that concern God's commands for us and our living out the life of Jesus, we are going to have to have a prophetic function. I don't see how we can avoid it" and "in this world ... we are under obligation to stand with the truth and ... we're fools if we think we are going to get popular because we did it."[25]

Indeed, Gerard's controversial work as pastor, politician, and protestor in Vancouver provides a rich case study of one expression of Pentecostal social engagement apart from what the national office of the PAOC decided to do or not to do. In October 1973, Gerard preached a series of sermons on prophecy to her Vancouver congregation, the Fraserview Assembly, that reveal the foundational thinking behind all of her public engagement. She was careful to point out that a prophet's role was not restricted to predicting future events or speaking about end times. In a series of four sermons entitled "Too Much Wilderness, Too Few Prophets,"[26] Gerard made clear her thinking about the need for believers to be engaged with the culture around them; in her mind, prophets were called to bring God's message not only to fellow believers but also to the culture around them. "We Bible believers today understand the urgency of the Great Commission," she told readers of her autobiography, "but are frequently guilty of taking an either/or approach when we should be saying, 'Yes, let us preach the good news for the salvation of the lost, *and* explore every possible means to act and speak prophetically to our contemporaries.'"[27] For Gerard, contemporaries included both believers and unbelievers.

The predicament that believers face in trying to be true to the admonition is how to be "in the world but not of the world." Recognizing that fellow believers might have trouble accepting not only her actions of social protest but her rationale for acting, Gerard explained: "I literally preached myself into politics, shocking as the idea may be to many conservative other-worldly evangelicals."[28] It is intriguing that Gerard drew this distinction between herself as a Pentecostal and a group she called "conservative other-worldly evangelicals." She expected that latter group to be uncomfortable, even "shocked," at her explanation for how she came to take up these very public acts of political involvement and protest.

For Gerard, having a presence in the world led her to enter municipal politics and take very public stances on questions of morality. Indeed, her convictions caused her to take actions that fellow believers could not condone. She was unequivocal in her opposition to abortion, willing to work with Roman Catholics when other Pentecostals would not, and, indeed, willing to cooperate with other like-minded allies to promote her causes. She invoked her own life story (Gerard's birth mother was a patient in a mental health facility, and therefore she was offered up for adoption at birth) as her best argument against abortion in an attempt to counter the logic that if a child was not "wanted," they should not be born. While many would have supported her stance on that question, as we have seen, it is clear that not everyone within PAOC circles was convinced that abortion should never be an option under any circumstances.

The second issue that Gerard took up was public nudity. Here she took actions that some other Canadian Pentecostals could not condone, especially her controversial action of going to the beaches in Vancouver where nude sunbathers greeted her and her entourage as they made their silent protest. The "clothing optional" beach in Vancouver, known as Wreck Beach, on Point Grey, had long had a place in the community, and Gerard was not protesting its existence. But, having heard from her constituents that the practice of nude sunbathing was spreading to other public beaches, Gerard decided to take a stand. She insisted that in order to protect public beaches for the use of families and concerned citizens, she needed to endure some unpleasant encounters and even personal harassment. Therefore, she led a silent protest march along the beach to make the point that not all of Vancouver's beaches were clothing optional and for the sake of "public decency," those limits needed to be respected.

A third example of Gerard's public protesting activity involved her objection to what she considered obscene content offered in Vancouver theatres. Yet when Gerard made it clear that she had actually viewed the film *Caligula*, that was going too far for many church folks who were uncomfortable with the fact that a Pentecostal pastor had exposed herself to the media content that she herself had declared "obscene." Gerard defended her action on that occasion, saying that it was disingenuous to protest against a film that she herself had not seen. Whether it was the actions she took to protest abortion, public nudity, or risqué theatre productions, Bernice Gerard was unusual for the degree of public engagement she took on these controversial issues and also because she did so as an elected municipal politician.

The fact that Gerard herself was controversial is hardly surprising. Given the context of Canadian social history during the 1970s, her resistance to the liberalization of sexual mores was sure to invite criticism from the public media and secular society. She freely admitted, for example, that in retrospect the media frenzy over her beach walk was understandable, even funny. Newspaper reports in Vancouver insisted that Gerard took a famous "walk on Wreck Beach," and they satirically reported on this, saying, for example, that "*barely* any one met her there." However, Gerard insisted she never went near the nude beach but only walked the public beach adjoining it. According to Gerard, that was the point – not to stop the nudists from enjoying their own area but to make a statement that the spread of nudity beyond that one beach was not acceptable. Gerard fully expected that her stance on these questions of morality would invite ridicule. As she explained, "non-believers ... were apprehensive of 'born again Christians' achieving political power, imagined that behind every born-again politician is a monolithic, oppressive, power-hungry church structure."[29]

A Vancouver journalist writing about Gerard in 1979 observed, "At the height of her career both as an evangelist and a politician, the thing Bernice Gerard fears most is that she will become a caricature of herself. It may already be too late."[30] Indeed, Gerard accepted that being ridiculed was part of the prophet's lot in life. As she recounted in her autobiography, "The truth is that Christians will be spoken against as evil-doers whether they deserve it or not." Her consolation, however, was that "Trouble because one is faithful to God is only a short-term problem."[31] Gerard recognized that opposition from unbelievers was to be expected; playfully, she even included a satirical cartoon in her autobiography to illustrate how she was regarded for her conservative stance as an alderman.[32]

More surprising is the opposition that Gerard endured from other evangelical Christians, and for her that was no laughing matter. While her own congregation was consistently supportive of her foray into municipal affairs, she was fully aware that some Christians felt differently. "Some of my Christian critics were particularly concerned that I, as a minister of the gospel in the political arena, would receive a great deal of persecution simply for who I was ... Their idea seemed to be that if we all keep reasonably quiet and inactive in community affairs, we will save ourselves a lot of trouble."[33]

Yet keeping quiet was not an option for Gerard because, as she explained in her autobiography, her involvement in public affairs, political life, and protest movements came from a place of deep conviction. She understood her involvement as the acts of one who was called of God as a prophet. Moreover, she lamented that "Unfortunately, Christians often shrink from the prophetic task and somehow see the 'condemning of ungodliness' as embarrassing to themselves and their church, and as an end in itself whereas righteous living is a part of God's redemptive action and a proper expression of His love (Ephesians 5:6–11) [*sic*]."[34] Bernice Gerard acted out of her own convictions rather than any directive coming from the PAOC national office. She represents an anomaly among PAOC pastors, not only because of her gender (PAOC would not officially ordain women until the late 1980s) but even more so because of her conviction that public engagement in the affairs of the city where she pastored was a central component of her call to ministry.

THE END OF PUBLIC INFLUENCE?

Canadian scholars are divided over the question of whether or not there is a "religious right" in Canada and what influence, if any, evangelicals have on social and political issues.[35] While it appears that the PAOC vacated the public sphere beginning with MacKnight's leadership in the late 1980s, it would be naive for readers to assume this is the case. Rather, it is more accurate to observe that public engagement rises and falls over time depending on the issue and that the social ties that develop between groups may or may not be enduring. Furthermore, we know that in Canada no single organization or person has been capable of completely capturing the imagination of evangelicals. None has been able to effectively organize and mobilize them in a unified way. The case of same-sex marriage from the late 1990s illustrates the point.

The movement towards legal recognition of same-sex marriages was shaped by several key events. In 1999, the Canadian government allowed for the extension of benefits to same-sex couples who were in a co-habiting relationship. Beginning in 2003, same-sex marriage was recognized first in Ontario and then in British Columbia, followed by Quebec in 2004. Several other provinces also recognized same-sex marriage. In 2005, the federal government introduced the Civil Marriage Act, which was passed by the House of Commons and the Senate, receiving royal assent in July of the same year. After the Conservative Party assumed office with a minority government in 2006, Prime Minister Stephen Harper promised to open the debate, but following a vote by the House of Commons, the motion was defeated. The response by Canadian churches varied, with mainline Protestant churches like the United Church of Canada affirming same-sex marriage.[36] The Roman Catholic Church and evangelical churches, including the PAOC, did not support the legislation and argued for a traditional definition of marriage between a man and a woman, as published in position papers written by the EFC.[37] Following the Ontario decision, a letter was sent in 2003 to PAOC ministers by William Morrow, general superintendent, to inform them of their view on marriage, which was recognized as between one man and one woman.[38] Interestingly, the letter referred to a new official position of the PAOC that acknowledged the need for a legal framework that recognized "various forms of adult inter-dependent relationships" but to find language other than marriage to do so. The letter encouraged members to take action in a variety of ways following the example of the EFC and the Roman Catholic Church to inform their constituencies and to write to members of Parliament. The letter also referred to a brief that was prepared for submission to the House of Commons Standing Committee on Human Rights and Justice to further explain their position. The PAOC stood firm in its opposition alongside these other socially conservative groups, stating, "The need to strengthen marriage and family relationships within congregations is obvious, especially in light of the recent legislations that blur definitions of marriage."[39] In 2004, the PAOC passed a resolution at its General Conference that stated, "A minister may decline to officiate at a wedding ceremony which is not in harmony with personal beliefs and convictions."[40] In the Statement of Fundamental and Essential Truths, the section on Marriage and Family says, "Marriage is a provision of God wherein one man and one woman to the exclusion of all others enter into a lifelong relationship."[41]

The inability of evangelicals to organize and influence the debate is based on a number of factors. For example, evangelicals typically have organized across a range of different denominations and groups, suggesting that while there are general tendencies to support issues like the preservation of the traditional family, evangelicals disagree on how to achieve this goal.[42] While evangelicals in Canada and the United States share a similar subculture supported by congregations, denominations, music, books, seminaries, and universities, the subculture between the two countries also shows differences. Where evangelicals differ in Canada and the United States is on social and political issues. Canadian evangelicals, for example, are more inclined to support a range of social issues that help refugees or policies that protect the environment. On questions about how comfortable Canadian evangelicals are with LGBTQ people, research shows that Canadian evangelicals have become more willing over time to show civility toward LGBTQ people. However, Canadian evangelicals, and the PAOC, show they are less inclined to affirm same-sex marriage, reflecting a certain tension between a diverse and inclusive society and traditional views of marriage and the family.[43]

While Canadian evangelicals are showing some level of change about LGBTQ people, they have not organized at any level to influence social change when it comes to the traditional definition of marriage. There are a number of reasons why this is the case. First, evangelicalism is not a large group in Canada, representing approximately 10 per cent of the population, with their primary focus on congregational life and not social and political concerns.[44] Second, like most Canadians, evangelicals are regionalized and separated by geography, making it difficult to engage for long periods of time, which is necessary for organizing and mobilizing, even with the use of digital technology.[45] Third, evangelicals do not represent a large voting block politically, even though they hold a conservative view on marriage.[46] Evangelicals in Canada, while showing some movement in the past decade toward supporting the federal Conservative Party, also have significant numbers aligning with the Liberal Party, the New Democratic Party, and the Green Party.[47] Evangelicals also tend to organize along the lines of special interest groups that cut across denominations and organizations, which has the effect of bringing people together but often only temporarily because of other commitments.[48] Finally, evangelicals have not done a very effective job in communicating their concerns in a way that does not come across as defensive and at times antagonistic, even homophobic, toward those they disagree with, especially in the LGBTQ community.[49] As a result, in spite of the claims sometimes made in the media, evangelicals have not been effective in exerting public pressure on the Canadian government and, further, do not represent a movement that is even remotely close to the religious right in the United States.[50]

PENTECOSTALS AND THE BODY

Pentecostalism is an embodied religion. One of the more contentious issues for Canadian society since the 1960s revolves around expressive individualism, choice, and the body.[51] In the context of the decline of religious influence and the secularization of the state, Pentecostals have responded. The response, however, is not simply explained as a failure to organize and mobilize its members to become politically active. What is of interest is the way in which Pentecostals have culturally constructed a sacred body over and against a secular body. The debates about abortion and same-sex marriage are examples of the types of bodies that Pentecostals believe violate a sacred notion of the body. Sacred bodies are those that are saved, sanctified, and filled with the Holy Spirit while they await the return of Jesus. Sacred bodies are at work sharing the good news of Jesus. Sacred bodies are not characterized only by what they do not do but also by what they do. Sacred bodies are constructed through rituals like those revolving around Spirit baptism and glossolalia, healing, water baptism, prayer, and exorcism. Sacred bodies are not simply constructed through doctrines and belief systems. They are imagined and lived daily through various practices and disciplines. And further, sacred bodies are always in context, and the specific debates about abortion and same-sex marriage define religious notions of bodies.

Pentecostals not only believe that the body is the "temple of the Holy Ghost," they also live their lives as if the body actually is a site for the dwelling of the Holy Spirit. Holy temples are defined by the various ways in which Pentecostals embody the culture of Pentecostalism. Pentecostals have a long history of requiring holiness, which included a range of restrictions. Over time, those restrictions have changed, but they included things like not drinking alcohol or smoking cigarettes. Restrictions revolved around where sacred bodies could be found and especially where they could not be found, including theatres and dance halls. Pentecostals regulated how bodies were dressed and how much flesh could be revealed, if any at all. On this question, restrictions were particularly detailed for women, with directives about modest fashion and limited use of makeup. Sacred bodies were sexually inactive until marriage, and divorced bodies were not allowed to remarry. Of course, some of these notions of the body have been relaxed, including allowing divorce, attending theatres, dancing, and dressing fashionably. Some Pentecostals now drink alcohol, whereas it was completely prohibited in the past.[52] Abortion is nuanced, although it appears that Pentecostals have become more restrictive than they were in the 1960s when abortion was thought of as a privilege. Views on same-sex marriage have not reached the point of acceptance that would involve full inclusion in the activities of the church, and the PAOC is certainly not affirming of marriage equality.

What the future of the PAOC may be as it attempts to come to terms with changing notions of the body is unclear. A comparative example with Australia may be instructive.

Mark Jennings conducted a study of LGBTQ people and the Australian Christian Churches (ACC), a Pentecostal denomination similar to the PAOC in history and size, with 280,000 members and 1,110 churches.[53] Jennings conducted a series of face-to-face interviews with LGBTQ people who attended ACC churches and with pastors. The interviews with the pastors included a series of questions about their views of LGBTQ issues, how the church was responding to debates about same-sex marriage, and how it was caring for LGBTQ members in their congregations. Jennings discovered that the pastors were mostly open to LGBTQ members in their congregations and were trying to find ways to demonstrate pastoral care for them. Some pastors spoke of genuine faith conversions among members from the LGBTQ community that was challenging for some congregations because they had never dealt with questions about homosexuality – for example, whether it was a choice or if people were born this way, whether or not they should be celibate, and whether homosexuals could be included as church volunteers. The response from pastors was ambivalent, with many opting for the position of "welcoming but not affirming." This view, however, created some tension among the Christians from the LGBTQ community who wanted to volunteer in the local congregation or to speak about their sexuality to those who were wholly devoted to Pentecostalism and also wanted to be affirmed in their sexuality. Some pastors, likewise, did not see any tension between the authentic spiritual experience of LGBTQ members and the ability to serve as a volunteer in the congregation. Some LGBTQ Pentecostals, however, were relieved from volunteer positions and responsibilities when it became an issue for the congregation. Some respondents to the survey said that this was an injustice and that they thought it was unfair. Jennings's research illustrates the tension among Pentecostal pastors on LGBTQ issues that will require some thinking for congregations and pastoral ministry in the PAOC.

While no parallel study exists with PAOC pastors, in 2017 the PAOC presented a document entitled "Pastoral Reflection on Human Sexuality" to its clergy to address LGBTQ issues.[54] It was a five-page document that was intended to be a discussion piece from the General Executive in response to requests from pastors seeking guidance on addressing questions about human sexuality, notably LGBTQ issues.

The document begins with a restatement of the PAOC's official view of marriage and the family, a traditional view that recognizes marriage as a lifelong relationship between one man and one woman. It then affirms its view on sexuality and humanity: all people are loved by God; one's identity is in Christ, not in their sexual orientation; all people are created in God's image; all humans are fallen and marred by sin, which includes their sexuality; sexual relations are to be expressed in marriage; congregations need to welcome all people; membership and leadership in congregations is limited to those who are celibate or to those who live holy lives in a faithful biblical marriage (heterosexual marriage); and, finally, that church leaders must be truthful and full of grace. The document also offered "pastoral counsel" for its clergy on how to preach and teach in a way that welcomes all people while affirming their biblical view of marriage. Pastors were also to be sure to clarify church policy on sexuality in a way that would avoid discrimination, to provide venues for confidential discussions about struggles with sexuality, to inform themselves about the struggles with sexuality for people's faith journeys, to provide resources for the congregation about sexual identity, to use respectful language in any interactions with people on LGBTQ issues, to refer any requests for marriage by LGBTQ people to the local church constitution and policies of the PAOC, to advise on dedicating children of same-sex couples, to respond to public displays of affection in worship services that are consistent for all members, and to respond always in love and encouragement. Finally, the document included a bibliography on human sexuality primarily written by evangelical authors. Generally, the document outlines the PAOC position, which is to "welcome but not affirm." In Canada, where marriage equality is recognized, no person in a same-sex marriage is breaking the law. And if Pentecostals believe that Pentecostalism is good news for all people, including members of the LGBTQ community, then they will have to come to terms with a cultural message that understands what that good news means for all people. And clearly for LGBTQ people, that message has to mean something other than "you are welcome, but your involvement must be limited unless you change."

Since the 1960s, the PAOC has gone through a number of changes that reflect the perceived threat that a growing secularity poses for Pentecostal interests. One of the flashpoints of this period was the legal changes introduced by the government to reduce the restrictions around abortion and to decriminalize homosexuality. In response, the

PAOC followed a predictable pattern of moral panic, as articulated by Goode and Ben-Yehuda. First, we observe that in response to social change, the PAOC expressed specific concerns over amendments to the law. The proposed law around abortion is a case in point. We also see a growing level of hostility toward the government as evidenced by the editorials and articles in *PT*. Even with the disagreement over the law, however, there was at first an effort among some in the PAOC to come to terms medically and theologically with abortion whereby a more measured response toward therapeutic abortion was voiced. Eventually, those moderate voices were muted, and the general consensus among PAOC clergy was that social change posed a serious threat, not only for Pentecostals but also for the country. Increased activism was supported by the constituency, and organized activities of the PAOC were funded in the Social Concerns Department, a new office alongside a full-time director and a budget to publicly engage social issues. There also appears to be a response by the PAOC that was out of proportion with the threat associated with the new law. This gave way to a level of volatility within the PAOC that resulted in a course correction. This does not mean that the PAOC completely retreated from public issues. Their concerns were always latent, or just outside of the purview of the Canadian public, but also capable of rising again as reaction to the Civil Marriage Act demonstrates. But the strategy of the PAOC was to form alliances with other organizations, most notably the EFC, with which it has maintained a long-standing relationship. The PAOC, however, has yet to articulate a compassionate and workable position for its clergy on how to provide pastoral care and inclusion for LGBTQ people in their congregations. The ambivalence surrounding the case in Australia over "welcoming but not affirming" seems to be the case for the PAOC as well.

6

Canada as a Mission Field

INTRODUCTION

In the 1960s, two central developments in Canadian social history mirror the PAOC's focus on domestic evangelistic efforts. As the Quiet Revolution unfolded in Quebec, outreach to French Canadians in that province became a focus, and as Indigenous activism arose in response to centuries of Canadian colonialism, Pentecostals brought renewed resources to their continuing work among Indigenous peoples. Once again, it is clear that the PAOC was echoing some of the concerns of broader Canadian society. And, like the majority anglophone population, the PAOC leadership soon learned that what was unfolding with Quebecers and Indigenous communities was complex.

In this chapter, we examine the assumption that Canada is a mission field and the particular ways in which English-speaking Pentecostals engaged Indigenous peoples and French-speaking people in Quebec. The efforts of English-speaking Pentecostals parallel a long-standing tradition of conflict and tension between English and French, Roman Catholic and Protestant, the settlers and Indigenous people. Viewing Canada as a mission field is a key aspect of the subculture's repertoire that extends colonial views and patterns. This case allows us to review an important discussion among scholars about the complexity of Pentecostalism, conversion, cultural interaction, and decolonization.

Pentecostalism at its core is a missionary movement with roots in nineteenth-century evangelicalism. Gary McGee has made a compelling case for understanding the historical and theological context of Pentecostal missionary efforts and the attempts to evangelize the world in the twentieth century.[1] What many Holiness and Methodist Christians believed in the late nineteenth century, however, was that they lacked the ability to complete the goal of preaching the gospel to the whole world. The radical evangelicals that emerged in the nineteenth century were reading the biblical accounts of the early church and asking how the church was able to grow so quickly. It was not long before some preachers, like Charles Parham in 1901, were making the link between evangelism and what the writer of Acts was saying: "you will receive power when the Holy Spirit comes upon you" (Acts 2). This empowerment to evangelize with the biblical support of "signs and wonders" or miracles was quickly embraced by many. Yet it was also controversial. For Parham and many American evangelicals, the relationship between speaking in tongues and missionary work was believed to be the supernatural ability to speak the language of the people God was sending you to evangelize, without prior knowledge of their language or need for language acquisition through traditional means of learning a second language. This understanding of tongues as a missionary language, or, technically, xenolalia, was rejected by some and later transformed into the classical Pentecostal doctrine of tongues as evidence of Spirit baptism. Classical Pentecostals, like the PAOC, still maintained that there was a relationship between tongues and missionary activity – namely, empowerment to do evangelistic work. Church growth through the work of empowered missionaries was believed to be a sign of God's miraculous activity in the world. When PAOC missionaries worked in Canada among French and Indigenous peoples, they encountered social realities that complicated their plans.

Pentecostal mission history is quite complex, as Allan Anderson argues.[2] While popular histories of Pentecostalism tend to focus on the efforts of particular American or European individuals to evangelize and start churches, Anderson points out that it was actually the work of local Indigenous peoples who facilitated the spread of global Pentecostalism with greater success than most popular histories recognized. With examples from India, China, and South Africa, Anderson retells the story of Pentecostal mission work that emphasizes the work of local people in the rapid growth of Pentecostalism. This is an important aspect for understanding the worldwide spread of Pentecostalism, and it has implications for understanding what also occurred in Canada, especially with the spread of Pentecostalism among Indigenous peoples. That spread took place largely in spite of the PAOC and its programs. Further, it also helps to explain what happened with the PAOC's missionary work in Quebec. For decades, the PAOC leadership had largely discredited or undervalued the work of francophone Pentecostals in relation to the work of national directors for Home Missions or district superintendents from eastern Ontario who were operating parallel programs in Quebec. Anderson writes about the success of many Pentecostal missionary efforts in spite of what he calls "signs and blunders" among missionaries who did not understand local cultural practices.[3] For Canadian Pentecostals, there are also blunders associated with views of superiority among anglophone Pentecostals towards francophone people. There were tensions between Pentecostals and Roman Catholics over proselytism, with different views about conversion, evangelism, and missionary work in Quebec. At the same time, there were paternalistic and racist views toward Indigenous peoples implicit in the adopted colonial patterns of missionary work, and yet there are also some accounts of rapid church growth and Indigenous leadership in spite of these problems.

HOME MISSIONS

Mission Canada is a department of the PAOC and the national mission-sending agency of the denomination. The PAOC states: "We have made a crucial decision as a Pentecostal family. We have determined to have a national mission agency that will enable us to reach Canada with the gospel in unique ways. There are many contexts where there is a gap; campuses, people groups, regions and communities where Jesus is inadequately represented. Mission Canada is committed to identify and equip those who will pursue their calling to fill these gaps."[4] Mission Canada has a particular focus on establishing congregations, ministries, and outreach to youth and children (especially those at risk) through chaplaincies on university campuses, urban projects especially among the poor, and working with cultural language groups (including Christian immigrants seeking affiliation with the PAOC and non-Christian immigrants whom they hope to evangelize), francophone Canadians, and Indigenous peoples. Specifically, the department envisions its role revolving around discipleship, social responsibility, and planting new congregations. The goals and objectives of Mission Canada largely focus on what the PAOC refers to as the "challenges" of a diverse and multicultural Canada.

The view of Canada as a mission field requires some historical context for understanding Pentecostal mission activity at home. The colonial history of North America, as territory claimed by the French and later British settlers, is the historical basis for understanding North America as a mission field for European Christians with the primary focus on converting Indigenous peoples. John Webster Grant's 1984 book, *Moon of Wintertime*, provides an early scholarly account of the interaction between European Christian missionaries with Indigenous peoples in North America since 1534.[5] Grant examines the aims and activities of missionaries and their interactions with Indigenous peoples, noting how Christianity was embraced but also the ambiguity of cultural interaction, including the particular problems associated with the decline of traditional culture, spirituality, and language and especially the residential school system. Continuing work on these questions adds complexity to understanding the consequences and repercussions of cultural losses by pointing to the power imbalances, abuses, and ongoing legacy of these relationships. Most recently, the report of the Truth and Reconciliation Commission (2015) drafted 94 "Calls to Action" as a means of beginning to address these atrocities,[6] and the National Inquiry on Missing and Murdered Indigenous Women and Girls invoked the language of "genocide" in its June 2019 final report.[7] Missionary activities of the Christian churches are implicated in the complex realities that are being brought to light through the reports mentioned above and ongoing scholarship on related questions.

While the Pentecostals have a shorter history of involvement among Indigenous peoples in Canada, they too embraced the missionary role, with some limited success. Grant identifies the affinities that exist between Pentecostalism and Indigenous spiritualities but also sounds a caution, saying, "The Pentecostals, whose charismatic approach has affinities with Indian concepts of communion with the spirits, have been especially successful in winning native converts and in developing native leadership. Confident in the truth of their message, however, few representatives of these groups seem to have sought to learn any lessons from the experience of earlier missions that began with equal enthusiasm and apparent success."[8]

The Pentecostal missionary impulse, including its successes and failures, is a product of the broader missionary activity of colonial Protestant Christianity. Werner Ustorf describes the modern Protestant missionary movement as one that is shaped by Victorian sensibilities and colonial encounters between Europeans and the rest of the world as they attempted to "unify the world through a twofold process involving modernization and Christianization."[9] By the middle of the twentieth century, the Christendom project collapsed, and the missionary movement was left to redefine itself. Pentecostalism, with its idea of Spirit-empowered mission, embraced the missionary challenge to evangelize the world, and while Canadian Pentecostals sent missionaries to Africa, Asia, and Latin America, they also continued the patterns of engaging Canada as a mission field, which included Indigenous peoples as well as French-speaking Roman Catholics.[10]

The earliest missionary work among Pentecostals in Canada is found in Ellen Hebden's work in Toronto when she opened up her "Faith Home" in May 1906 (see chapter 2).[11] Hebden's mission focused on ministering to people in need and providing a place of respite for missionaries coming home on furlough. Her ministry was typical of the types of faith mission homes among evangelical Protestants, especially Methodist and Holiness women in the late nineteenth and early twentieth centuries, and these became important for Pentecostals too.[12] James Opp examined the relationship between faith homes, healing, and women in Victorian Canada, accounting for the connection between the domestic environment of faith healing and the home as a spiritual space set apart from the world of men, politics, and industry.[13] Women regularly worked in faith homes, offering spiritual and physical health while writing healing narratives in devotional works, testimonies, letters, newsletters, and prayers. Hebden also practised the writing of healing narratives in her own newsletter, *The Promise*, which told stories of her experience of Spirit baptism, speaking in tongues, and the growing number of people who were attending her meetings. Hebden, following her Pentecostal experience, also believed that God was empowering Christians for missionary work. She encouraged leaders to seek the baptism of the Holy Spirit and to go out into the world empowered with that message. The Hebden Mission played a key role in funding early Pentecostal mission work in Canada among Indigenous people and around the world. She wrote about the missionary activities of people she supported, including Charles Chawner, who had a vision of evangelizing Africa.[14] The Hebden Mission raised funds for the Chawners beginning in 1907 as well as for numerous missionaries who went to South Africa, North Africa, China, Japan, India, Mongolia, and the Six Nations Indian Reserve near Brantford, Ontario. In 1907, revival meetings in Winnipeg included a number of Cree people who embraced the Pentecostal message. The Hebdens also held three "Pentecostal Workers Conventions" in 1908, 1909, and 1910 with key Pentecostal speakers like William H. Durham from Chicago. The conventions served to network the early Pentecostal movement and to inspire those in attendance to evangelize the world through the support of Pentecostal missionaries in Canada and overseas.

By the time the PAOC was formed in 1919, there were already fourteen Pentecostal churches in operation in Canada and fifteen missionaries serving overseas with some connection to the Hebden Mission.[15] In the 1920s, the PAOC financially supported the Chawner family, including the son, Austin Chawner, for his work among people from Mozambique working in the mines of South Africa. While there was no distinct "Home" or "Foreign" missionary department in the PAOC, missionary receipts for the PAOC were collected for work in Canada and abroad and reported in *The Pentecostal Testimony* (*PT*) with details from all affiliated congregations as giving for home and foreign missions. Missionary receipts decreased in the 1930s during the Great Depression, and fewer missionaries were supported. Special programs to raise funds for bicycles for foreign missionaries began in the 1930s and later transformed into the "Wing the Word" program for Pentecostal youth to raise money to purchase vehicles for missionaries. The PAOC adopted "the indigenous church idea" policy at its General Conference in Toronto in 1933 with the view of self-governing, self-propagating, and self-supporting congregations.[16] While the origin of the policy is not explicit in the PAOC documents, it may have taken its inspiration from the nineteenth-century Protestant mission work of Rufus Anderson, secretary of the American Board of Commissioners for Foreign Missions. The idea was developed and adopted for Pentecostals by Assemblies of God missionary Melvin Hodges in the 1950s and published as *The Indigenous Church*.[17]

Missionary secretaries for the PAOC included Robert E. McAlister (1919–32), Alfred G. Ward (1932–38), Charles M. Wortman (1939–44), and George R. Upton (1945–66). However, it was not until the 1940s that the PAOC made an organizational change for its work in Canada. In 1941, *PT* reported that a new department, "The Home Mission and Extension Department," was established with the approval of a motion at the 1940 General Conference held in Toronto.[18] The resolution stated: "RESOLVED, that a new department be created to be known as the Home Mission and Extension Department, aimed at reaching the unevangelized in our country especially the non-English speaking people."[19] More specifically, the object of Pentecostal evangelism at home, according to an article in

PT, included: "Fishermen, canners, loggers, trappers, settlers along the British Columbia coast line, and elsewhere; Foreign born settlers in sections of Canada. Chinese and Japanese in cities. Ukrainian, Russian, and other European, in cities, towns and country, districts; Untouched districts in older parts of Canada; and Eskimos. Indians [*sic*]."[20]

A 1941 editorial said, "It has been difficult to get our people to realize that there are thousands in our own Canadian land who never hear the Gospel and that we should take enough interest in them to pray and give that they might have someone to go to them."[21] Throughout the 1940s, the PAOC reported on a variety of home mission activities that included the "gospel boat" that travelled the coast of British Columbia, evangelistic meetings aimed at French-speaking Roman Catholics in Quebec, and calls for Pentecostals to support evangelism among Indigenous peoples. Pentecostal ministers like Arthur Townsend regularly reported in PT about home mission work. For example, Townsend wrote about his evangelistic work in the Cariboo region of British Columbia among Indigenous peoples, starting new congregations in remote regions of the province, and efforts to do mission work along the coast. Townsend said, "The command is: 'Go ye into ALL the world.' Sometimes we forget that Home Missions comes under this command. But, when one is situated among 'B.C. heathen' the need is readily and plainly seen. We have heathen at home! Are you praying for them and supporting the Home Missions' Extension Fund?"[22]

Salome Cressman, writing about French Canada in 1942, said "The eyes of many of our people are turning toward French Canada as a new mission field."[23] Cressman wrote about how French Canada was neglected and that the need was great for Pentecostals to respond. The mission was identified as the large number of disaffiliated Roman Catholics who at one time belonged "but finding nothing to satisfy, left that organization."[24] Cressman wrote about the large numbers of people who still belonged to the Roman Catholic Church, although "bound by the error and superstition of Rome." The author appealed to Pentecostals to respond to the new mission field with money and prayer and for workers to hear the call to come to French Canada. One Pentecostal minister highlighted in the article was W.L. Bouchard, who was noted for his successful evangelistic efforts in Montreal among Roman Catholics, the establishment of French-speaking congregations, and the French Bible school, Berean Bible Institute.[25]

However, it was not until the 1960s that the PAOC administration separated the two roles of Home Missions and Foreign Missions from the responsibility of the missionary secretary. At that time, C.H. Stiller was appointed as the Home Missions and Bible Colleges director (1963–66) and then as the general secretary-treasurer (1967–71), while Carmen W. Lynn was director of Overseas Missions (1967–80).[26] The Home Missions department expanded throughout the twentieth century and, through the efforts of Pentecostal leaders, engaged French-speaking Roman Catholics with new programs and efforts that created conflict between French-speaking Pentecostal pastors and English-speaking Pentecostal leaders. English-speaking Pentecostals also attempted to evangelize Indigenous peoples, and while some claims were made among English-speaking Pentecostals about the success of their efforts, much of the PAOC growth among Indigenous peoples happened through the work of Indigenous peoples themselves and not necessarily through PAOC programs. Two key individuals who shaped the Home Missions department and offer specific case studies for a discussion about conversion and culture are the focus of this chapter. Robert Argue (1967–82) and Gordon Upton (1983–92) served as directors for Home Missions during a period of social change in Canada. Their work illustrates the way in which Pentecostal mission was conducted in Quebec and among Indigenous peoples since the 1960s.

QUEBEC

The view of Canada as two solitudes is represented by more than 200 years of anglophone–francophone relations. From the Royal Proclamation of 1763 to the Quebec Act of 1774 and from the Constitutional Act of 1791 to the Rebellions of 1837–38, the relationship between the English and French was characterized by two nations attempting to come to terms with their differences. The Act of Union in 1840, which brought Lower Canada and Upper Canada together as a single province, however, did not reduce the tensions, with anglophone leaders securing power in the new union. By the 1860s, political leaders debated the value of the Act of Union and attempted to implement a new federal system with other British North American colonies. In 1867, a federation of four provinces with a central government located in Ottawa came into being and launched the new Dominion of Canada, although with lingering tensions between anglophone and francophone peoples. Even after Confederation in 1867, further tensions were evidenced in the Manitoba Act of 1870 over language issues and funding for Roman Catholic schools, and when Alberta and Saskatchewan became provinces in 1905, they followed the lead of Ontario in not allowing the use of French in schools by the 1920s. Further disagreement occurred over the involvement of Canada in British wars, most notably the South African Boer War and the conscription crises during World War I and World War II. Postwar prosperity benefitted both anglophone and francophone populations, but significant social change characterized the 1960s in Quebec, including the Quiet Revolution with its Quebec nationalist sentiments and Vatican II, which brought about significant social and religious change for Roman Catholics.

The political, social, and cultural shifts during this period between anglophones and francophones are intertwined with Protestant and Roman Catholic relations. The nineteenth century in particular was characterized by the growing power and expectation of the Roman Catholic Church to represent the concerns of francophone people in support of the political elite following the unsuccessful rebellions of 1837–38. In the period from the Act of Union until the Quiet Revolution, the Roman Catholic Church played an important role in shaping the identity of the Québécois, with the church impacting most of social life from the family to farm, work, unions, education, politics, and religion, all while fostering strong anti-Protestantism in the province. Protestants held deep prejudices against the French Roman Catholic Church with anti-Catholic sentiment. Protestants acting on their missionary impulse clashed with Catholics in their attempts to establish churches, conduct evangelism, use secular buildings for religious purposes, and gain access to media like radio and newsprint for advertising religious events.

The presence of French Protestants in the nineteenth century is explained by the Huguenots who left France following persecution and eventually expulsion. In the first half of the nineteenth century, French Protestant growth was due to the work of Swiss missionaries, Henriette Feller and Louis Roussy, and the founding of the Grande Ligne Mission in 1835 with the purpose of evangelizing francophone Roman Catholics. Other missions soon followed, including those by the Presbyterian Church in the 1840s and the Church of England in Canada with its Montreal Association in Aid of Colonial Church and School Society in the 1850s. One important person in the nineteenth century was Charles Chiniquy, a former Roman Catholic who converted to Protestantism. In the 1870s, Chiniquy worked with the

Presbyterians and claimed large numbers of converts, although there is some question about the number of people who left the church and whether or not they represented a shift from Roman Catholic to Protestant churches or emigration to the United States. Still, while evangelization proved to be difficult in Quebec, the Protestant missionaries claimed to have made an impact with the building of churches and schools, citing evangelization as the reason for their growth. However, by the turn of the twentieth century, the Protestants were questioning the financial costs of running churches in Quebec and the real success of evangelism. New fields were appealing, with waves of immigration on the Prairies, leaving the challenge of Quebec as a mission field for other groups like the Pentecostals.[27]

Pentecostalism first arrived in Quebec through the work of C.E. Baker, a former Methodist lay preacher who embraced the Pentecostal message in 1911 through the work of R.E. McAlister. Baker became a regular preacher in a number of evangelistic campaigns in Ottawa, and in 1913 his preaching found some reception among English speakers in Gatineau, Quebec, across the Ottawa River. In this same time frame, prayer meetings were held in Montreal by Kydd Byrne on Van Horne Street. In 1916, Baker came to Montreal to preach at the Mission on Van Horne Street where a British Methodist minister of French ancestry, Philip LeBrocq, embraced the message of the Pentecostal preacher. LeBrocq played a prominent role in the establishment of the first French Pentecostal meetings in Montreal in 1919 while working with Baker, who led the anglophone church.

In 1920, Baker and his growing congregation, Evangel Pentecostal Church, invited Aimee Semple McPherson to come to Montreal to hold evangelistic meetings. McPherson preached for three weeks at St Andrew's Church where it was reported that the building was often full to capacity and people had to be turned away. The English press reported on the events in the *Montreal Gazette* and *The Montreal Daily Star*, but no reports appeared in *Le Devoir* or *La Presse*. Michael Di Giacomo attributes the silence in the francophone newspapers to the tensions between Protestants and Roman Catholics.[28] Di Giacomo also writes, "The impact of her Montreal campaign for francophone Pentecostal and evangelical expansion is undeniable."[29] Di Giacomo argues that McPherson's campaign made a significant impact on the growth of Pentecostalism in the province with the conversion of key francophones who became Pentecostal leaders. For example, Louis Roussy Dutaud was instrumental in transforming the francophone

Pentecostal meetings at Baker's church into its own congregation in 1921, *La première église de pentecôte française.* Dutaud died in 1931, and the congregation reached its peak in the 1940s when it served about 300 people. By the 1960s, French Pentecostals had established eighteen congregations, a retirement home, a Bible school known as *L'Institut biblique bérée*, *Académie chrétienne de Montréal*, radio and television programs, and *La Conférence française*, a unique district of the PAOC, officially recognized in 1949. As early as 1945, French Pentecostals were seeking permission from the Eastern Ontario and Quebec District for an autonomous Francophone District. In 1949, when *La Conférence française* came into being, it had its own officers, constitution, and by-laws and was under the supervision of the Foreign Missionary Department of the PAOC. This period of growth and development came through the leadership of Emile Lassègues and Walter Bouchard and a number of francophone pastors in Quebec.[30] And yet, in spite of the work conducted by the francophone Pentecostals during this period, even with the heightened Roman Catholic and Protestant tension, the PAOC was unsatisfied with the developments, which became a major point of conflict between Robert Argue, PAOC director of Home Missions and Bible Colleges, and *La Conférence française.*

Robert Argue, nephew of the prominent Pentecostal leader Andrew Harvey Argue, was born in Winnipeg in 1916.[31] His early life was shaped by the Pentecostal movement and Calvary Temple in particular, influencing his educational choices, which included North Central Bible Institute and Central Bible Institute of the Assemblies of God. Argue completed a BA at Wheaton College and after serving in the Assemblies of God, US, returned to Canada in a variety of ministries, including director of Bethel Bible Institute in Saskatchewan following the Latter Rain incident in the late 1940s. After successfully navigating the Bible institute through that turmoil, Argue took up pastoral ministry at Evangel Pentecostal Church in Montreal. For eight years, he pastored Evangel where the congregation experienced growth and doubled to 1,200 people in the early 1960s. In 1966, Argue was elected as the executive director of Home Missions and Bible Colleges. Argue represented an important transition in leadership in the office and its approach to Quebec. During the 1960s, Quebec experienced the Quiet Revolution and Vatican II and the transformation of Quebec from a province dominated by the Roman Catholic Church to one with secular social institutions. As the Roman Catholic Church was beginning to experience decline in social authority, Catholics were also starting to slip out of the pews. Protestants, including the Pentecostals, were also finding that evangelism and church growth was difficult, with a decline in the number of people identifying as Pentecostal. Those new social realities in Quebec's increasingly secular society were the cultural backdrop to the PAOC's next steps in the province.

Argue saw this as an opportunity to re-engage Quebec as a mission field, and in 1968 he launched a major evangelistic effort during the summer months with young people to distribute Bibles, preach in churches, and visit people from door to door. *Dominion Outreach*, a publication of the PAOC (1962–69), contained articles in 1968 that described social change in Quebec and the spiritual need of francophone people as an opportunity for evangelism: "Where else in the world is the need so great? Over five million people within the borders of Quebec need Christ!"[32] Explaining the urgency of reaching Quebec, a PAOC leader asserted, "Quebec is at the cross-roads. A vacuum is being created in the hearts of hundreds of thousands of French Canadians as they endeavour to assess the amazing changes in their faith and practice. The inroads of secularism and materialism have greatly eroded the traditions of the past. The future is clouded by the uncertainties of science and government."[33]

The PAOC worked in conjunction with Evangel Church in Montreal, Evangel Church in Toronto, and the missionary organization Youth with a Mission, founded in the US by former Assemblies of God minister Loren Cunningham.[34] The evangelistic outreach took place in the summer of 1968, but it was clear that Argue was not satisfied with the efforts. In the 1970 annual business meeting of *La Conférence française*, Argue took the opportunity to scold the French pastors for not supporting the national office program.[35] Throughout Argue's tenure, he would face criticism and opposition from the francophone leaders who did not agree with his assessment or his view that they were part of the problem for the lack of growth in Quebec. One particular initiative by Argue, known as FLITE (French Language Intensive Training for Evangelism), encouraged anglophone pastors to move to Quebec, and through the acquisition of French language skills, they would engage in evangelism and plant new French churches. The program, however, was not without its problems, in part because the PAOC, and Argue specifically, failed to recognize the deep cultural differences between English and French Canada.

FLITE began in 1969 as part of Argue's strategy for evangelism and church growth in Quebec. Argue visited PAOC colleges to encourage students to study French and respond to the call to come to Quebec. He also corresponded with PAOC pastors and in June 1968 wrote: "A crash course in conversational French will be taught this coming year at Berea Bible Institute, Montreal ... Here is an opportunity for those called of God to French Canada to quickly learn the language. A few scholarships are offered. Write me today if you feel God calling to Quebec."[36] One student, David Whittaker, responded, and in 1969–70 he commenced his language instruction, which was a general conversational course. Argue faced numerous challenges, including lack of support from *La Conférence française* as well as the refusal to offer French language courses at *Institut biblique Bérée*. Undeterred, Argue made arrangements with *Institut biblique Béthel*, a non-Pentecostal interdenominational college in Lennoxville, Quebec, for language instruction. The arrangement lasted from 1969 to 1973 when theological differences between *Institut biblique Béthel* leaders came about through the growing influence of the Catholic charismatic movement and Pentecostals feeling less welcome. For the 1973–74 program year, Argue made arrangements for FLITE students to attend Laval University, Quebec City, to learn the French language as non-francophones. The relationship with Laval University lasted for fourteen years until the FLITE program came to an end.

Throughout Argue's tenure, tensions with *La Conférence française* were discussed annually in the standing Home Missions committee meetings, revealing his frustration with the francophone pastors. Without their cooperation, Argue arranged for parallel ministries in Quebec through the Eastern Ontario and Quebec District, which only exacerbated the situation, with questions raised about administrative responsibilities between the two districts (French and Eastern Ontario and Quebec). In 1975, it was finally recognized that *La Conférence française* was distinct from other language districts such as the German and Slavic Branch Conferences and "that the comparison of French Canada to an overseas field could no longer be sustained."[37] A new constitution was drafted to reflect the unique relationship between the PAOC and the francophone Pentecostals.[38] The FLITE program came under the direction of the Eastern Ontario and Quebec District and its new French Ministries Division. Throughout the 1970s, the francophone Pentecostals defended their work and record of church planting in Quebec and sought further administrative reorganization, including amalgamation with the French Ministries Division. The Eastern Ontario and Quebec District, however, proposed the consolidation of *La Conférence française* within its jurisdiction in 1989–90. The idea was rejected by the francophone leaders, who sought a unilingual French District in Quebec. Finally, in 1995, *La Conférence française* and the Eastern Ontario and Quebec District agreed to consolidate into one district with the promise of the creation of a Quebec District, which came into existence in January 2000 to provide administrative leadership for francophone and anglophone churches in the province. However, the long-standing tension and frustration among francophone Pentecostals was also the catalyst for key Pentecostal congregations and leaders to leave the PAOC.

While the PAOC was strategizing to evangelize in Quebec, some Pentecostals were on another path, engaging in dialogue with the Roman Catholic Church. In 1972, Pentecostals were invited to the Vatican for a dialogue with Roman Catholics on how to promote mutual understanding and respect between Roman Catholics and Pentecostals.[39] The dialogue focused on a number of issues, including the nature of religious experience, the role of the church and its relationship to evangelism and culture, the persecution of Pentecostals by Roman Catholics, and conflict over proselytism. Ronald Kydd, a former Bible college professor and pastor in the PAOC, was a participant in the dialogue from 1990 to 1998. Reporting on the annual meeting in 1996, Kydd said, "The fact that members of these two Christian communities have begun such a discussion shows growth in mutual trust and the maturing of a fragile relationship established in 1972. It also leads to the hope that they will find ways to bridge the gap, end the competition, and engage in common witness."[40] Ironically, the dialogue was not embraced by many Pentecostals, including the PAOC where suspicion was raised about ecumenism, the Roman Catholic Church, and numerous other issues.[41] For those who hesitated to be involved, it was a question of maintaining boundaries. Given the long history of anti-Catholic attitudes, many Pentecostals in the PAOC simply could not embrace what seemed to be a breach of their carefully constructed definitions of insiders and outsiders to their organization. Randall Holm said, "Given the historical inimical attitude of Canadian Pentecostals toward Roman Catholicism in general, Kydd's participation with the Roman Catholic–Pentecostal dialogue and his invitation to take part in these discussions has set him apart as a scholar of Pentecostalism, and a major Canadian Pentecostal thinker on the international and ecumenical stage."[42] However, for many in the PAOC, it meant that Kydd was making dangerous ties with those outside the PAOC fold, and it did not help to shift the view of Roman Catholics in Quebec as a mission field. Negotiating the relationships between the PAOC and Roman Catholics would lead to deep differences of opinion among Canadian Pentecostals.

INDIGENOUS PEOPLES

According to the 2016 Canadian census, Indigenous peoples in Canada (including Inuit, Métis, and First Nations) accounted for about 1.6 million people or roughly 5 per cent of the national population. The Indian Act, which only relates to First Nations peoples who appear in the Indian registry, is administered by the federal government. However, all Indigenous peoples are recognized as having special rights according to the Constitution Act, 1982. With more than 600 First Nations, more than fifty Inuit communities, several regional Métis organizations, and other Indigenous peoples who do not fit colonial categories, Indigenous peoples are far from homogenous. Reflecting unique histories, cultures, languages, politics, and spiritualties, Indigenous peoples and their societies are dynamic, not static. Throughout Canada's colonial history, the relationship between settlers and Indigenous peoples has included serious atrocities. Missionaries too have interacted with Indigenous peoples following typical patterns of mission programs, means of conversion, and the operation of residential schools in cooperation with the Canadian government that has had a significant detrimental impact on Indigenous communities. Much of the paternalism and racism throughout Canadian society was extensive in the churches. Indigenous peoples were also divided by religion between those who maintained traditional spiritualties and those who identified with Christianity, most notably Roman Catholicism, Anglicanism, and Pentecostalism.[43]

Missionaries played a key role alongside governments in building hospitals and residential schools, which brought clergy, doctors, nurses, and teachers into the mission.[44] Three types of schools included day schools on the reserves, boarding schools, and industrial schools for learning trades. The residential school system was initiated in 1883 after an American model, operating until the 1990s, with the goal of assimilation.[45] The number of residential schools operated by faith groups in 1923–24 was Roman Catholic, thirty-nine; Church of England, twenty-one; Methodist, six; and Presbyterian, seven. The schools all received financial support from the federal government, and by the end of the 1930s, the number of faith-based and government-run schools totalled 239 day schools, thirty-four boarding schools, and fifteen industrial schools.[46] Complaints over the schools included inadequate funding, poor quality of education, lack of food, physical and sexual abuse, high mortality rates, exploitation, discrimination, and condemnation of Indigenous culture.[47] The residential school system failed Indigenous people and became the focus of a series of public apologies from churches and, in 2008, the federal government. For decades, the government and churches heard complaints about the education system, abuse, violence, racism, discrimination, and a host of issues around broken families and disrespect for traditional culture. Even when the residential school system came to an end, rumours persisted about the abuse, which was followed by denial and reports of cover-up. The 1990s was a period of disbelief and denial among Canadians when investigations into the residential school system revealed the extent of emotional, sexual, and physical abuse.[48]

While the Pentecostals did not operate residential schools, Pentecostals from Indigenous reserves did attend the schools, including Matthew Coon Come, who was elected Chief of Canada's Assembly of First Nations in 2000. When Coon Come was elected, the focus of the media was not so much on his political views or his fight for Indigenous rights, which were already well known. Rather, it was that Coon Come was a Pentecostal.[49] Since the 1950s, Pentecostal growth had been accelerating among Indigenous peoples, with key leaders emerging from Indigenous Pentecostal churches. In 1931, about 0.08 per cent of Indigenous people identified as Pentecostal, growing to 4 per cent in 1991, which was almost four times the rate of Pentecostalism in the rest of the Canadian population. In 2001, it was reported that 19,000, or 3.4 per cent of "Registered/Treaty Indians," identified as Pentecostal, and another 35,000 Canadians with some Indigenous ancestry also claimed to be Pentecostal (see table 6.1).

The PAOC reported that they had 100 Indigenous congregations by the end of the 1980s, after which there began a pronounced slowing in the rate of growth of Pentecostalism in Canada, including Indigenous Pentecostals. Between 1945 and 1980, Pentecostalism grew largely because of Indigenous leaders and not because of any specific

Table 6.1
Percentage Distribution of Indigenous Peoples as Pentecostal, 1931–2001

1931	*1941*	*1961*	*1971*	*1981*	*1991*	*2001*
0.08	0.1	1.1	2.1	3.3	4.0	3.4

Source: Derived from Statistics Canada, 1931, 1941, 1961, 1971, 1981, 1991, 2001.

PAOC program, according to Robert Burkinshaw.[50] Burkinshaw argues that Indigenous Pentecostals played a prominent role in the development of Pentecostalism through their own evangelistic efforts. He reports on the efforts of the PAOC as early as the 1930s to evangelize along the BC coastline, which included logging, mining and fishing camps, small towns, and settlements. By the 1940s, a "gospel boat" ministry was launched, and a plea from the Home Missions department was made to help fund the ministry, which would also focus on Indigenous peoples. Soon, several boats were added, and the funding for these "gospel boats" was added to the Home Missions budget. While only a few conversions were reported by the end of the 1940s, one small congregation was started at Alert Bay on a small island near Vancouver Island. By the 1950s, numerous revivals were reported among Indigenous peoples and spread quite quickly along the coast, creating some interest in the PAOC, especially for John Nygaard, a PAOC missionary.

Reports of meetings that were packed with Indigenous peoples, experiences of healing, and testimonies of conversion with a powerful move of the Holy Spirit were quickly spreading. According to Burkinshaw, "Evidence suggests that these revivals were characterized by a great deal of native initiative, despite the PAOC's official interest and its investment in personnel and finances in outreach to natives."[51] In some cases, the PAOC missionaries were critical of the singing and preaching by Indigenous Christians. Important Indigenous Pentecostals in this period included Stacey Peters, Harry Hunt, George Kallappa, James Kallappa, Paul Clayton, William Gladstone, Paul Mason, and Marion Johnson. While Native initiative and leadership was prominent throughout the 1950s, the PAOC eventually took a more prominent role in organizing and institutionalizing the movement throughout the 1960s and 1970s, with administrative responsibilities, policies for Indigenous preachers, including appropriate credentials, reports on congregational activities, and Bible school programs. In the 1980s, Peggy Kennedy worked to develop new congregations in the BC

Interior, especially the Cariboo region, and a focus on Native theological education.[52] Throughout this period, the PAOC continued to employ colonial patterns and critical attitudes toward Indigenous Pentecostal leaders while ignoring the realities of the trauma of residential schools and the racism that many experienced. In the midst of the developments, PAOC leaders worked to establish and maintain their own organizational culture and, in doing so, failed to recognize and respect Indigenous cultures and ways.

In the 1980s, the PAOC supported the development of a National Native Leadership Council (NNLC), sponsored by the National Home Missions Department, to wrestle with issues of interest to Indigenous communities. In 1986, the NNLC brought together key Native leaders for a "free exchange of concerns between native people and leaders" on church leadership, education, evangelism, healing, spiritual gifts, native spirituality, and pastoral issues.[53] Gordon Upton, former executive director of Home Missions and Bible Colleges for the PAOC, wrote about Indigenous peoples as "Canada's Forgotten People" in a 1987 *PT* article highlighting the poverty and despair in Native communities.[54] Upton wrote about social problems like alcoholism, unemployment, violence, and suicide in these communities as comparable to those in Third World countries. He also pointed to a resurging hope as God was "reaching down and granting new life and liberty to increasing numbers of native Canadians."[55] However, Upton was largely silent about the issues around colonialism, racism, and paternalistic attitudes toward Indigenous peoples. In the 1990s, the NNLC started to address church leadership issues as well as social and political issues like Native self-government, religious freedom, AIDS, and family dysfunction, although there was no direct discussion of the residential school system.[56] However, Pentecostals did participate in a "Sacred Assembly" in Ottawa in 1995 where Christians across Canada gathered to discuss and pray about how Aboriginal people were treated in residential schools.[57] By the end of the 1990s, the growth of Pentecostalism among Indigenous peoples was slowing, leaving scholars to ponder the question of why Indigenous peoples initially embraced Pentecostalism and why this had declined. On this question, John Webster Grant suggested that Pentecostalism was initially embraced because of its affinities with Indigenous spirituality, and other scholarship on Indigenous peoples and Pentecostalism confirms the links between traditional spiritualties and a Pentecostal focus on the spirit world, including the Holy Spirit and evil spirits.[58]

However, there may be other explanations beyond parallel spiritual world views. Clint Westman's research among Cree Pentecostals in northern Alberta focuses on the relationship between Pentecostalism and the political agency of Indigenous peoples, which allows for engagement on social issues around land claims and economic development.[59] Similar views about Pentecostalism and its role in mobilizing political action are noted among the Crow people in the US.[60] One other explanation for the spread of Pentecostalism has to do with the Indigenous principle or the focus on self-governing, self-propagating, and self-supporting congregations. While the PAOC adopted the "indigenous idea" as early as the 1930s, there is some question about whether or not it was ever put into practice. Angela Tarango argues that the Assemblies of God, US, also adopted the Indigenous principle and that the appropriation of it by Native Americans was central for local leadership, autonomy, and the transformation of Indigenous Christianity.[61] However, aspiring to follow the Indigenous principle and actually practising it are two different things. Graham Gibson's research into the problems of ministry training for Indigenous leaders in the PAOC highlights questionable education practices in Indigenous contexts.[62] Following four years of leadership in the Native Bible College in northern Ontario, Gibson stated that the PAOC needed to listen more closely to Indigenous voices that were frustrated with a paternalistic theological education and a system that was in need of radical Indigenization. In spite of these calls for far-reaching change, the PAOC has yet to respond to Indigenous issues in a way that recognizes its role as settlers in a colonial society. It has yet to demonstrate a working relationship with Indigenous congregations in the PAOC that understands the importance of Native culture, language, spirituality, the land, and healing and reconciliation. Incorporating those Indigenous cultural values into its own organizational culture represents a real challenge because it calls upon the PAOC to rethink some of its past decisions about boundary-making and shared authority.

In 2008, Prime Minister Stephen Harper made the first public apology for the role the Canadian government played in the residential school system in which children were separated from families, deprived of basic human needs, abused and neglected, and forced to assimilate through the eradication of Indigenous language and culture.[63] The prime minister stated, "The government recognizes that the absence of an apology has been an impediment to healing and reconciliation. Therefore, on behalf of the government of Canada and all Canadians,

I stand before you, in this chamber so central to our life as a country, to apologize to aboriginal peoples for Canada's role in the Indian residential schools system."[64] In the apology, Harper went on to recognize wrongs committed, leading to the implementation of the "Indian Residential Schools Settlement" to move toward healing and reconciliation.

Responses from the evangelical churches in Canada included an official letter from Bruce Clemenger, president of the Evangelical Fellowship of Canada (EFC). In a letter addressed to Prime Minister Harper, Clemenger said, it "is a significant initiative which I believe will contribute substantially to the process of reconciliation between Canada and its First Nations people."[65] Ray Aldred, chair of the Aboriginal Ministries Council for the EFC said, "The residential school experience has shaped the relationship between Aboriginal and non-Aboriginal in Canada. The hurt was particularly felt by those who were in the residential school system."[66] Aldred said that good could come out of the apology if non-Indigenous Canadians continued to address the issues raised in the apology needed for reconciliation and healing. Aldred also pointed to three steps that Canadian evangelicals needed to take to be agents of reconciliation. These steps included acknowledging the sin of the residential school system by telling the truth; developing a theology of suffering that begins with listening to those who were violated; and developing a shared plan for reconciliation and restoration.[67]

Matthew Coon Come, a Pentecostal, former national Chief of the Assembly of First Nations and former Grand Chief of the Grand Council of the Crees of Quebec, responded to the apology by the prime minister, revealing that he had been taken from his parents and forced to attend a residential school where he experienced abuse: "As a former residential school survivor, I have waited a long time for this day. And I accept the apology. Each survivor must make his or her own decision. I decided a long time ago that I would move forward. I want broad change, but that change must start with me ... It is time for me to move on. And to continue being Cree, in defiance of everything the federal government intended for me and my people. And to continue asserting our peoples' human rights to self-determination, to our cultures and to our resources and lands."[68] Coon Come's statement reveals a complex mix of accepting the apology and asserting ongoing resistance.

Clearly, as Coon Come's statement demonstrates, Pentecostalism among Indigenous peoples is complex, and its adoption can be attributed in part to some affinity between traditional Indigenous spirituality and Pentecostal views of the spirit world. And yet it is also attractive because Indigenous efforts to spread Pentecostalism reveal a certain level of autonomy in spite of tensions about the role of the Home Missions Department. It is critical to recognize both the PAOC's failure to employ a self-governing Indigenous church model and the colonial patterns and attitudes of Home Missions. Nevertheless, Indigenous Pentecostals have demonstrated independence in their congregations and extended that agency to address issues around self-governance, resources, land, and cultural preservation. The way forward must involve a process of decolonization whereby the institutional structures of settler organizations, including Home Missions, are dismantled. This will require a new relationship with Indigenous peoples, including greater autonomy and recognition for the work of Indigenous Pentecostals. Working these issues out with Indigenous partners is yet another example of the complexity of negotiating cultural realities for the PAOC.

CULTURE AND CONVERSION

The view of Canada as a mission field and the various roles that the PAOC played, including those of its denominational leaders and missionaries, was ambiguous in many ways. In some ways it perpetuated colonial patterns and unequal relations rooted in racism as observed in the tensions between anglophones and francophones, Protestants and Roman Catholics, and Indigenous peoples and settlers. In other ways, Pentecostals in Quebec, for example, were able to negotiate a new, separate district that allowed them greater autonomy in the province. This was not without some controversy, however. As for Indigenous Pentecostals in the PAOC, they are still working out these issues as they relate to colonial patterns of settlement, missionary activity, cultural identity, and the authority of the denomination as it is currently structured. Questions about the role of the PAOC and its shifting boundaries that define who is in and who is out are clearly illustrated in this chapter. Furthermore, the organizational identity of the PAOC was questioned by Quebec Pentecostals and Indigenous peoples who challenged the anglophone majority, assuming their culture was equal to the organization's identity. The response of the PAOC to francophones, Roman Catholics, and Indigenous peoples was also rooted in a cultural repertoire of conversion supported by its denominational magazine, *The Pentecostal Testimony* (PT).

Testimony, the public recounting of a conversion narrative, is an important cultural tool that serves to legitimize the PAOC's work among francophones, Roman Catholics, and Indigenous peoples. Since its first publication in 1920, *PT* has focused on stories of conversion from across Canada. Testimonies were at one time (and perhaps still are in some PAOC congregations) ritualized in the Sunday congregational meeting. In some cases, a special speaker would address the congregation from the platform either during the sermon or at some other point to tell the story of how they came to Christ. The typical pattern followed a narrative around what one's life was like before meeting Christ, how they met Christ, and what their life has been like since then. For Pentecostals, some aspect of the narrative included the baptism in the Holy Spirit with speaking in tongues, healing, or some other miraculous event. Congregations would also regularly practise the offering of public testimonies from the pews, which were meant to be spontaneous whereby anyone could stand up and share what the Holy Spirit was doing in and through them in the previous week. Testimonies served to encourage people, motivate them, provide evidence of the work of the Holy Spirit, and socialize the young into what was expected or normative about the Pentecostal experience. They could also be risky because the leadership and congregation never knew what someone might say, but that was always both the strength and weakness of these congregational stories.

While Pentecostal stories of conversion were shared in the congregation and through *PT*, they primarily focused on the individual's experience of conversion. However, our understanding of conversion is far more complex and according to sociologists includes other levels like organizations, societies, and cultures.[69] Questions about culture and conversion at the level of the individual include why people join new religious movements like the Pentecostals. Explanations for why individuals converted to Pentecostalism have focused on ideas like deprivation, personal attachments of friendships and family, and the role of social networks. At the level of organizations, questions about conversion were often asked in relation to the process of secularization and why the mainline Protestant churches were declining while evangelical Protestant churches were growing. Market model explanations focused on the success of some churches that organizationally met the need for religion among people in the marketplace. The winners in the religious marketplace were organizations like the Pentecostals who maintained a high demand for strictness and orthodox faith in contrast with the low demand among so-called liberal churches. At the societal level, sociologists explored the social and cultural context for understanding why large groups of people, especially in Africa, Asia, and Latin America, converted to Pentecostalism. One of the main issues here is understanding how societies go through periods of social change that disrupt the culture, leading large numbers of people to convert.[70] Conversion in this case is linked to the disordering of society and the need for some social cohesion that religion offers. All three levels have something to say about conversion, and in Canada it appears that while some individuals convert and some organizations appear to do better in a secular context, the declining demand for organized forms of religion at the societal level is making it increasingly difficult even for Pentecostals to grow. Viewing Canada as a mission field based on older patterns of colonial interaction and anglophone superiority met with mixed results for PAOC initiatives among Indigenous people and French Canadians. The changing cultural landscape means that the PAOC goals of mission and conversion will be challenged as it seeks to maintain its subculture, social boundaries, and organizational identity.

Theologians have also had something to say about mission and conversion. David Bosch, for example, wrote about the many different forms that mission takes, including mission as solidarity with the poor, mission as social justice, mission as liberation, mission as evangelism, mission as contextualization, and mission as common witness among Roman Catholics.[71] Bosch's theological treatment of mission challenges the one-dimensional view in the PAOC that mission is primarily about evangelism and conversion. If Canada is a mission field, then mission will look different from what was imagined in the twentieth century. While evangelism was the primary focus of conversion narratives found in *PT*, some Pentecostals, like the Roman Catholic dialogue partner Ron Kydd and Indigenous leader Matthew Coon Come, engaged in other forms of mission, including mission as common witness and mission as social justice. We suggest that a conversation about mission as partnership and mission as decolonization is also needed, which may lead to some form of organizational conversion.

7

Immigration and Religious Diversity

INTRODUCTION

The Royal Commission on Bilingualism and Biculturalism (1963–69) brought about a range of social and cultural changes in Canadian society. The commission set out to study the bicultural and bilingual nature of Canada during a period of unrest over language and culture, leading to the development of the Official Languages Act and the Department of Multiculturalism. Seven volumes were published by the commission, which focused primarily on anglophone and francophone issues and the role each played in the so-called founding of the country. However, not all Canadians responded enthusiastically to the commission, as reported in a government publication entitled *The Cultural Contribution of the Other Ethnic Groups*, which noted that "other" Europeans, especially northern, eastern, and southern Europeans, wanted to be recognized equally as builders of the country.[1] The view of Canada as a bilingual and bicultural country soon evolved into a vision of a polyethnic and multicultural society that recognized a commonwealth of many nationalities within the framework of its two founding peoples. Indigenous people, however, were not included in the commission's mandate.

Multiculturalism in Canada has a number of meanings that illustrate the complexity of the term.[2] Often, multiculturalism is used simply to describe the demography of Canadian society, highlighting a range of ethnically diverse peoples that have migrated over the centuries. Multiculturalism can be used prescriptively to promote a set of ideals that not only encourage diversity but serve as a sort of moral order for how Canadian social institutions ought to operate.

Multiculturalism also contains a practical component that facilitates the lived expression of particular ethnic groups and the cultural practices they celebrate within homes, cultural centres, street parades, and stages across the country. What is most often debated, however, is the political aspect of multiculturalism that includes a range of policies and government initiatives that relate to, among many things but not solely, immigration. In this chapter, we focus on how the Pentecostal Assemblies of Canada (PAOC) responded to the growing numbers of immigrants from Asia, Africa, and Latin America in the 1990s. We discuss the PAOC's focus on new immigrants as sources of church growth in relation to earlier patterns of interaction with European immigrants and black Pentecostals. We also examine the response of the PAOC to non-Christian religions following 9/11 and the challenge of religious diversity, which represents a tension for Pentecostals between inclusion and exclusion.

BRANCH CONFERENCES AND BLACK CHURCHES

The PAOC responded strategically and pragmatically to the migration of Pentecostals from other European countries by allowing them to organize as Branch Conferences in the 1930s, as long as there was no conflict doctrinally or organizationally. In this way, the PAOC could expand by welcoming new members even as it continued to reinforce boundaries around its views of orthodoxy and organizational authority. Branch Conferences were defined as: "A unit in the General Conference organization equivalent to a District Conference in General Executive membership and relationship ... A Branch is distinguished from a District Conference in that its territory of operation is not geographical, but is confined to ministry among certain races or language groups. Its geographical area of operation may therefore overlap or coincide with that of one or more District Conferences."[3] Branch Conferences operated somewhat independently, like the District Conferences, within the general framework of the PAOC, controlling their own camps, programs, and budgets.

This was an important organizational feature of the PAOC in its early formation, with ethnic congregations of the PAOC grouped into Branch Conferences. They operated like the geographical District Conferences but were formed around ethnicity and were especially important for French-, German-, Finnish-, and Slavic-speaking Pentecostals. In Canada, black Pentecostals formed their own denominations with organizational links to Pentecostals in the United States. Following the 1960s, the development of Branch Conferences was discontinued, coinciding with the growth of immigration from non-European countries. Black churches, however, were organized around links with black Pentecostal denominations in the United States like the Church of God in Christ. The PAOC, through its department Mission Canada, focused on language and cultural groups as avenues for evangelism but mostly, in spite of its claims, for assisting new immigrant Pentecostals who were seeking to affiliate with the denomination. The history of the relationship of the PAOC with Branch Conferences and black churches is instructive for a number of reasons that are not simply related to church polity but also to the changing demographics of Canadian society and the development of multiculturalism.

Between 1931 and 1971, the ethnic origin of Pentecostals in Canada shows that most Pentecostals were British, followed by other European and French. For example, in 1931, 69 per cent of Pentecostals had a British ethnic background, 2 per cent French, and 28 per cent other European (see table 7.1). The other Europeans were mostly German, Scandinavian, Dutch, and Italian. Scandinavians included people with Norwegian, Swedish, Danish, and Icelandic ethnicities. Some ethnic groups, like the Dutch Pentecostals, while larger than the Finnish, never established their own Branch Conference. The Italian Pentecostals established a separate denomination, the Italian Pentecostal Church of Canada (now the Canadian Assemblies of God) yet with close ties to the PAOC.[4] Table 7.2 shows the percentage of Pentecostals within specific ethnic groups so that in 1931, 0.3 per cent of those with a British ethnic background identified as Pentecostal, growing to 1.5 per cent in 1971. Pentecostals experienced growth among the French, German, Scandinavian, and Dutch between 1931 and 1971, while the Italian Pentecostals decreased.

By 1941, three Branch Conferences had formed, including the Slavic Conference (1931), the Finnish Conference (1939), and the German Conference (1940). The French Conference was organized in 1949. Thomas Miller wrote that the Branch Conferences formed because of language differences, which is partially correct but does not fully account for the organizational appeal of forming a Branch Conference.[5] While a common language, for example, brought German-speaking Pentecostals together, there was also, constitutionally, a level of

Table 7.1
Percentage Distribution for Ethnic Origin of Pentecostals, 1931, 1941, 1961, 1971

	1931	*1941*	*1961*	*1971*
British	69	67	65	67
French	2	3	4	3
Other European	28	28	26	24
Other	1	2	5	6
Total	100	100	100	100

Source: Derived from Statistics Canada, 1931, 1941, 1961, 1971.

Table 7.2
Percentage Distribution of Ethnic Groups as Pentecostals, 1931, 1941, 1961, 1971

	1931	*1941*	*1961*	*1971*
British	0.3	0.7	1.2	1.5
French	0.01	0.04	0.1	0.1
German	0.6	1.0	1.4	1.6
Scandinavian	0.8	1.5	1.7	2.0
Dutch	0.4	1.0	1.2	1.2
Italian	0.7	1.1	0.4	0.4

Source: Derived from Statistics Canada, 1931, 1941, 1961, 1971.

autonomy, financially and organizationally, for the Branch Conference. Branch Conferences established their own congregations, camps, mission programs, and, in some cases, leadership training. The point is, while some groups formed Branch Conferences around language, not all ethnic Pentecostals followed the same pattern.

The largest and, arguably, the most successful, was the German Branch Conference. The origin and growth of German Pentecostalism in Canada had two important sources, which included the migration of German-speaking Pentecostal leaders in the early twentieth century and, second, the role of revival meetings by those German Pentecostals that saw German immigrants join them.[6] Important figures, Julius Schatkowski, August Kowlaski, and Oskar Jeske played prominent roles in organizing and expanding Pentecostalism among German immigrants.[7] Some German-speaking pastors were trained in Europe at the International Bible Institute in Danzig, Poland, including Wilhelm Kowalkski, Aflons Mittelstaedt, Reinhold Hildebrandt, Matthian Baumgartner, and Christian Green.[8]

Pentecostal ministry in Canada among German-speaking peoples initially developed independently of the PAOC. In 1919, Rev. George Schneider, a German-speaking pastor from Edmonton, Alberta, began tent meetings where many German Christians were filled with the Spirit. Feeling persecuted for their new experiences, they left their Lutheran churches to establish new congregations, and in 1919 the first German Pentecostal congregation was established in Wiesenthal, near Leduc, Alberta.[9] By 1934, there were ten congregations in Alberta.[10] Feeling the need for closer ties with other Pentecostals, the Germans established their own organization, later joining the PAOC as an official Branch Conference in July 1940. The affiliation of the German Pentecostals also benefitted the PAOC by incorporating more resources into the denomination. Following the World Wars, the Pentecostal movement in Canada continued to grow with the migration of German-speaking Pentecostals from Austria, West Germany, and Poland, experiencing rapid growth in the cities of Edmonton and Winnipeg. During the 1950s and 1960s, the German Branch Conference expanded by planting new congregations in Ontario and British Columbia. Expansion also allowed for organizational changes in the 1970s with the hiring of full-time administrators for their new office in Kitchener, Ontario. By the 1980s, however, growth among German Pentecostals was slowing, and that trend generated a number of challenges and debates about the future of the Branch Conference and German-speaking congregations. The decline also corresponded with smaller numbers of German immigrants, growing numbers of Pentecostals arriving from Africa, Asia, and Latin America, and a shift in policy about Branch Conferences.

The relationship between the predominately white Pentecostals and the black Pentecostals, however, reflected a different history. The racial history that divided Pentecostals in the United States was also reflected in Canada through the close tie between the PAOC and the white Assemblies of God and with the separation of black churches from white churches. The PAOC was also a member of the Pentecostal Fellowship of North America, a network of historical white denominations. Charles Parham, who was considered the initiator of the doctrine of Spirit baptism in the United States with the evidence of speaking in tongues, taught the doctrine to his students in a Bible school in Kansas. He had experienced speaking in tongues in 1901. William Seymour, the African-American preacher who was the leader of the Azusa Street revival meetings in Los Angeles (1906–09) learned about the doctrine from Parham while attending one of his classes. Parham, shaped by the racial divisions of the United States and a sympathizer of the Ku Klux Klan,[11] allowed Seymour to attend the class as long as he was separated from the white students. Seymour sat in the hall and listened to Parham teach with the door slightly ajar. Shortly after the Azusa Street revival began, Parham visited Seymour in Los Angeles and was shocked to discover that the meetings were interracial and included blacks, whites, Mexicans, and people from Asia. Parham thought this was scandalous, and not long afterwards the meetings began to decline, with white Pentecostals separating from the black Pentecostals, forming separate churches and organizations. The racial tensions among Pentecostals in the United States had implications for Canada where racial policies excluded blacks from PAOC ministry but also meant that black Pentecostal churches in Canada largely formed with links to American black churches like the Church of God in Christ and the Church of God of Prophecy.

The largest Pentecostal church in North America is the African-American denomination, the Church of God in Christ (COGIC), founded by C.H. Mason in 1907.[12] The success of COGIC in Canada is largely due to the work of C.L. Morton (1897–1962) and his son C.L. Morton, Jr (1942–), who established the Mount Zion church in Windsor, Ontario. Morton's ancestors settled in southwestern Ontario and were part of the Holiness movement in which his maternal grandmother had a charismatic experience that shaped the family. As a teenager, Morton had his own conversion experience and began attending a white Pentecostal church in Chatham. At age seventeen, he was preaching and assumed pastoral duties a year or so later when the senior minister resigned. Morton also served in a white Pentecostal church in Brantford, Ontario. However, when World War I broke out and conscription was introduced, Morton refused to serve because it was against his religious beliefs. Morton was tried, convicted, and sentenced to three years in the Kingston Penitentiary. Morton served nine months until he was released along with other conscientious objectors.[13]

Upon his release, Morton moved to Detroit and joined a COGIC congregation. However, it was not long after arriving in Detroit that he was sent to West Virginia to lead a congregation. After three years of preaching, he felt he was called by God to go back to Canada and establish a church in his home country. Around 1925, he began preaching in Windsor, with little success for the first three years, holding revival meetings in Amherstburg, Ontario, where seventy-five people were baptized in the Detroit River. Morton opened another church in 1928 in Harrow, a small farming community east of Amherstburg. He also began radio broadcasts around the same time in Chatham and Windsor. The success of his radio ministry allowed him to build a new building for Mount Zion Full Gospel Church at 795 McDougall Avenue in 1939. Morton also planted a church in Buxton, Ontario. Morton unexpectedly died of a heart attack on 15 November 1962, turning the ministry of the Canadian COGIC over to his son. Other black Pentecostal churches included the Church of God of Prophecy in Canada, which established its first congregation in Swan River, Manitoba, in 1937.[14] By the 1990s, there were thirty-eight Church of God of Prophecy congregations in Canada, with a membership of 3,107 people and 100 clergy.

In the 1930s and 1940s, controversy surrounded the PAOC and one of its ministers. Concerned about how an interracial marriage might impact his ministry, the PAOC leaders passed a motion at the 1934 General Conference that said, "WE RECOMMEND that this conference go on record as unfavorable to the intermarrying of the colored races with the white, especially among our workers, and in so doing it will seriously affect their standing with the Pentecostal Assemblies of Canada."[15] In the 1941 PAOC yearbook, there appeared in a section titled "Workers (Rules Governing)" a prohibition concerning "the intermarrying of the coloured races with the white, especially among our workers."[16] The prohibition was last published in 1945 when the yearbook then became a list of ministers, missionaries, and local assemblies. The General Constitution and By-Laws included the paragraph until 1943, after which no new editions of this document were published and the issue of interracial marriage is not mentioned. There is also no reference to the removal of this prohibition in the General Conference minutes. We can only speculate that the decision to drop the rule was made internally sometime after 1945. The specific issue that initiated the decision revolved around a credentialed minister who married a white woman after being warned by the PAOC that doing so would jeopardize his ministry. The minister disagreed with the policy and married the woman in spite of the objection and went on to have a prominent ministry in Canada, although as an independent Pentecostal. The role that systemic racism played through PAOC policy was also reflected in its membership in the Pentecostal Fellowship of North America. That organization for Pentecostals finally disbanded in 1994 at the so-called "Memphis Miracle" where white Pentecostal denominations apologized to African Americans for years of racism and exclusion.[17] It is clear that the PAOC in the first half of the twentieth century was in agreement with the broader culture on issues about racial segregation, specifically prohibiting mixed-race marriage for its leaders. Those cultural assumptions later shifted as Canadian societal attitudes toward race liberalized.

NEW IMMIGRANT PENTECOSTALS

In the 1990s, there were a number of discussions among evangelicals about the decline of Christianity and the need to address those concerns with new evangelistic efforts. Books like *Reinventing Evangelism* by Don Posterski asked questions about pluralism, secularism, and social change in Canada and how traditional patterns of engaging culture were not effective.[18] If churches were going to grow, they needed to come up with new strategies. Church planting conferences and seminars were promoted by the PAOC, and many pastors attended conferences that focused on the challenges of Canadian culture and immigration. One discussion among evangelicals focused on new immigrants as sources of church growth. The assumption was that new immigrants were non-Christians, in need of evangelism, and if churches would consider Canada as a mission field, then they could focus their efforts on those people arriving from Africa, Asia, and Latin America.[19] However, the main problem with this logic is that the vast majority of Africans, Asians, and Latin Americans coming to Canada were already Christians. And many of these immigrants were already Pentecostals who believed God had called them to Canada to evangelize Canadians who were succumbing to secularism.[20]

Evangelicalism did experience growth in the 1990s, precisely because new immigrants were already Christians, not because they were evangelized after arriving in Canada. Ethnic congregations represented transfer growth from world Christianity in regions outside of the Global North. The Global South represents one of the most important developments in Christianity, not only as its centre and geographic location but also its theological and ethical impulse.[21] However, in Canada there is already some evidence that the growth of evangelicalism, largely from immigration, is beginning to slow in some denominations.[22] This has not discouraged evangelicals or the PAOC from engaging new immigrants and non-Christian religions in ways that raise questions about multiculturalism, inclusion, exclusion, and the process of boundary-making.

Canadian Pentecostalism continues to change and be influenced by recent developments in migration. Since the 1970s, when immigration strategies focused on recruiting more immigrants from Asia, Africa, and Latin America, Pentecostalism in Canada became increasingly culturally diverse. What this means for Pentecostals in Canada is that Pentecostalism is culturally diverse and going through a process of de-Europeanization whereby the majority of the PAOC, once predominately British, is declining. Ethnic and cultural congregations from Africa, Asia, and Latin America in the PAOC represent increased diversity (see table 7.3). Furthermore, the visible-minority status of Pentecostals in Canada is increasing, with black Pentecostals representing the largest group (see table 7.4).

New immigrant Pentecostals also maintain important networks with other Pentecostals outside of Canada. Networks reveal new practices and priorities for immigrant congregations, illustrating the changing nature of boundaries in global society as people, money, ideas, and Pentecostalism flow back and forth, and over and above, traditional borders.[23] The flows of Pentecostalism exemplify the ease with which Pentecostalism travels the globe. Pentecostal immigrants in Canada not only travel widely across borders, they also carry between home and host countries beliefs and practices that serve as a type of social capital. Key transnational networks, for example, are important for immigrant Pentecostals like the Koreans, who work together in Canada and around the world, facilitated through Yoido Full Gospel Church, Korea. Global conferences also serve to link Pentecostals together where they share resources, pray together, worship, and support one another in their work. These networks also support new denominational ties whereby resources like pastors are shared and recruited to serve in immigrant congregations in Canada.

Still, new immigrant Pentecostals have struggled to be recognized as full partners in the PAOC.[24] The work required to gain recognition is illustrated through many misunderstandings, which they have worked toward resolving. For example, in the 1990s denominational leaders did not understand to what extent these new immigrants already identified as Pentecostal with established viewpoints,

Table 7.3
Total Number of PAOC Congregations by Ethnic/Cultural Group, 2015–2017

Congregations by Ethnic/Cultural Group	*2015*	*2016*	*2017*
Aboriginal	79	78	77
Afghan	0	0	1
African	4	4	4
Arabic	2	2	2
Asian	1	1	1
Chinese – Cantonese	11	10	10
Chinese – Mandarin	4	4	4
Egyptian	1	1	1
English	699	688	698
Fijian	6	6	6
Filipino	21	23	23
Finnish	7	6	6
French	83	84	82
German	8	8	7
Ghanaian	7	8	8
Greek	1	1	1
Haitian	4	3	3
Hindi	1	1	1
Hungarian	1	1	1
Indo-Canadian	2	2	2
Japanese	1	0	0
Korean	21	20	18
Malayalam	3	3	3
Native Inuit	2	1	1
Nepali	1	1	1
Nigerian	1	1	1
Polish	6	6	6
Portuguese	12	9	9
Punjabi	1	1	1
Romanian	1	1	0
Slavic	15	15	15
Spanish	47	47	44
Tamil	11	11	11
Urdu	2	2	1
West Indian	2	2	2
Yugoslavian	2	1	1

Source: PAOC Statistics, 2018.

Table 7.4
Visible-Minority Population for Pentecostals in Canada, 2001

Minority Group	*Total*
Chinese	2,595
South Asian	4,310
Black	47,595
Filipino	3,545
Latin American	5,730
Southeast Asian	535
Arab	150
West Asian	125
Korean	685
Japanese	330
Other Visible Minority	3,040
Multiple Responses	1,270
Total	69,910

Source: Derived from Statistics Canada, 2001.

theologies, mission practices, organizational polities, theological training, ministry experience, and social networks. Furthermore, denominational leaders were unsure how to incorporate new immigrant Pentecostal leaders into their existing structures. However, ongoing discussion has resulted in changes in districts that include the development of leadership positions in cultural ministry for new immigrant pastors.[25] Negotiating these arrangements with newly arrived Pentecostals demonstrates that the PAOC's engagement is not limited to its interactions with those outside the church but also with fellow Pentecostals, all in an effort to establish orthodoxy, authority, and organizational coherence.

One particular leader is Jacob Joo, who came to Canada from South Korea in the 1980s to study at Eastern Pentecostal Bible College. Upon graduation, Joo was the pastor of the Pentecostal World Mission Church in Toronto and also affiliated with Yonggi-Cho's Full Gospel Church in Seoul, Korea.[26] Initially, this dual affiliation created problems for the PAOC as they attempted to navigate the new reality of global Pentecostal networks. However, this was not an issue for Joo or the members of his congregation where the benefits of the social ties with the home church in Korea enhanced his ministry in Canada.

The relationship with Korea provided Joo with an established network of pastors, congregations, and worldwide support. Annually, Korean clergy would travel to Korea and receive support and encouragement as they shared with one another news about their work. The link with Yonggi-Cho's church also offered Joo an important connection for new immigrants arriving in Toronto. As Joo explained, the name "Pentecostal" was sometimes questioned among Koreans while "Full Gospel" made sense contextually. The affiliation allowed Joo to maintain an important dual Canadian and Korean affiliation.[27]

The congregation in Toronto shared a building with a United Church of Canada congregation until 2003 when the Koreans purchased their own property. Along with the move, they renamed themselves the Full Gospel Mission Church. The congregation renovated a former 50,000-square-foot warehouse into a worship space with offices, classrooms, and multi-purpose rooms. By 2007, the congregation had well over 200 people attending the Korean-language service and about 100 people attending the English-language service. They also shared the building with other recent arrivals, including a Russian-speaking congregation and a Guyanese congregation, both of which formed shortly after the move to their new facility. For Joo, the relationship with these two congregations was important and reflected his congregation's mission and vision of ministry. Their relationship with the Russian-speaking congregation mirrored another aspect of their ministry. The Korean congregation had an affiliation with a Korean missionary in Ukraine, and therefore supporting a Russian-speaking congregation in Canada was a sign of God working through them both in Toronto and Ukraine.

The unique relationship between the Toronto congregation and the Korean missionary in Ukraine began as early as the mid-1990s when Joo and members of his congregation travelled to Ukraine to support another Korean pastor. Joo explained that the pastor had an "Elijah call" on his life whereby he was to be like the ancient prophet and bring the word of God to Russian-speaking Ukrainians and to plant 1,000 churches. Joo and his congregation assisted in starting thirty-five new churches and a theological college in Ukraine where they partnered with third-generation Russian-speaking Koreans to plant these churches. This ministry endeavour reflects two important historical points. First, much research has focused on the flows of people into Europe and North America when in fact there are other migrations in other regions of the world that are just as significant, one being the flow of people from Korea to Russia.[28] Different waves of Koreans have migrated north for economic reasons, settling in the far eastern regions since the nineteenth century. Koreans, once in Russia, migrated west and settled, with a sizable population in Ukraine. Second, the story reflects a religious shift, with Korea moving from a missionary-receiving country to a missionary-sending country in the world.[29] With accelerated globalization, the Russian-speaking ethnic Koreans came to partner with a missionary from Korea and a Korean pastor from Toronto. The mission work, however, is not aimed at new immigrants but at Russian-speaking Ukrainians whereby ethnic Russian-speaking Koreans translate the work of the Korean missionary into Russian with the assistance of Koreans from Toronto.[30]

Korean Pentecostalism in Toronto also reflects the concerns of its members over the tensions between North Korea and South Korea and issues about re-unification. During a Sunday worship gathering in 2007, Joo preached about the anniversary of the end of the Korean War and the tensions between North and South Korea. For his sermon, he showed a variety of slides from the war and offered both a political and a theological interpretation. Preaching from Matthew 12:25 – "Every kingdom divided against itself will be ruined, and every household or city divided against itself will not stand" – he focused on the divisions within Korea that led to the war between North and South. Joo spoke about the role Christians could play through prayer for unity and reconciliation. Joo said that if the churches do not show unity, how can the two Koreas do so? Korean unity was not simply an illustration of a theological idea but had social and political dimensions. Furthermore, the entire sermon focused on the anniversary of the end of the war, the problems of war, and the division between North and South Korea.

In the 2000s, the congregation faced new concerns over the growing numbers of second-generation members. The youth pastor, a young adult in his early twenties, was wrestling with how to work with the youth and their parents. Born in Canada to parents who emigrated from Korea in the mid-1970s, he graduated from the University of Toronto and started a career in the high-tech industry while volunteering at the church with the youth group. Following a short-term mission trip to Ukraine and Kazakhstan in 2001, he sensed that God was calling him into ministry. The youth pastor resigned from his job and began working at the church while attending seminary. During his tenure as a youth pastor, he experienced a number of challenges from the parents and the youth. The various issues revolved around language, education, parental expectations, and differences between parents and their children over Korean and Canadian culture.

For example, the youth pastor had to deal with tensions between the 1.5-generation youth and the second-generation youth over the use of English and Korean for youth activities.[31] Most of the 1.5-generation youth were not as competent in English as the second generation and preferred to speak in Korean. The second-generation youth were not as competent in Korean and preferred to speak English. The youth pastor attempted to resolve the tension by creating two youth groups – one that was English-speaking and the other that was Korean-speaking. Some parents of the 1.5-generation youth, however, wanted their children to be better English speakers and did not want a separate Korean-speaking group, while another set of parents thought speaking Korean was preferred, since they were intending to return to Korea once their children's education was completed. The youth pastor said, "There was a conflict, so in the end we decided to just merge the two youth groups together and make it one and as a result of that move a lot of the Korean-speaking students left the church. I guess they wanted to find another church that was predominantly Korean and where the service was in Korean. So it's still an issue that we haven't really resolved. I think we haven't really put much thought into it and how we can resolve the issue ... this whole language issue."[32]

A second concern revolved around what was perceived by parents as a distraction or temptation for their children over Canadian culture that was in tension with Korean Christian values. "I guess the concern is the future, their future, and a lot of the students right now just ... I don't know what it is. I think there are a lot of factors involved. Distractions and temptations and lack of discipline and so, many of them are struggling with school and not really taking their future seriously and thinking about their career, and so I think that's one concern that I have as a youth pastor."[33]

He also talked about the pressure he faced from parents who expected him to be a "parent" or, more specifically, a "father" to their children. Along with running a weekly youth meeting, retreats, and other activities, he said parents expected him to offer spiritual, academic, and future professional advice. Parents usually couched the expectation in a discussion about their own inability to communicate with their children because of the differences between English and Korean culture. The youth pastor agreed that it was partly about language differences but also a cultural expectation for Korean pastors to be more than a spiritual influence and said, "I'm not sure if this happens in other churches, like non-Asian churches, but there's an expectation that parents place on the youth pastor to raise their kids, you know, to be their father. So not only being their spiritual father, their shepherd, but also being their father – getting involved in their academic life and personal social life. And I think the line isn't really clear, and so because the parents have a hard time communicating with their children they expect me as the youth pastor to communicate the importance of education and studying hard in order to be successful in the future. So I think there's an expectation placed on me to do that."[34]

A decade later, another set of questions was being discussed not only among academics but increasingly in the Canadian public sphere over immigration, security, terrorism, religious diversity, and multiculturalism. In an interview with Jacob Joo in 2017, he was asked a series of questions about religious diversity and multiculturalism to try and understand his view on these issues. Joo expressed a common tension among evangelicals over inclusion and exclusion. That is, Joo was trying to come to understand how the exclusive claims he believed about Jesus being the only way for salvation could be reconciled in a society that valued multiculturalism and religious diversity, at least in theory.

> I think politically and socially speaking, multiculturalism seems to be working in Canada. I think the key word in multiculturalism is tolerance. I guess you have to tolerate other peoples' faith, values – appreciate other people ... as long as you keep that (tolerance) you are ok ... Intolerance is the bad word, it seems like in Canada. But when it comes to a spiritual and evangelistic perspective, I think there is subtle, maybe it is not really subtle, but explicit pressure not to evangelize. Evangelism is almost a crime. I mean ... because it's almost like intolerance, you know. You cannot, you should not, evangelize other people's faith because that shows that you are narrow-minded. It shows that you are right and the other the person is wrong. So I think there is, the climate in Canada that, evangelism is a no-no.[35]

Joo's comments reflect the view that multiculturalism is a sort of antidote to intolerance, but he also believes that for him to express his religious views, he must evangelize and tell others about Jesus. And yet there is for him a level of tension about evangelism because to claim Jesus is the only way is believed to be intolerant. Following a discussion about tolerance and whether that means acceptance or just leaving one another alone and never interacting, he moved on to discuss what he thought about religious diversity and whether or not he had any interactions in the city with people of other faiths, particularly Muslims and Hindus. Joo's response illustrated the tension he felt between what he thinks are the exclusive claims of Christianity and whether or not he can sincerely interact with non-Christians without compromising his faith.

> I don't want to be too narrow-minded. I don't want to be too stupid in saying this, but we have to be wise. But at the same time, I cannot give up my faith that Jesus is the only way to salvation, and other people, including Hindus, Muslims, they must believe in Jesus Christ for salvation … But at the same time, I don't believe in attacking other religions. I respect other religions. I allow them to express their own faith … I mean of course we have to evangelize … I don't want to attack them … We don't want to be branded as Islamophobic or homophobic and stuff. We want to be kind, and we want to be gentle. And we want to respect them. But I don't want to lose the focus that ultimately, they need to be saved … I am not sure Pentecostals can ever change that tenet of faith – that Jesus is the only way. It is not only the denominational tenet of faith, but it is also my personal tenet of faith.[36]

Conversely, Joo felt that if there is any intolerance in Canada, it is expressed toward Christians and that religious freedom is often granted to non-Christian religions.

> I think there is an anti-Christian spirit in a sense. I guess they're attacking more Christians. But, you know, there is monotheism and polytheism, and if you are polytheistic they are not exclusive. Whatever God you believe that is fine. Hinduism, Buddhism, they are all OK. But we have a monotheistic religion with Judaism, Islam, and Christianity. I mean, they are exclusive. They make exclusive claims. Jews, they believe in Yahweh and you have to be Jewish to be saved. Islam, they believe in Allah and Mohammed. We believe in Jesus Christ. And it seems like

> society is not attacking Jewish people. They are not attacking Islam for their exclusiveness. But it seems like they are attacking Christian exclusive claims. So I don't know why there is such an anti-Christian spirit that opposes our Christian faith. But they would not attack Islam for their own faith, or Jewish people. Why Christians?

However, as he talked about this initial claim, he shifted his comments to recognize the intolerance experienced among other religions.

> I sympathize with those Muslims living in Canada and the States because they feel threatened. Especially in the States right now. And you know, people attack them verbally on the streets because they are wearing hijabs and stuff. But, you know, if you look at, turn it upside down, if you are living in those countries and if you are Christian and if you are attacked on the street because you are Christian, I mean, you'd be scared, terrified, right? I sympathize with them because they're Muslim. Just because they are Muslims they should not be attacked like that … There are good people. There are bad people. There are good Christians, and there are bad Christians. In the same way, there are good Hindus, and there are bad Hindus. Good Muslims and bad Muslims, I guess. But I don't believe in attacking other religions, Hindus or Muslims, especially since this is more a Christian country. There are predominately more Christians than Hindus and Muslims, and because they are minorities they feel more threatened and they feel marginalized, and we have to, we need to embrace them, help them to feel at home … Not being anti-Muslim, anti-Hindu in the name of Christ. I think that is really a bad way of evangelism.[37]

Joo's comments reflect one of the major problems of identifying the goal of multiculturalism as tolerance. Tolerance, however, does not have the objective of integrating religious groups into Canadian society, nor does it further the interests of the state for equality. Rather, tolerance simply becomes a form of acceptance, albeit at arm's length from those one disagrees with and not a basis for mutual understanding.[38]

The intersection of immigration, ethnicity, and religion in Canada shaped the PAOC in very specific ways, accounting for its interactions with immigrants, growth, and organizational practices. Waves of migration during the first half of the twentieth century were primarily from Europe, and it is not surprising that Pentecostalism in Canada was shaped by these patterns. The PAOC also provides a window into the racial tensions between blacks and whites, not just from a distance as cousins of the American Pentecostal movement but also present in its history. Further changes in the cultural character of Canada as it adopted a multicultural policy with new sources of immigration from Africa, Asia, and Latin America have challenged the organization's assumptions about the religious identity of new immigrants and the diverse practices of Pentecostalism. The PAOC benefitted from these social changes as new ethnic congregations appeared across the country, primarily in the urban areas. And yet immigration also included non-Christians, which the PAOC attempted to come to terms with following 9/11.

RELIGIOUS DIVERSITY AND INCLUSION/EXCLUSION

Reginald Bibby observed that there are four responses by Christians in Canada to religious diversity. First, there are those Christian groups, like the United Church of Canada, who *celebrate* religious diversity and welcome it. Second are those groups, like some evangelicals and most progressive Christians, who *accept* religious diversity, recognizing that the dominance of Christianity is over and the churches have to learn to live in a new post-Christian society. Third, there are those Christian groups, like most conservative evangelicals, who attempt to *use* diversity as an opportunity for evangelism in a new Canada that must be considered a mission field. And fourth, there are those Christians who *reject* diversity and view the loss of Christian Canada as unfortunate but see no need to evangelize or change newcomers, wishing that life had not changed.[39] Bibby does not offer any examples for the fourth category, and it would probably be fair to say that his observations are less empirically defined and that the range is more like a method for categorizing responses on a continuum from embrace to reject. The observation we make is that Pentecostals in Canada are mostly in the middle of the continuum and, more specifically, that the PAOC aligns with Bibby's third category of those who hope to capitalize on diversity as a means of church growth.

Peter Beyer has argued that with globalization there is pluralization, meaning that religion does not decline or disappear in the world but takes on a range of forms in new contexts.[40] Migration is one important social context that brings religions closer together geographically but not necessarily closer in mutual understanding. Beyer's theoretical work on religion and globalization focuses on a range of ideas that offers some insight into how Pentecostals in Canada are responding to non-Christian religions. Beyer argues that there are a series of interactions that one can observe with religions in global society that highlight tensions over the nature of the world, the role of religion, issues about authenticity and authority of religion, and debates about orthodoxy and orthopraxy. For Beyer, the interactions take place at the following levels: 1. Interactions at the level of Subsystems (e.g., Religion and Political Spheres); 2. Interactions at the level of Religions (e.g., Christianity and Islam); 3. Interactions at the level of Religious Tradition (e.g., Pentecostals and Roman Catholics); 4. Interactions at the level of Religious Family (e.g., Classical Pentecostals and neo-Pentecostals). When discussing the response of Canadian Pentecostals to new immigrants of non-Christian religions, our observations are at the level of Religions whereby the debates among Pentecostals revolve around questions about the orthodoxy, orthopraxy, and orthopathy of non-Christian religions and, more specifically, about their authenticity as "true" religions and authority in Canadian society.[41] In short, this relates to defining and maintaining boundaries.

One further theoretical point shapes our understanding of Pentecostals and religious diversity in Canada, and that is the historical work of Roland Robertson. Robertson has outlined a range of historical phases for understanding globalization as a process that has brought the world to its current phase of increased worldwide connectedness and our awareness of the world as a single place. The historical phases relevant for this chapter include what Robertson calls "the uncertainty phase" from 1960 to 2000, which was characterized by new social movements, technological developments, and, among other characteristics, increased tension over polyethnicity and multiculturality.[42] Robertson refers to the most recent phase following 9/11 as the "millennial phase," which is characterized by increased levels of fear; apocalypticism; security; reconstruction of self-identities, including bodies; threats to human life, including environmental issues; and religious inclusion/exclusion.[43] It is this last point about inclusion/exclusion that characterizes globalization and is present in the discourse in the PAOC about immigration and non-Christian religions. Two key sources offer us insight into the response, including a denominational position paper on social change and religious diversity and articles from *The Pentecostal Testimony* (PT), which published two special editions post-9/11 on non-Christian religions.

In 2004, Irving Whitt and James D. Craig wrote an extensive document (236 pages) called "A Philosophy of Missions for the Pentecostal Assemblies of Canada." The paper, presented to the Executive leaders of the PAOC for discussion, states that "The purpose of this study is to set forth on behalf of the Pentecostal Assemblies of Canada a philosophy or a system of foundational beliefs concerning Christian missions. This is an attempt to provide a biblical, theological, historical and missiological perspective on a number of key issues affecting the missions endeavour."[44] The paper discusses at length the challenges of social change in Canada and includes what the authors refer to as "landmines." The metaphor of landmine suggests danger or a threat and includes globalization, multiculturalism, pluralism, and their impact on the PAOC. Further, the authors argue that these threats are related to a potential crisis for the PAOC and require a response. Throughout the document, the challenge presented to the PAOC focuses on how to address these concerns as an organization, including evangelism, prayer, and the efforts of congregations to work together to defend their Christian values. The response demonstrates the view of the PAOC that multiculturalism and ethnic diversity are a threat while boundary-making in the subculture defines who is in and who is out.

Whitt and Craig focused on fifteen issues grouped into three themes: 1. Theological/Missiological Issues; 2. Functional/Organizational Issues; and 3. Personnel/Resource Issues. A series of recommended policies and positions on each of the issues was reviewed and critiqued by the World Missions Committee and an advisory group between 2001 and 2003 before seeking final approval from the General Executive in 2004. The paper is broad and examined in detail questions about the historical background of PAOC mission work, the biblical and theological rationale for missions, the role of districts and local congregations, and the role of "Missions in Canada." More specifically, the Missions in Canada discussion revolved around how the PAOC understood Canada as a mission field, national strategies to be formulated and implemented, the organizational structure of the PAOC, and specific groups and ministries that ought to be its focus.

There are several points that require some attention. First, the authors view pluralism as problematic because it represents a contrary world view influenced by postmodern thinking. The paper discusses the views of postmodern thinkers like Jean-François Lyotard and a range of criticisms about the value of rationality in the modern world and the relativism associated with personal experience. While not embracing postmodernism, the authors suggest that Pentecostalism might have an opportunity to engage Canadians who have been influenced by a postmodern world view because Pentecostalism also values some postmodern qualities like personal experience. Whitt and Craig recommended to the PAOC that they take seriously the postmodern shift and come to understand its implications for ministry. Second, they recommended that PAOC congregations adjust their ministry to engage emerging generations of young people who have taken on the values of postmodernity.[45] The authors state, "The missional church sees itself as a community of both Christ-seekers and Christ-followers. It recognizes that postmodern people place a high value upon the concepts of journey and inclusion. For many, belonging to a Christian community will preceed [*sic*] believing or personal faith in Christ since they value inclusion and relationships over adherence to doctrinal confessions and formal membership in an organization."[46]

Related to the PAOC concern about postmodernism and pluralism is another challenge: "other-faiths and religions."[47] The challenge for the PAOC was discussed around several issues, including the resistance of non-Christian religions to the efforts of missionaries. Migration was also a problem with the movement of people from countries that were predominately non-Christian to Canada contributing to its multicultural nature. Furthermore, the growth of non-Christian religions, "once on the wane," state the authors, is now making the entire world a "multicultural/multifaith tapestry" so that PAOC ministry is not geographically defined.

Whitt and Craig add that "While Christian missionaries have circumvented the globe, people of the world's major religions have remained solidly resistant. Once they were the objects of missionary outreach in far-off lands. Now they are the neighbours next door. Consequently, the Western Christian church has the opportunity to engage the non-Christian world as never before."[48]

The impact of pluralism, relativism, and multiculturalism is a "landmine" for the PAOC and requires, according to the authors, a new approach for engaging Canadian diversity: "While people of many religions now surround us, Christians are challenged to rethink their faith in the context of a pluralistic society that is espousing religious relativism and preaching a doctrine of tolerance. This has eroded the church's convictions about the lostness of people without Christ and with it the urgency of missions."[49] The recommendations made to the PAOC about non-Christian religions include: 1. intentionality (duty of the church to be missional); 2. sending of missionaries (a corporate responsibility); 3. crossing barriers (not limited to geography); 4. witnessing to those of other religions (exclusivity of the gospel and salvation); 5. power evangelism (Pentecostal emphasis on healing, signs and wonders, spiritual warfare prayer to confront evil forces, liberation); 6. reconciliation (people to God); 7. incorporation (making disciples and gathering into congregations as empowered communities); 8. redemption (to improve the social and economic situation of others); 9. lifestyle (living an exemplary life); 10. extending the Mission of Jesus (all Christians need to be empowered by the Spirit for mission); and 11. incarnational (mission as form of service).[50]

Whitt and Craig take time to make some distinctions between inclusion, exclusion, and pluralism. They argue that exclusivism makes specific assertions about Christianity and that salvation cannot be found in other religions. Inclusivism, they argue, is like exclusivism, with a view of the uniqueness of Christianity but also with a more open view about the role of non-Christian religions and salvation. However, according to the authors, pluralism is problematic with its view of many paths for salvation that are not limited to Christianity.[51] In an attempt to articulate a position that moves away from the inclusion/exclusion debate, the authors suggest that "particular" versus "universalistic" may be more appropriate for theological discussions about Pentecostal engagement with non-Christian religions, opting for the particularity of Christian faith. As the authors state,

> We recognize that while on the one hand pluralist positions represent the old universalism, avidly propounded by those referred to as liberal, on the other hand inclusivism has become a popular position held by a number of evangelicals, that according to our understanding does not offer viable theological support. As such we cannot support an "inclusivist" theology that is wildly agnostic, suggesting the salvific potential in other religions. Neither would we classify ourselves as exclusivist or restrictivist, because of the negative labeling and punitive implications. However, because of the particularity of the Gospel and the revelational design of God's redemptive plan, we would subscribe to a view

> identified as particularistic, recognizing the latitude and scope of this theological position.[52]

Notwithstanding the theological nuances around the debates internally about non-Christian religions, including the different options of inclusivisim/exclusivism or universalistic/particularistic, the PAOC in adopting a particularistic position has stated clearly that inclusivism is more problematic than exclusivism. Even if we are to understand the range of responses somewhere on a continuum between inclusion and exclusion, the PAOC response of particularity is toward the end of the exclusion pole. The specific ways that the PAOC writes about world religions in Canada illustrates how they view other faiths and their continuous process of defining who is inside and who is outside the boundaries of orthodox belief.

We investigated *PT* between 1999 and 2016 to see what the PAOC published on non-Christian religions with the purpose of understanding the cultural discourse surrounding "other faiths." The dates allow us to get some sense of what was published before and after 9/11. Our findings show that during this period twenty-five articles were published on "other faiths," including two editorials and two special editions. In 1999, two articles were published, including one written by Irving Whitt entitled "New Millennium – New Mission." The article is especially relevant for understanding many of the initial ideas that Whitt elaborated on in the position paper discussed above, including the changing nature of Canada. The second article was published in May 1999 and briefly talked about the plurality of religions as part of the "new age." In 2000, no articles were published on "other faiths." In June 2001, Irving Whitt wrote an article entitled "Pentecostal Response to Islam" that primarily focused on the missionary work of Pentecostals in "the Muslim world" in which Whitt discussed how some Muslims had converted following a dream or vision of Jesus. Whitt also argued that theologically, Pentecostals have differed from evangelicals on the nature of authority and revelation, recognizing that God does speak to people outside of the Bible, which in his view was one reason that Pentecostalism had grown throughout the world.[53]

However, in 2001, following 9/11, a special edition with eleven articles and an editorial was published, called "Rethinking Missions." While the articles were most likely all written before 9/11, the timing of the special issue cannot be ignored. The editorial focused on how the PAOC was coming to terms with religious diversity in Canada through its "Priority One" campaign, which was "To make disciples everywhere by the proclamation of the Gospel of Christ in the power of the Holy Spirit; to establish local congregations and to train spiritual leaders."[54] More specifically, it discussed the denomination's commitment to fulfil its mandate, assess the financial and personnel needs, maximize resources, and secure funding for engaging non-Christian people.

Whitt's lead article was entitled "Rethinking Religion?" and covered briefly a range of ideas from the view that all religions are equal, that religious freedom in Canada means that people can hold different religious views, the growing numbers of immigrants who are non-Christians, and how the PAOC needs to rethink not only the changing nature of religion in Canada but also Pentecostal ministry in a multi-faith context. The next eight articles followed a pattern that first outlined the basic beliefs of a religion, followed by an article that told the story of someone who converted from that religious belief to Christianity. For example, "Understanding Buddhism" offered a brief history of the religion and some of its basic principles, including the four noble truths. The following article, "From Buddhist Incense to Christian Praise," told the story of a Buddhist convert in Thailand and the role that the PAOC missionaries played in the conversion. Other articles focused on Islam, Hinduism, and animism. The final article, "Is Anybody Answering?" written by the General Superintendent Bill Morrow, pointed to the challenges of mission work in a diverse multi-faith context. Morrow identified two challenges: the many Canadians outside of Christianity who do not believe in the truth of Jesus and second, the inclusivity and exclusivity of the gospel, which means the good news of God's love is for everyone, but exclusion means you can only be saved through Jesus. Morrow wrote: "I have just two simple but significant questions to ask. Do we still believe in the inclusive call of Christ to salvation? Do we still believe in the exclusivity of the gospel?"[55] These articles serve to define the boundary between Pentecostals and other faith groups as cultural repertoires that generate cultural cohesion for those in the PAOC.

Between 2002 and 2006, the number of articles on world religions declined, with two articles in 2002, one article in 2004, and another in 2006. Three of these four articles focused on the PAOC's instructions for readers about how to interact with Islam. In 2007, there was another special issue called "Understanding World Religions" with six articles and an editorial. The editorial, written by Linda Gibson, focused on how she got to know her new neighbours who were Muslims and, she wondered, "what we would have in common with this young couple?" Gibson describes sharing coffee together, visiting on the front porch, work, and family. She also talked about sharing her faith with her neighbours and, for this special edition, how other Pentecostals could learn about the many different religions of their Canadian neighbours while sharing the claims of Christianity. The special edition followed a pattern similar to that of the previous special edition with articles on Islam, Buddhism, and Hinduism that described histories and basic beliefs followed by stories or "testimonies" of Pentecostals who evangelized their neighbours.

Two articles in 2007 dealt with specific issues about inclusion/exclusion and tolerance. First, Graham Gibson wrote "Why Can't We Be More Tolerant as Christians?" asserting that while everyone is talking about tolerance, many Christians are confused about it because they do not understand that not all religions lead to God. Gibson argued that to be tolerant of other faiths is not the Pentecostal position, which is about the exclusivity of the gospel. He argued that not all religions are the same when it comes to beliefs and practices, non-Christian religions do not make the same claims as Christianity, all people are lost because of sin, being religious does not count, the Bible does not say there are many ways to God, the unevangelized cannot be saved with the revelation they may find within their religion, and true conversion requires confession of faith in Christ. Bill Griffin's article, "How Come Religion Seems So Complicated?" discussed the problems associated with religion, asking, "Can you believe that religion is still a central player in 21st century wars?"[56] Griffin was troubled over the absolute claims of radical Muslims that lead them to die for their beliefs. He admitted he did not know how to respond to them. And yet he critiqued the view that religious pluralism would help us to solve our problems, especially if we accept that all religious views are sincere with all roads leading to the same place. Griffin argued that for Pentecostals, all roads do not lead to the same destination and stated, "Centuries ago Jesus Christ made a statement in response to a question by His disciple Thomas that is as disconcerting to many today as it was then: 'I am the way and the truth and the life. No one comes to the Father except through me' ... And there it is – religious exclusivism in its clearest form. Jesus claims there is no other way to get to the Father but through Him."[57] Between 2008 and 2016 only one article was published on "other religions," entitled "A Conversation with the Nations" by an anonymous author, which focused on the work of Pentecostal missionaries with Muslims. It was written as a form of "testimony," telling a story about numerous conversions intended to inspire its readers to pray for Pentecostal missionaries and the principles that feature their approach to religious diversity.

Clearly, Pentecostals in the PAOC believe that pluralism and religious diversity are problems. First, for Pentecostals pluralism is a "landmine" that undermines the work of the PAOC. Second, pluralism requires a response articulated in the exclusive claims of Christianity. Third, making exclusive claims is related to an inclusive gospel that justifies the activities of Pentecostals. Fourth, other religions are not true and are philosophies, ideologies, and superstitions that need correction and conversion. Finally, conversion is justifiable as an act of transforming someone's life from error to truth and from darkness to light.

Theoretically, the response of the PAOC to religious diversity also reflects the various views and observations of scholars. First, the PAOC fits Bibby's observation that Pentecostals use diversity to serve organizational aims. However, these aims also raise other issues about inclusion and exclusion and universality and particularity. While there appears to be an increased awareness within the PAOC about religious diversity, it is mostly thought of as a threat to Christianity, as evidenced in the response that is framed around Robertson's observation about inclusion/exclusion in Canadian society. Finally, the PAOC response to religious diversity raises questions about the authenticity and authority of all religions in global society, most notably the view among Pentecostals that non-Christian religions are not true expressions of authentic religion or authoritative in any way like Christianity. The many issues raised by Pentecostals in the articles that discuss the histories and beliefs of non-Christian religions also focus on how they do not represent orthodoxy, orthopraxy, and orthopathy.

Multiculturalism has proved to be a challenge for the PAOC. Ironically, Pentecostals have assumed that immigration has primarily meant the arrival of non-Christians to Canada, and they have misunderstood the implications of the changing ethnic composition of Pentecostalism and the transnational networks immigrants maintain. At the same time, new immigrants, many of whom are Pentecostal, have served to invigorate the PAOC and have contributed to its growth. The relative vitality of evangelicalism generally, and Pentecostalism in particular, is largely due to the migration of Christians from Africa, Asia, and Latin America. Immigrants have proved to be an important source of transfer growth. The main challenge of new immigrants for the PAOC revolves around incorporating new immigrants into the structure of the organization and allowing them leadership roles. Maintaining social ties with Pentecostals outside of Canada is also a challenge for the denomination but one that has changed over time. The main issues for the PAOC in the future will be the de-Europeanization of Canadian Pentecostalism and whether or not the denomination will be able to restructure as more Pentecostals move to Canada. Multiculturalism also raises other challenges for the PAOC while they are still attempting to come to terms with religious diversity and how to live with their new neighbours. Pentecostals within the PAOC have responded to religious diversity in an exclusive manner, arguing that their beliefs, practices, and religious sentiments are superior. This position justifies their views of non-Christian faiths but also illustrates boundary-making and the process of generating cultural cohesion. While 9/11 moves further into the past, ethnic diversity and the transnational quality of Pentecostalism in Canada will challenge the PAOC to reimagine what it means to be Pentecostal. Ongoing immigration and the growth of non-Christian religions will challenge the PAOC to engage multicultural Canada in ways that will in turn raise questions about its own authority and the process of maintaining boundaries in a diverse and multi-religious society.

Conclusion

After the revival, Pentecostals organized. What was once a movement of renewal among Protestant Christians became, within twenty years, an institutionalized church. The Pentecostal movement started out as a more or less spontaneous phenomenon, but at the same time it had links with faith homes, congregations, denominations, and mission agencies. The early Pentecostals were loosely organized, and what they had in common was not a doctrinal statement but a commitment to shared experiences of something new that they believed had been lost in their churches. New religious movements, like other social movements, are characterized by a mixture of organization and spontaneity, and the Toronto Hebden Mission was a case in point. New movements commonly hold the view that the previous order needed to change and what was about to replace it, a new social order, was not just a hope but could become a reality. Pentecostals hoped for the Kingdom of God, and they believed it was coming soon. Signs and wonders, spiritual gifts, and a growing number of Pentecostals made that reality seem imminent. Many Canadian Pentecostals, including Ellen Hebden, did not believe that membership was required or that a denominational structure was necessary. Those who shared in the experience of the Holy Spirit made up the community of believers, and the community was open to all who would come, including women and men, the young and the old, the poor and the rich, from all over the world. It was a liberating message for those who joined. One did not need a mission agency to approve one's calling, nor did one need a denomination with a credentialing board to license one to preach. Women of all ages were called, and they established faith homes, congregations, and mission work wherever the Spirit took them. Authority was not found in the institution; it rested with the followers, who were filled with the Spirit. While many outside the ranks wondered what they were all about or doubted they would ever amount to anything, Pentecostals set about to organize. After the revival, a new Canadian church was in the making.

Some historians and sociologists, as discussed in chapter 1, have observed a tension between religion as movement and religion as organization that tends to value the primitive over the pragmatic or the charismatic impulse over institutionalization. These views suggest that the primitive or the charismatic impulse are a pure form that represents an earlier period of authenticity, authority, and vitality, and yet the charismatic impulse of religious movements is always unstable, as Weber reminds us.[1] While religious movements can call upon a so-called "glorious past," they are also filled with what Allan Anderson calls "signs and blunders." This is true of the early Pentecostals, who believed that Jesus was coming soon and therefore missionaries did not need to learn the languages of those to whom they were called to preach. Rather, they believed that God would miraculously equip them through spiritual gifts, including the gift of languages, to be able to speak in tongues that people would understand and, by hearing the word of God, convert. Some early twentieth-century missionaries, as Anderson reminds us, made significant errors in judgment and lost their lives or returned home discouraged after they realized they could not communicate.[2]

On the other hand, organization does entail the transformation of the movement's internal culture to create another cultural form. That new organization will continue to draw upon the culture of the movement, but organization means that the movement will now work within boundaries created by policies, boards, budgets, and statements of faith. Members must adhere to those directives in order to remain insiders. Using Penny Edgell's work, we have explored how the PAOC underwent a series of episodes that tested those boundaries and established the authority of organizational structures, including the district and national offices. Organizations do not just set limits. They also mobilize members and resources into a system that attempts to maximize the group's cultural capital so that the organization grows. And the Pentecostal Assemblies of Canada (PAOC), which formed in 1919, did grow. It grew at a tremendous rate. Not all Pentecostal denominations in Canada experienced growth the way it did. So, what made the difference? Was it "sound theology" and the "blessing of God" on the PAOC?

In spite of the providential explanations insiders offered, claiming that it was the Spirit who made all things grow, we do know that the leaders of the PAOC brought their organizational skills and business acumen to the cause. They organized and did it well. Saying that it was all the Spirit's doing is a cultural repertoire, utilized in a particular way to carry on the internal culture of the movement within the structures of the organization. The 1919 charter was an important first step for the PAOC, but it was not until 1925 that a larger group of Pentecostals came together under that charter to make the PAOC a truly Canadian church with congregations in every province from east to west.

Coincidentally, 1925 was also when the United Church of Canada formed, bringing together the Congregationalists, a large group of Presbyterians, and the Methodists who did not leave to join the Pentecostals. The United Church of Canada had a vision to be a national church, and much attention was given to its role in shaping Canadian society.[3] Much less attention was given to the Pentecostals. Almost 100, the United Church has followed a history very different from that of the PAOC, but both denominations have ended up where most did not think they would. The influence of the United Church has declined, while the PAOC has moved from the margins of Protestantism in Canada to the centre. There is no denying the reach and influence of the PAOC with its numbers of clergy, congregations, adherents, and budgets. In saying this, we do not intend to suggest that somehow the PAOC is the "winner" and the United Church is the "loser," to use the language of religious market theorists.[4] As Sam Reimer and Michael Wilkinson have demonstrated in their national study of evangelical Protestants, they too are showing signs of decline.[5]

The culture of evangelical congregations, once robust and characterized by vitality, is facing some very real challenges, including the slowing of growth, which is due to aging members and lower birth rates. Growth is largely dependent upon immigration and the transfer of Christians from Africa, Asia, and Latin America. Evangelical churches in Canada are also losing their youth at rates that have alarmed evangelical leaders. Evangelical churches were often referenced by sociologists like Reginald Bibby as strong because of their youth and children programs.[6] Bibby argued that the mainline churches needed to adopt their playbook and follow the evangelicals' example for retaining their youth and children. But what happens now that the evangelicals themselves are also dealing with problems in retaining their young people? Reimer and Wilkinson also point out that evangelical churches in Canada have an aging clergy that will be retiring in the next decade. While these older clergy have said they are very happy with their ministry, younger pastors have stated they are not as happy in ministry, and some have considered leaving ministry. When this is coupled with declining enrolments in Bible colleges, seminaries, and graduate schools of theology, evangelical churches will have to deal with a potential clergy crisis. Finally, Reimer and Wilkinson observe that evangelical congregations are also operating in a cultural context that is less inclined to see the value of organized religion, with some people opting for no religion or defining themselves as spiritual but not religious.[7] As Canadian society changes, the churches will have to deal with these signs of decline, including the PAOC.

In this book we have argued that the culture of Pentecostalism as structured and organized in the PAOC has its own unique qualities and characteristics. It has developed throughout the twentieth century, drawing upon some aspects of Canadian culture, including business models in step with periods of prosperity in the Canadian economy and family ministry models designed to cater to postwar nuclear families. Those strategies have enabled the PAOC to establish a particular identity that appealed to particular segments of the population. Over time, the organizational culture has met challenges from within by Pentecostals like those from the Latter Rain movement who were not prepared to submit to denominational authority. The PAOC has also wrestled with its relationship to the larger Canadian culture – for example, when its Social Concerns Department attempted to address what it perceived were the negative aspects of social change, especially changes in the legal system about divorce, marriage, and sexuality. As the PAOC engaged changes in other spheres of society, it found its public voice for a period of time but later withdrew to reconsider what it gained or lost in doing so. Forays into "home missions" revealed that the PAOC struggled with Canadian diversity, as illustrated by its efforts to establish congregations among French Quebecers and Indigenous peoples. Globalization brought new tensions for the PAOC, and it raised questions about multiculturalism, immigration, and religious diversity. A cultural analysis has allowed us to make specific observations about the subculture and its interactions with other social institutions in Canada, the fluid nature of Pentecostal identity over time, and the symbolic boundaries it draws upon to give meaning for the PAOC as it builds a Canadian church.

In this book, we have considered what happened with Pentecostals after the revival. What appeared to begin as a largely spontaneous renewal movement quickly gave way to organizational structures as the leadership agreed that there were advantages in systems and channels of authority. After the revival, a new Canadian church emerged. As the PAOC begins its next 100 years, the denomination is undertaking ambitious plans for growth that include refreshing its doctrinal statement and dreaming about another time of revival. It remains to be seen how this church, whose statistical strength and material resources give it a pre-eminent position at the centre of religious life in Canada, will navigate the process of defining both its internal culture and its relationship to Canadian culture in the twenty-first century.

Appendix

This statement appeared in the February 1926 issue of *The Pentecostal Testimony* (pages 2–3):

On May 17th, 1919, the Pentecostal Assemblies of Canada were granted a Dominion Charter. This meeting had to do largely with the work in Eastern Canada as Western Canada, previous to this date, was recognized as a district of the General Council, U.S.A. On November 23, 1920, Eastern Canada and Western Canada united as one body. At the same meeting Eastern Canada assumed the relationship of a District Council to the General Council, U.S.A., retaining, of course, our standing in Canada as a distinct Canadian body. By doing so the Pentecostal Assemblies of Canada accepted the statement of fundamental truths approved by the General Council, not as a basis of fellowship or a creed, but as a basis of a united ministry.

A STATEMENT OF FUNDAMENTAL TRUTHS APPROVED BY THE GENERAL COUNCIL OF THE ASSEMBLIES OF GOD

According to our Constitution we have the right to approve of all Scriptural truth. The Bible is our all-sufficient rule for faith and practice. Hence this Statement of Fundamental Truths is not intended as a creed for the Church, nor a basis of unity for the ministry alone (i.e., that we all speak the same thing, I Cor. 1:10; Acts 2:42). The human phraseology employed in such statement is not inspired nor contended for, but the truth set forth in such phraseology is held to be essential to a full Gospel ministry. No claim is made that it contains all truth in the Bible, only that it covers our present needs as to those fundamental matters.

1. The Scriptures Inspired

The Bible is the inspired Word of God, a revelation from God to man, the infallible rule of faith and conduct, and is superior to conscience and reason, but not contrary to reason (2 Tim. 3:15, 16; 1 Pet. 2:2).

[2.] The One True God [sic – not numbered]

The one true God has revealed Himself as the eternally self-existen [*sic*], self-revealed "I AM;" and has further revealed Himself as embodying the principles of relationship and association, i.e., as Father, Son and Holy Ghost (Deut. 6:4; Mark 12:29; Isa. 43:10, 11; Matt. 28:19).

3. Man, His Fall and Redemption

Man was created good and upright; for God said, "Let us make man in Our image and in Our likeness." But man, by voluntary transgression, fell, and his only hope of redemption is in Jesus Christ the Son of God (Gen. 1:26-31; 3:1–7; Rom. 5:12–21).

[4.] The Salvation of Man [sic – not numbered]

(a) Conditions to Salvation.
The grace of God that brings salvation to all men has appeared through the preaching of repentance toward God and faith toward the Lord Jesus Christ; whereupon man is saved by the washing of regeneration and renewing of the Holy Ghost, and, having been justified by grace through faith, he becomes an heir of God according to the hope of eternal life (Titus 2:11; Rom. 10:13–15; Luke 24:47; Titus 3:5–7).

(b) The Evidence of Salvation.
The inward evidence, to the believer, of his salvation, is the direct witness of the Spirit (Rom. 8:16). The outward evidence to all men is a life of righteousness and true holiness (Luke 1:73–75; Titus 2:12–14); the fruit of the Spirit (Gal. 5:22); and brotherly love (John 13:35; Heb. 13:1; 1 John 3:14).

5. Baptism in Water

The ordinance of Baptism by burial with Christ should be observed as commanded in the Scriptures, by all who have really repented and in their hearts have truly believed on Christ as Saviour and Lord. In so doing, they have the body washed in pure water as an outward symbol of cleansing while their heart has already been sprinkled with the blood of Christ as an inner cleansing. Thus they declare to the world that they have died with jesus [*sic*] and that they have been raised with Him to walk in newness of life (Matt. 28:19; Acts 10:47, 48; Rom. 6:4; Acts 20:21; Heb. 10:22).

6. *The Lord's Supper*

The Lord's Supper consisting of the elements, bread and the fruit of the vine, is the symbol expressing our sharing the divine nature of our Lord Jesus Christ (2 Pet. 1:4); a memorial of His suffering and death (1 Cor. 11:26); and a prophecy of his second coming (1 Cor. 11:26); and is enjoined on all believers "until He comes."

7. *The Promise of the Father*

All believers are entitled to, and should ardently expect, and earnestly seek the promise of the Father, the baptism in the Holy Ghost and fire, according to the command of our Lord Jesus Christ. This was the normal experience of all in the early Christian Church. With it comes the enduement of power for life and service, the bestowment of the gifts and their uses in the work of the ministry (Luke 24:49; Acts 1:4; 1:8; 1 Cor. 12:1–31. [*sic* – no closing bracket]

8. *The Full Consummation of the Baptism in the Holy Ghost*

The full consummation of the baptism in believers in the Holy Ghost is indicated by the initial physical sign of speaking with other tongues as the Spirit of God gives them utterance (Acts 2:4). This wonderful experience is distinct from and subsequent to the experience of the new birth (Acts 10:44–46; 11:14–16; 15:7–9) [*sic* – no period] The speaking in tongues in this instance is the same in essence as the gift of tongues (I Cor. 12:4–10, 28), but different in purpose and use.

9. *Entire Sanctification the Goal For All Believers*

The Scriptures teach a life of holiness without which no man shall see the Lord. By the power of the Holy Ghost we are able to obey the command, "Be ye holy for I am holy." Entire sanctification is the will of God for all believers, and should be earnestly pursued by walking in obedience to God's Word (Heb. 12:14; 1 Pet. 1:15, 16; 1 Thess. 5:23, 24; 1 John 2:6).

10. The Church a Living Organism

The Church is a living organism; a living body; yea the body of Christ; a habitation of God through the Spirit, with divine appointments for the fulfillment of her great commission. Every true believer and every true local assembly are integral parts of the General Assembly and Church of the First-born, written in heaven (Eph. 1:22, 23; 2:22; Heb. 12:23).

11. The Ministry and Evangelism

A divinely called and a Scripturally ordained ministry is the command of the Lord for the evangelization of the world and the chief concern of the Church (Mark 16:15–20; Eph. 4:11–13).

12. Divine Healing

Deliverance from sickness is provided for in the atonement, and is the privilege of all believers (Isa. 53:4, 5; Matt. 8:16, 17).

13. The Blessed Hope

The Resurrection of those who have fallen asleep in Christ, the rapture of believers who are alive and remain, and the translation of the true church, this is the blessed hope set before all believers (1 Thess. 4:16, 17; Rom. 8:23; Titus 2:13).

14. The Imminent Coming and Millenial Reign of Jesus

The premillennial and imminent coming of the Lord to gather His people unto Himself, and to judge the world in righteousness while reigning on the earth for a thousand years is the expectation of the Church of Christ.

15. The Lake of Fire

The devil and his angels, the beast and false prophet, and whosoever is not found written in the Book of Life, and fearful and unbelieving, and abominable, and murderers and whoremongers, and sorcerers, and idolators [*sic*] and all liars shall be consigned to everlasting punishment in the lake which burneth with fire and brimstone, which is the second death (Rev. 19:20; Rev. 20:10–15).

16. The New Heavens and New Earth

We look for new heavens and a new earth wherein dwelleth righteousness (2 Pet. 3:13; Rev. 21 and 22).

Notes

INTRODUCTION

1 *Canadian Journal of Pentecostal-Charismatic Christianity* is a peer-reviewed online journal founded in 2010. The final edition was published in 2019. https://journal.twu.ca/index.php/CJPC/index.

CHAPTER ONE

1 Reimer and Wilkinson, *A Culture of Faith*.

2 Mark Chaves distinguishes three types of religions organizations: congregations, denominational organizations, and religious non-profits. He states: "By *congregations*, I mean the relatively small-scale, local collectivities and organizations through which people routinely engage in religious activity: churches, synagogues, mosques, temples. Religion-producing organizations that are not congregations mainly include denominational organizations that serve, are supported by, or have authority over local congregations: Catholic dioceses, mission agencies, regional and national offices of denominations, and so on." Chaves, "Religious Organizations," 1,523. Also see Chaves, *Congregations in America*, 202–11.

3 The United Church of Canada reported an average weekly attendance of 125,623 people for 2017. See https://www.united-church.ca/sites/default/files/resources/united-church-statistics.pdf, accessed 4 February 2019. For an analysis of the decline of the United Church of Canada, see Clarke and Macdonald, *Leaving Christianity*.

4 The PAOC grants the following credentials for leaders who serve in a range of positions in the organization: Ordained, Licensed Minister,

Recognition of Ministry, and Ministry Related. The term "clergy" refers to all ministry personnel who serve in an official capacity for the PAOC.

5 See Pentecostal Assemblies of Canada, "What Is the 2020 Initiative?"

6 Ibid.

7 Kulbeck, *What God Hath Wrought*, ii.

8 Ibid.

9 A.G. Ward, "Foreword," in Kulbeck, *What God Hath Wrought*, v.

10 Ibid.

11 Atter, *The Third Force*, 3rd edn. Atter's book was adopted as the standard Bible college textbook by PAOC colleges, and this explains why multiple editions were published.

12 Rudd, *When the Spirit Came upon Them*, 15.

13 Atter, *The Third Force*, v.

14 Ibid., 304.

15 Miller, "About the Author," *Canadian Pentecostals*, 4.

16 While Miller did not provide the reference for Moberg's work that he had in mind, it is likely that he was referring to Moberg's *The Church as a Social Institution* (1962) which appeared in a revised edition in 1984. In that book, Moberg discussed theories about church life cycle.

17 Miller, *Canadian Pentecostals*, 15.

18 Ibid., 17–18.

19 Ibid.

20 James MacKnight, in Miller, *Canadian Pentecostals*, 11.

21 Rudd, *When the Spirit Came upon Them*, 13.

22 Ibid., 14.

23 Ibid. To establish the authority of what he hoped to communicate, Rudd cited Dr Craig Bloomberg, professor of New Testament at Denver Seminary and former research fellow at Tyndale House, Cambridge University.

24 Ibid., 16.

25 Ibid., 17.

26 Ibid., 355.

27 Ibid.

28 Ibid., 357.

29 McKenzie, "A Timeless Story," 9.

30 Wells, "Conclusion," *Picture This!*, 219.

31 Ibid., 215.

32 Ibid., 218.

33 Ibid., 213.

34 Cerillo, Jr, and Wacker, "Bibliography and Historiography of Pentecostalism in North America."

35 Dayton, *Theological Roots of Pentecostalism*. On the roles of women, see Marks, *Revivals and Roller Rinks*; and Whiteley, *Canadian Methodist Women*.

36 Atter reminded readers that "Revivals broke out in many other lands. In some cases, these were entirely independent of, and unknown to the North American brethren, coming as a direct visitation from heaven without any American contacts." At the same time, Atter concedes that some other sites of global revival were sparked by "the influence of the Azusa Street Revival in Los Angeles." Atter, *The Third Force*, 43.

37 Anderson, *An Introduction to Pentecostalism*; on Canada as part of the global story, see Wilkinson and Althouse, "Like a Mighty Rushing Wind."

38 Miller, "The Canadian 'Azusa'"; Stewart, "A Canadian Azusa?"; and Sloos, "The Story of James and Ellen Hebden."

39 Stewart, "A Canadian Azusa?" 35.

40 Yong and Alexander, eds, *Afro-Pentecostalism: Black Pentecostal and Charismatic Christianity in History and Culture*.

41 Ramirez, *Migrating Faith: Pentecostalism in the United States and Mexico in the Twentieth Century*.

42 Medina, "Discerning the Spirit in Culture: Toward Pentecostal Interculturality."

43 Wilkinson, *The Spirit Said Go*; Wilkinson, "Canadian Pentecostal Diversity: Incorporating the Many Voices."

44 Stewart, "Re-visioning the Disinherited"; Althouse, "Waxing and Waning of Social Deprivation as a Model for Understanding the Class Composition of Early American Pentecostalism."

45 Wacker, *Heaven Below*, 10.

46 Ibid., 268.

47 Ibid., 266.

48 Ibid., 269.

49 For further details on the development of the sociology of religion in Canada, see Wilkinson, "History of English-Speaking Sociology of Religion in Canada." On the development of sociology and Pentecostal studies, see Wilkinson, "Sociological Narratives and the Sociology of Pentecostalism."

50 Weber, *The Protestant Ethic and the Spirit of Capitalism*.

51 The sectarian and churchly nature of Christianity was further developed into church-sect theory to explain how some sectarian

groups changed over time from a position of opposition toward society to one that was more accepting. While this theory has offered important insights into sectarian religious groups, it is not the focus of this book. We are not solely interested in the sectarian qualities of early Pentecostalism. Rather, we focus on the social processes by which Pentecostalism is organized, its organizational identity in the PAOC, and the symbolic boundaries it imagines over time, illustrating the various ways it negotiated broader cultural trends through a range of interactions. For an earlier discussion about secularization and sectarian religion, see Wilson, *Religion in Secular Society*. Wilson expands on the work of Weber, Troeltsch, and Niebuhr, some of the earlier theorists to work with this model.

52 Weber, *Economy and Society*, vols 1 and 2, 241.

53 O'Dea, "Five Dilemmas in the Institutionalization of Religion."

54 Poloma, *The Assemblies of God at the Crossroads*.

55 Poloma, *Main Street Mystics*.

56 Martin, *A General Theory of Secularization*.

57 Martin, *Tongues of Fire*; Martin, *Pentecostalism: The World Their Parish*.

58 Wilkinson, *Canadian Pentecostalism: Transition and Transformation*.

59 Reed, "Denominational Charismatics."

60 Donald S. Swenson, "The Canadian Catholic Charismatic Renewal."

61 Beyer, "Movements, Markets and Social Contexts."

62 Finke and Stark, *The Churching of America*; Stark and Finke, *Acts of Faith*.

63 Berger, *The Desecularization of the World*.

64 See Bruce, *God Is Dead*; Bruce, *Secularization*. The debate was quite intense among sociologists and is represented in the following articles: Stark, "Secularization, R.I.P."; Bruce, "Christianity in Britain, R.I.P."

65 Miller and Yamamori, *Global Pentecostalism*.

66 Ibid., 37.

67 Edgell, "A Cultural Sociology of Religion."

68 For an assessment of key thinkers like Douglas and Berger on a cultural analysis approach, see Wuthnow, *Cultural Analysis*; Wuthnow, *Meaning and Moral Order*; and Bourdieu, *Outline of a Theory of Practice*.

69 For an example of analyzing the culture of congregations, see Reimer and Wilkinson, *A Culture of Faith*.

70 Edgell, "A Cultural Sociology of Religion," 253.

71 For an approach that examines the embodied nature of Pentecostalism, see Wilkinson and Althouse, eds, *Pentecostals and the Body*.

72 Edgell, "A Cultural Sociology of Religion," 257.

73 Ibid.

74 Ibid.

CHAPTER TWO

1 Wright, "20th Century Belongs to Canada."

2 Even into the late twentieth century, the unfortunate phrase "Peopling an Empty Land" was used to describe the process of populating the West with immigrants. See Bothwell, Drummond, and English, *Canada 1900–1945*, 55.

3 Ibid., 81.

4 Bumsted and Bumsted, *A History of the Canadian Peoples*, 272.

5 Detailed population statistics for the City of Winnipeg can be found in Artibise, *Winnipeg: A Social History of Urban Growth*, ch. 9.

6 Opp, "Re-imaging the Moral Order of Urban Space," 33.

7 For a useful discussion about Pentecostal eschatology in the context of social reform, see Althouse, "Apocalyptic Discourse and a Pentecostal Vision of Canada."

8 Allen, *The Social Passion*; Gray, *Booze*; and Cook, "*'Through Sunshine and Shadow'*."

9 PAOC Archives, Pentecostal Oral History Project, Transcript of Interview with Walter McAlister on R.E. McAlister by James D. Craig.

10 Reed, "*In Jesus' Name*", 105.

11 The view among many early Pentecostals was that speaking in tongues, more technically, xenolalia, was the ability to speak a second language for the purpose of evangelism as a spiritual gift. Pentecostals believed that the Spirit would supernaturally speak through them in a language they did not learn and that there was a sense of urgency for Christians to take the gospel to the whole world. The debates about sanctification, Spirit baptism, and various signs of this experience among Pentecostals were a continuation of nineteenth-century discussions primarily among Methodists and the Holiness Movement. See Dayton, *Theological Roots of Pentecostalism*.

12 The first doctrinal statement, adopted from the Assemblies of God, US, was published in *The Pentecostal Testimony* in February 1926. The statement went through several revisions, beginning with the 1928

version published in the PAOC Yearbook, reflecting the controversies over trinitarian views. Other revisions occurred throughout the twentieth century. The PAOC has more recently engaged in a process of consultation with its stakeholders in order to "refresh" the statement once again. See the Appendix for the 1926 version of the statement of faith.

13 Vondey, *Pentecostal Theology*.

14 "How Pentecost Came to Toronto," *The Promise*, May 1907, 1.

15 Rudd, *When the Spirit Came upon Them*, 77.

16 Dayton, *Theological Roots of Pentecostalism*; Butler, *Canadian Winds of the Spirit*.

17 R.E. McAlister, "Healing in the Atonement," *The Good Report*, May 1911, 8.

18 Ibid.

19 R.E. McAlister, "Called to Suffer for Jesus," *The Good Report*, May 1911, 6.

20 "Confession of Faith," *The Good Report* May, 1912, 3.

21 Miller, *Canadian Pentecostals*, 108.

22 Ibid.

23 Reed, *"In Jesus' Name"*, 87.

24 F.J. Ewart, "Defending Heresies," *The Good Report*, vol. 1, 3 (1912), 12.

25 Ibid.

26 Wilson, "McAlister, Robert Edward."

27 Editor [R.E. McAlister], "Error Persecutes Truth," *The Good Report*, vol. 1, 3 (1912), 14.

28 For a full recounting of the events of 1913 and their significance, see Reed, *"In Jesus' Name"*, 77–107.

29 Brumback, *Suddenly from Heaven*, 204–210, cited in Miller, *Canadian Pentecostals*, 111.

30 Miller, *Canadian Pentecostals*, 112.

31 Thomas A. Robinson, "Oneness Pentecostalism," in Wilkinson, ed., *Canadian Pentecostalism*, 46.

32 Miller, *Canadian Pentecostals*, 112.

33 Ibid.

34 R.E. McAlister, "The Basis of Unity," *Truth Advocate*, vol. 1, 3 (1912), 14.

35 Wilkinson, "Charles W. Chawner and the Missionary Impulse of the Hebden Mission."

36 "A Cry from the Dark Continent," *The Promise*, February 1909, 4.

37 "Lama Gersha," *The Promise*, October 1909, 1.

38 "Truly God Is Good," *The Promise*, March 1910, 5.
39 Ibid., 6.
40 Miller, *Canadian Pentecostals*, 43; Miller, "The Canadian 'Azusa'."
41 E.K.H [Ellen K. Hebden], "Thirteen Days with God," *The Promise*, vol. 14, October 1909, 1.
42 Ibid.
43 Courtney, "The 1909 and 1910 Canadian Pentecostal Camp Meetings in Markham, Ontario."
44 Rudd, *When the Spirit Came upon Them*, 324.
45 Wakefield, *Alexander Boddy: Pentecostal Anglican Pioneer.*
46 Miller, *Canadian Pentecostals*, 105.
47 "God Appointed Convention," *The Promise*, vol. 15, March 1910, 2.
48 "Organization," *The Promise*, October 1909, 1.
49 Miller, *Canadian Pentecostals*, 113.
50 "God Appointed Convention," *The Promise*, vol. 15, March 1910, 1.
51 Ibid.
52 Ibid., 2.
53 Ibid.
54 Ibid., 1–2.
55 R.E. McAlister's first wife died in May 1910. He remarried in 1911, but his second wife died in 1921. McAlister married for a third time on 8 February 1922 in Kitchener, Ontario, to Laura Arnold, a former PAOC missionary to Liberia. Meanwhile, two of his children died as infants: Lorraine McAlister died in March 1917 at six days of age; and Paul Edward McAlister died at eight days of age in October 1924 from complications of circumcision. When R.E.'s second wife, Lillie, died in 1921, Chambers wrote a letter to other Pentecostal workers asking them to contribute to the expenses of the medical care and the burial. He intimated that R.E. was shocked by the loss, describing him as having a heavy and sore heart from "the blow" he had sustained. According to Chambers, R.E.'s "own words are 'God has taken everything out of me and left nothing'" but that he was "being wonderfully sustained" and "the one who has given the blow is pouring in oil and wine and is going down into the valley with our brother in the most blessed way I have ever witnessed." PAOC Archives, G.A. Chambers to "The Dear Saints & Co-workers in the Gospel," 1 February 1921.
56 Mittelstadt, "'Canada's First Martyr'"; Dempster, "The Canada–Britain–USA Triad."
57 Miller, *Canadian Pentecostals*, 44.
58 Miller, "The Canadian 'Azusa'."

59 Miller, *Canadian Pentecostals*, 44. Miller's suggestion that the Hebdens were tied to the "Latter Rain" is curious because that movement, known as the "New Order of the Latter Rain," only emerged in the 1940s, well after both Hebdens had died. Miller's reference here may be to "latter rain theology," which was articulated by early Pentecostals, but it is more likely that he intended to offer a caution regarding the excesses of individuals who claimed authority in their prophetic ministries, especially when they refused to submit to PAOC leadership.
60 Sloos, "The Story of James and Ellen Hebden."
61 Ibid., 200.
62 Ibid., 202.
63 "Organizations," *The Promise*, March 1910, 1.
64 Ibid.
65 Ibid.
66 Miller, *Canadian Pentecostals*, 44.
67 George A. Chambers, "In Retrospect," *The Pentecostal Testimony*, November 1934, 7.
68 Miller, *Canadian Pentecostals*, 105.
69 Ibid.
70 J. McAlister, "Independence vs. Co-operation or Is Independence the Will of the Lord for Us?" *The Pentecostal Testimony*, July 1926, 13.
71 Ibid.
72 Ibid.
73 James Hebden died in 1919, and Ellen Hebden died in 1923 after a long illness.
74 Miller, *Canadian Pentecostals*, 114.
75 Griffin, "1919: Ninety-Nine Years and Counting," 33.
76 PAOC Archives, General Conference fonds, Minutes of the First General Assembly of the Pentecostal Assemblies of Canada, Kitchener, ON, November 25–28, 1919, 4.
77 Ibid.
78 Griffin, "1919: Ninety-Nine Years and Counting," 37–8.
79 Ibid., 41.
80 In a similar way, the American Assemblies of God adopted an overlay of Presbyterian structures at the executive level while remaining congregational at the local level. Poloma, *The Assemblies of God at the Crossroads*, 123–7.
81 Griffin, "1919: Ninety-Nine Years and Counting," 42.
82 Thietart, "Chaos Theory and Organization." For an extended discussion on the relationship between organizational theory and religious

organizations, see Scheitle and Dougherty, "The Sociology of Religious Organizations."

83 "Decently and in order" refers to St Paul's admonition to the Corinthian Church on the proper use of spiritual gifts in the church. See I Corinthians 14.

CHAPTER THREE

1 Kulbeck, *What God Hath Wrought*, 33.
2 Nicholas, *The Modern Girl.*
3 Cook, *The Secret Life of Soldiers*, 47–52; Humphries, "War's Long Shadow"; Vance, *Memory, Meaning, and the First World War.*
4 McGinnis, "The Impact of Epidemic Influenza"; and Bogaert, "Military and Maritime Evidence of Pandemic Influenza in Canada during the Summer of 1918."
5 Comacchio, *Nations Are Built of Babies.*
6 Miller, *Canadian Pentecostals*, 121.
7 Ibid.
8 Edgell, "A Cultural Sociology of Religion."
9 Ziefle, *David du Plessis and the Assemblies of God*, 24.
10 Kulbeck used the term "architect": *What God Hath Wrought*, 11. Miller called R.E. McAlister a "founding father of Canadian Pentecostalism," *Canadian Pentecostals*, 15.
11 See Introduction.
12 Kulbeck, *What God Hath Wrought*, 38.
13 Miller, *Canadian Pentecostals*, 120.
14 PAOC Archives, General Conference fonds, "Minutes of the United Conference of the Pentecostal Assemblies of Canada," Resolutions Committee, Saskatoon, 1 August 1927.
15 See Introduction.
16 Flatt, *After Evangelicalism*, 24.
17 Ibid. Flatt cites United Church of Canada Board of Evangelism and Social Service, *Annual Report 1935–36*," 26.
18 Watson Argue, "Were You at the Cross." *The Pentecostal Testimony*, April 1929, 16–17.
19 Charles Elmo Robinson, "What Must Such a Member Do?" *The Pentecostal Testimony*, 1 November 1940, 11.
20 Ibid.
21 A.H. Townsend, "Touch Not God's Anointed," *The Pentecostal Testimony*, 15 June 1948, 9.

22 Hogan, "Print and Organized Religion in English Canada," 287.
23 Miller, *Canadian Pentecostals*, 119.
24 Sneath, "Imagining a Mennonite Community," 217–18.
25 Ibid., 210.
26 Ibid., 215. Sneath concludes: "To the outside observer, the periodical may appear to offer little; its conventions of speech and cultural scripts of weather, crops, and greetings to a seemingly endless, faceless list of individuals, seem to make for lackluster reading. However, the *Post* is not meant for outside observers. For the adherents of this community this is the story of their lives, and the ostensibly arbitrary details of weather and names are the threads that sustain the community. In many respects, this community is not imagined at all. Its members are just as tangible, their experiences just as recognized, their burdens as shared, and their voices at least as loud, as if every member of this community lived in the same literal village and sat at the same table."
27 *The Pentecostal Testimony*, October 1937, 26.
28 Kee, *Revivalists*.
29 The four titles were: *The Beauty of the Cross*, *Strenuous Days*, *Prevailing Prayer*, and *Practical Christian Living*.
30 *The Pentecostal Testimony*, October 1937, 26.
31 Zelma Argue published a total of 235 articles between 1920 and 1969. Of those, 175 (70 per cent) were published in *The Pentecostal Evangel*, 43 (20 per cent) in *The Pentecostal Testimony*, and 17 (less than 10 per cent) in *The Latter Rain Evangel*. Her publications in *The Latter Rain Evangel* only appeared between 1927 and 1939 when it ceased publication.
32 Gerson, "Publishing by Women."
33 Ambrose, "Zelma and Beulah Argue."
34 Ambrose, "Establishing a Gendered Authority through Pentecostal Publications."
35 Zelma Argue, "Paving the Way for a Miracle," *The Pentecostal Evangel*, 19 September 1936, 2–3.
36 Kulbeck, *What God Hath Wrought*, 49. With the 1924 start date, Kulbeck is including a short course Bible school that operated out of the Drummond Street Evangel Church in Montreal during the year before the Winnipeg school was established.
37 Ibid., 49–50.
38 Ibid., 49–74; Miller, *Canadian Pentecostals*, 201–15.
39 Kulbeck, *What God Hath Wrought*, 49–50.

40 Craig, "'Out and out for the Lord,'" 14.
41 Althouse, "The Influence of Dr. J.E. Purdie's Reformed Theology on the Formation and Development of the Pentecostal Assemblies of Canada"; Craig, "Out and out for the Lord; Guenther, "Pentecostal Theological Education"; Ross, "James Eustace Purdie: The Story of Pentecostal Theological Education."
42 For example, see Poloma, *The Assemblies of God at the Crossroads*; Stephenson, *Dismantling the Dualisms for American Pentecostal Women in Ministry*.
43 Mittelstadt, "Canada's First Martyr."
44 Zelma Argue, "The Outlook of the Unregenerate World," *The Pentecostal Testimony*, January 1922, 2. For an explanation of "eschatological pacifism," see Brock, *Pacifism in Europe to 1914*, 472. Also see Althouse and Waddell, eds., *Perspectives in Pentecostal Eschatologies*.
45 G.A. Chambers, "Should Christians Go to War?" *The Pentecostal Testimony*, November 1935, 14; December 1935, 13; January 1936, 6; and February 1936, 10.
46 Miller, *Canadian Pentecostals*, 42; Hocken, "Chambers, George Augustus."
47 Althouse, "Canadian Pentecostal Pacifism."
48 Miller, *Canadian Pentecostals*, 247.
49 R.A.N. Kydd, "Buntain, Daniel Newton (1888–1955)."
50 D.N. Buntain, "If I Were Caught in the Draft," *Pentecostal Testimony*, 1 September 1941, 4.
51 Ibid.
52 PAOC Archives, Western Bible College fonds, J.E. Purdie to Rev. D.N. Buntain and C.M. Wortman, April 20, 1944.
53 PAOC Archives, Western Bible College fonds, H. Wuerch to Dr. Perdie [*sic*], July 29, 1942.
54 PAOC Archives, Western Bible College fonds, Purdie to McPherson, October 15, 1942.
55 PAOC Archives, Western Bible College fonds, Leslie Tausendfrende to Dr. J.E. Purdie, July 16, 1942.
56 PAOC Archives, Western Bible College fonds, Purdie to Tausendfrende, July 20, 1942.
57 PAOC Archives, Western Bible College fonds, Purdie to C.M. Wortman, January 17, 1945.
58 Miller, *Canadian Pentecostals*, 159.
59 Kulbeck, *What God Hath Wrought*, 49–50.

60 C.B. Smith, "An Explanation Concerning Bethel Bible Institute," *The Pentecostal Testimony*, 15 November 1947, 9.
61 Ibid., 9, 21, 22.
62 Donald Gee, "Sobriety with Spiritual Gifts," *The Pentecostal Testimony*, 1 August 1949, 3–4; A.H. Argue, "The Gifts of the Spirit and Their Value," *The Pentecostal Testimony*, August 1949, 6; E.S. Williams, "Spiritual Gifts," *The Pentecostal Testimony*, 15 May 1949, 3–4; C.B. Smith, "An Explanation of Our Position Relative to Spiritual Gifts," *The Pentecostal Testimony*, 15 June 1949, 2; C.A. Ratz, "Leaving the Principles of the Doctrines of Christ," *The Pentecostal Testimony*, 15 June 1949, 3–4.
63 PAOC Archives, R.E. McAlister fonds, R.E. McAlister, "The Manifestations of the Spirit," Toronto: Full Gospel Publishing House, n.d. [1949–50]; *The Truth Advocate*, R.E. McAlister, editor, vol. 1, issues 1 & 2 [June 1949 & October 1949]; Advertisement, "Just off the Press – Manifestations of the Spirit," by R.E. McAlister, *The Pentecostal Testimony*, 15 October 1950, 6.
64 Blumhofer, *Restoring the Faith*, 206.
65 C.B. Smith, "A Resolution," *The Pentecostal Testimony*, 15 November 1949, 2.
66 Thomas Miller asserts that the rapid growth offers a partial explanation. Miller, *Canadian Pentecostals*, 259. In making that argument, Miller is in step with and citing a historian of the American Assemblies of God: Brumback, *Suddenly from Heaven*, 330–31.
67 Edgell, "A Cultural Sociology of Religion."

CHAPTER FOUR

1 Owram, *Born at the Right Time*.
2 See Chaves, "Denominations as Dual Structures."
3 Stephen, *Pick One Intelligent Girl*; Keshen, *Saints, Sinners, and Soldiers*; Pierson, *They're Still Women after All*.
4 Ethel Bingeman, a registered nurse, served as a missionary to Liberia from 1915 to 1933 when she returned to Canada because she was ill. After she regained her health, she travelled extensively throughout Canada to speak at missionary conventions and taught at the Western Bible College in Winnipeg where she was director of personal work, home nursing, and first aid. She transferred to Toronto in 1944 to become national director of the WMC and matron of the Bethel Missionary Rest Home, a PAOC house used as a temporary residence

for missionaries leaving for and returning from overseas work. Bingeman resigned from the WMC in 1956 and married the Rev. R.J. Jamieson, a pioneer missionary to the West Indies since 1905. Rev. Jamieson died in 1961 at age 93, and Ethel died in 1975.

5 Ethel Bingeman, "Report of the Work of the Women's Missionary Society to the General Conference," *The Pentecostal Testimony*, 15 October 1948, 11, 14.

6 Ibid.

7 Ibid. Incidentally, the terminology that was given to the women's work varied. In the article cited here, three different titles were given to the work, including "Women's Missionary Society," "Home and Foreign Missions Women's Auxiliary," and "Women's Missionary Council." Eventually, the group came to be known as "WMC" or Women's Missionary Council, though it is not clear if this was a formal decision or simply an agreed-upon convention.

8 "Missionary Action Girls," *The Pentecostal Testimony*, September 1955, 29. The groups were sometimes referred to as "Pioneer Missionary Action Girls" or "P.M.A.G."

9 Gladys Lemmon, "From the Director's Desk – Missionary Women's Council," *The Pentecostal Testimony*, January 1960, 24 and August 1960, 24. The goal of creating these groups for every PAOC congregation was expressed as early as January 1955. See *The Pentecostal Testimony*, January 1955, 29.

10 "Love's Reward," *The Pentecostal Testimony*, June 1960, 6, 24.

11 Ella Parmenter, "Step up to the Wall!" *The Pentecostal Testimony*, April 1965, 24.

12 "Next Generation of Women in Ministry Please Stand Up!" *The Pentecostal Testimony*, June 1991, 2.

13 G.R. Upton, "Men of Vision Organize First Men's Missionary Council at Calvary Temple, Winnipeg," *The Pentecostal Testimony*, 15 June 1951, 8–9.

14 G.R. Upton, "Why Men Should Teach," *The Pentecostal Testimony*, September 1955, 22.

15 Harold Underhill, "Keeping up with the Ladies," *The Pentecostal Testimony*, 1 June 1950, 7.

16 Ibid.

17 PAOC Archives, Men's Ministry Committee fonds, "Minutes of the Meeting Appointed by the General Executive regarding the matter of organizing Men's Fellowships in our churches," 11 February 1954. The minutes record that four people were present at the meeting: W.E.

McAlister, C.M. Wortman, James Montgomery, and G.R. Upton. It was at this meeting that the decision was made to coordinate the efforts through the national office.

18 "Men's Fellowship," *The Pentecostal Testimony*, June 1955, 11.

19 The first issue of *Real Living* was published in the summer of 1963, with plans to publish quarterly. Copies of the magazine are housed in the PAOC Archives.

20 "'MF Emblem'," *The Pentecostal Testimony*, June 1957, 27.

21 PAOC Archives, General Conference fonds, James Montgomery, "Sunday School, Youth Departments, Testimony Press: Report to the PAOC General Conference," 1966.

22 B.T. Parkinson, "Crusading in a Changing Canada," *The Pentecostal Testimony*, 1 July 1961, 30.

23 Several versions of Montgomery's personal testimony can be found in the PAOC Archives, James Montgomery fonds, including James Montgomery correspondence with Rev. Ronald Kidd, 17 March 1976 and 23 June 1976, 13 pages; Transcription of T.W. Miller Interviewing Rev. James Montgomery, 29 July 1984, 18 pages; and James Montgomery, "The Memoirs of James Montgomery," June 1987, 13 pages.

24 PAOC Archives, Pentecostal Oral Histories Project, James Montgomery interviewed by Thomas Miller, 29 July 1984.

25 The number of Sunday Schools reporting was based on those that filed reports with the national office. The decline in number of Sunday Schools between 1960 and 1962 may represent a change in the reporting structure more than a reflection of actual declining numbers. The numbers reported for 1962 and 1964 were rounded off in the reports, indicating that they are most likely estimates, not actually reported numbers. No exact number of Sunday Schools was reported in the 1970 General Report, but one assumes the number may have declined by two, given that the PAOC had 743 assemblies that year, not 745. A note included in the report for 1970 pointed out that "Enrollment would be 120,000–130,000 if Newfoundland and Ethnic Churches were included."

26 PAOC Archives, General Conference fonds, "Christian Education Department Executive Director Report to General Conference," 1970, 22.

27 "Pentecostal Crusaders: Why Have Boys' and Girls' Crusaders?" *The Pentecostal Testimony*, April 1960, 30.

28 PAOC Archives, James Montgomery fonds, K. Parks, "Sunday School," n.d. [but with references to 1969 in the text, it is likely that this report is from that same year].

29 "Pentecostal Crusaders: Why Have Boys' and Girls' Crusaders?" *The Pentecostal Testimony*, April 1960, 30.
30 Ibid.
31 The James Montgomery fonds in the PAOC Archives includes several files of material, including correspondence with other youth organizations, handbooks, curriculum guides, and advice about how to go about establishing such groups.
32 "Pentecostal Crusaders: Why Have Boys' and Girls' Crusaders?" *The Pentecostal Testimony*, April 1960, 30.
33 PAOC Archives, Pentecostal Crusaders fonds, "Early Crusader File – The Organization and Working Plans of Our Youth Group, Zion Evangelistic Fellowship, Rhode Island."
34 B.T. Parkinson, "Crusading in a Changing Canada," *The Pentecostal Testimony*, July 1961, 30.
35 "Our Helmets!" *The Pentecostal Testimony*, February 1961, 30.
36 B.T. Parkinson, "Crusading in a Changing Canada," *The Pentecostal Testimony*, July 1961, 30.
37 Ibid.
38 Ibid.
39 Advertisement for Crusaders, *The Pentecostal Testimony*, September 1961, 30.

CHAPTER FIVE

1 Earl Kulbeck, "Canada Marks Another Birthday," *The Pentecostal Testimony*, July 1969, 2, 28.
2 Bowen, *Christians in a Secular World*.
3 For more on the 1960s in Canada, see Palmer, *Canada's 1960s*.
4 See Stewart, *The New Canadian Pentecostals*.
5 Hutchinson and Wolffe, *A Short History of Global Evangelicalism*, 244–6.
6 Goode and Ben-Yehuda, "Moral Panics: Culture, Politics, and Social Construction."
7 Ibid., 152.
8 Ibid., 165.
9 Emerging scholarship about 1969 complicates the popular view that massive social change can be traced to this one legislative change because sustained change and progress on several of its key issues took decades to emerge. See Hayday and Kelm, "Reconsidering 1969: A 'Turning Point' for Canada?" along with articles in that same issue on topics including abortion and homosexuality.

10 Louis Tamminga, "A Christian Testimony Regarding Abortion," *The Pentecostal Testimony*, August 1969, 6–7.

11 David Mainse, "More Prophesies Fulfilled – Revival is a Must," *The Pentecostal Testimony*, February 1971.

12 C.R. Stiller, "Therapeutic Abortion from the Medical Viewpoint," *The Pentecostal Testimony*, August 1971, 4–5, 26; Virgil L. Gingrich, "Therapeutic Abortion from a Theological Viewpoint," *The Pentecostal Testimony*, August 1971, 6–9.

13 Gingrich, "Therapeutic Abortion from a Theological Viewpoint," 8–9.

14 PAOC Archives, General Conference fonds, General Conference, 1968 report.

Resolution No. 19 – Letters to be sent re Omnibus Bill –
WHEREAS there is a need for the affirmation of Biblical principles as the only basis for a successful national or personal life, and
WHEREAS the "Omnibus Bill" said to be proposed this Fall, 1968, by Justice Minister Turner proposes changes in laws relating to lotteries and homosexuality which this Conference would deem to be contrary to the laws of God laid down in Scripture,
THEREFORE BE IT RESOLVED that this Conference through its General Office indicate to both the news media and by letter to every member of Parliament our serious and conscientious objection to the proposed legalization of lotteries and homosexuality, and
FURTHER, that we urge our government to apply such limits to the law regarding abortion as to ensure the sanctity of life;
AND FURTHER BE IT RESOLVED that this Conference request our General Office to send a letter to each pastor requesting that he and his people be encouraged to participate in a gigantic nationwide write-in campaign, voicing their objections to the above-mentioned changes in the Criminal Code; such letters to be directed to the Prime Minister, the Minister of Justice and their own local Member of Parliament.
M and S (Barber-Dynna)
Considerable discussion followed from the floor.
Amendments were M and S (Ewald-Counsell) as follows:
(1) To be added to Paragraph 4, "… and to safeguard the Canadian people from the irresponsible use of the privilege of abortion for selfish pursuits."
(2) To be added at the conclusion of the Resolution – "AND FURTHER BE IT RESOLVED that a Commission be appointed to arrive at a decision on abortion which may act as guidance for our ministry and people."
Discussion followed. The Motion was CARRIED as AMENDED.

15 PAOC Archives, General Conference fonds, General Conference 1978, Resolution #14 – (GEC-018), National Committee on Moral Standards.

16 PAOC Archives, General Conference fonds, General Conference 1980, Resolution #24 – (MS-110) re. Title of Committee on Moral Standards.

17 Hudson T. Hilsden, "Evangelism and Social Concerns in Partnership," *The Pentecostal Testimony*, September 1990, 4–6.

18 Ibid., 5.

19 Ibid.

20 PAOC Archives, Social Concerns Department fonds, Hudson T. Hilsden, "Submission to the Members of the Legislative Assembly of Ontario concerning the Amendment to Bill 7 to include Sexual Orientation in the Ontario Human Rights Code," July 1986.

21 Hilsden, "Oh Canada! God Keep Our Land!" *The Pentecostal Testimony*, 1 July 1989.

22 In 1988, following a similar plan in the Assemblies of God, US, James MacKnight organized the "Total Church Evangelism Strategy Committee" to coordinate the direction of the PAOC for the 1990s. From this committee, the PAOC implemented the "Decade of Destiny" as a strategy for its pastors and congregations to pray for Canada and to seek ways to evangelize. The 1990s was a period of organizational adjustment for the denomination, with new financial plans, a new mission statement, national conferences like the Congress on Pentecostal Leadership in 1993, and construction of a new national office. See Miller, *Canadian Pentecostals*, 397–412. The numerical and financial growth of the 1970s, however, was beginning to show signs of cooling in the 1980s, and the PAOC did not anticipate the further decline that characterized the 1990s.

23 Kydd, "Canadian Pentecostalism and the Evangelical Impulse."

24 Stackhouse, *Canadian Evangelicalism in the Twentieth Century*; and Stewart, *The New Canadian Pentecostals*.

25 Summit Pacific Library Archives, Bernice Gerard collection, Sermon Notes, "Two Much Wilderness, Too Few Prophets," Fraserview Assembly, October 1973. Sermon series Part I.

26 Ibid., Parts I–IV.

27 Gerard, *Bernice Gerard*.

28 Ibid., 183–4.

29 Ibid.

30 John Faustman, "Avenging Angel in 'Loose City,'" *The Vancouver Courier*, 25 July 1979.

31 Gerard, *Bernice Gerard*, 184.

32 The cartoon, originally published in the *Vancouver Sun*, depicted the "Snafouver Business License Department" reception desk at city hall like a church where applicants for liquor licences had to "take a pew" to wait while the clerk "invoked the wisdom of the mayor and Alderman Gerard" before issuing any document. Summit Pacific College Library Archives, Bernice Gerard collection, Photo Album and Scrapbook.
33 Gerard, *Bernice Gerard*, 184.
34 Ibid., 186.
35 Malloy, "Canadian Evangelicals and Same-Sex Marriage."
36 Hutchinson, "Focusing, Framing, and Discerning"; and Pamela Young, "It's all about Sex."
37 Solange Lefebvre and Jean-François Breton, "Roman Catholics and Same-Sex Marriage in Quebec"; and Malloy, "Canadian Evangelicals and Same-Sex Marriage."
38 PAOC Archives, General Superintendent fonds, 27 June 2003.
39 PAOC Archives, General Conference fonds, General Conference Report, 2004, 29.
40 Ibid., 51.
41 PAOC, Statement of Fundamental and Essential Truths, 2014, 5.
42 Reimer, *Evangelicals and the Continental Divide*; Reimer, "'Civility without Compromise.'"
43 Reimer, "'Civility without Compromise,'" 71–86.
44 Reimer and Wilkinson, *A Culture of Faith*.
45 Malloy, "Between America and Europe."
46 Malloy, "Canadian Evangelicals and Same-Sex Marriage."
47 Hutchinson and Hiemstra, "Canadian Evangelical Voting Trends by Region, 1996–2008."
48 Stackhouse, "Bearing Witness."
49 Haskell, "'What We Have Here is a Failure to Communicate'."
50 Simpson, "The Politics of the Body in Canada and the United States"; Bean, Kaufman, and Gonzalez, "Why Doesn't Canada Have an American-style Christian Right?"
51 Michael Wilkinson, "Pentecostalism, the Body, and Embodiment"; Wilkinson, "The Transformation of Religion and the Self in the Age of Authenticity."
52 Stewart, Gabriel, and Shanahan, "Changes in Clergy Belief and Practice in Canada's Largest Pentecostal Denomination."
53 Jennings, "A Silence Like Thunder."
54 PAOC Archives, General Executive fonds, "Pastoral Reflection on Human Sexuality," 7 February 2017.

CHAPTER SIX

1 McGee, *Miracles, Missions, and American Pentecostalism.*
2 Anderson, *Spreading Fires.*
3 Anderson, "Signs and Blunders."
4 "About Mission Canada," PAOC, https://paoc.org/canada/about, accessed 25 October 2018.
5 Grant, *Moon of Wintertime.*
6 See Truth and Reconciliation Commission of Canada, "Calls to Action." Access to this and all of the reports issued or created by the Truth and Reconciliation Commission are available on the website for the National Centre for Truth and Reconciliation, hosted by the University of Manitoba: http://nctr.ca/reports.php, accessed 21 June 2019.
7 See "Reclaiming Power and Place: The Final Report of the National Inquiry into Missing and Murdered Indigenous Women and Girls."
8 Grant, *Moon of Wintertime*, 201–2.
9 Ustorf, "Protestantism and Missions," 393.
10 There is very little written on the missionary nature of Canadian Pentecostalism. Irving Whitt completed a doctoral dissertation at Fuller Theological Seminary in which he reviewed the historical context of early Pentecostalism and the missiological nature of the PAOC. See Whitt, "Developing a Pentecostal Missiology in the Canadian Context."
11 Stewart, "A Canadian Azusa?"
12 Dayton, "The Rise of the Evangelical Healing Movement in Nineteenth Century America"; Wacker, *Heaven Below*; R.M. Riss, "Faith Homes"; Curtis, "Houses of Healing."
13 Opp, *The Lord for the Body*, 58–63.
14 Wilkinson, "Charles W. Chawner and the Missionary Impulse of the Hebden Mission."
15 Miller, *Canadian Pentecostals*, 43–4.
16 Ibid., 224.
17 McGee, *Miracles, Missions, and American Pentecostalism*, 163–5; Tarango, *Choosing the Jesus Way*, 31–40.
18 "Home Mission Extension Department," *The Pentecostal Testimony*, 1 February 1941, 1; "A Forward Move in Canada," *The Pentecostal Testimony*, 1 February 1941, 14.
19 Ibid.
20 Ibid.
21 "Home Mission Extension Department," *The Pentecostal Testimony*, 1 September 1941, 3.

22 A.H. Townsend, "Home Missions," *The Pentecostal Testimony*, 15 May 1941, 16.
23 Salome Cressman, "French Canada," *The Pentecostal Testimony*, 1 December 1942, 6–7.
24 Ibid.
25 Ibid.
26 Miller, *Canadian Pentecostals*, 417.
27 Zuidema, *French-Speaking Protestants in Canada*.
28 Michael Di Giacomo, "Aimee Semple McPherson."
29 Ibid., 162.
30 Thomas, "Pentecostal Predominance in French Evangelicalism in Quebec, 1921–1963."
31 "General Officers Leave Executive Posts," *The Pentecostal Testimony*, December 1982, 2; PAOC Archives, Executive Officers Committee fonds, "Robert M. Argue – Information Sheet," prepared for retirement, 1982.
32 Keith Parks, "Why a Quebec Outreach?" *Dominion Outreach*, April 1968, 2.
33 F.H. Parlee, "Quebec Literature Crusade Formed," *Dominion Outreach*, April 1968, 4.
34 PAOC Archives, General Conference fonds, Robert Argue, "District Conference Report – Home Missions, Bible Colleges, and Men's Fellowship Departments," 1968, 3–4.
35 Di Giacomo, "FLITE," 59.
36 PAOC Archives, Quebec District fonds, Robert Argue, circular letter to PAOC pastors, June 1968.
37 PAOC Archives, French Conference fonds, "Administrative History of the French Conference."
38 Ibid.
39 See Hollenweger, "Roman Catholics and Pentecostals in Dialogue"; McDonnell, "Pentecostals and Catholics on Evangelism and Sheep-Stealing"; Kärkkäinen, "An Exercise on the Frontiers of Ecumenism"; Murphy, *Pentecostals and Roman Catholics on Becoming a Christian*.
40 Kydd, "Roman Catholic/Pentecostal Dialogue in Italy."
41 See Ziefle, *David du Plessis and the Assemblies of God*; and Murphy, *Pentecostals and Roman Catholics on Becoming a Christian*.
42 Holm, "I'm Still There!" 75.
43 See Truth and Reconciliation Commission of Canada, *Canada's Residential Schools: The History Part 1, Origins to 1939*; Truth and Reconciliation Commission of Canada, *Canada's Residential Schools:*

The History Part 2, 1939 to 2000; and Bradford and Horton, *Mixed Blessings*.

44 See Grant, *Moon of Wintertime*, ch. 8. The general pattern of mission work in North America revolved around the missionary working in tandem with the movement of settlers and Indigenous peoples, eventually moving farther north and west from the landing points along the St Lawrence River to established mission posts. The mission post was organized around Indigenous peoples and later the reserve and typically included a church building for worship. There would be daily calls for morning prayer, the celebration of the mass for Roman Catholics, catechism classes in the afternoon, evening prayers, further teaching or preaching, and choirs for children. The Methodists and Anglicans followed a similar pattern with daily prayer, afternoon classes, and evening prayer meetings supervised by the missionaries. For the Methodists, the class meeting was incorporated into the pattern, and Anglicans held small group meetings with the missionary. The mission post included a range of activities for children and youth, and for Protestants, temperance societies were established. Regular evangelistic meetings were conducted alongside a tightly scheduled life in the mission post. Missionaries spoke with authority on numerous issues beyond the religious. Among Roman Catholic and Protestant missions, there was some discussion of Indigenous leadership, but opportunities were limited or never granted.

45 Truth and Reconciliation Commission of Canada, *Canada's Residential Schools: The History Part 1, Origins to 1939*; Truth and Reconciliation Commission of Canada, *Canada's Residential Schools: The History Part 2, 1939 to 2000*; and Miller, "The State, the Church, and Indian Residential Schools in Canada," 110–12.

46 Truth and Reconciliation Commission of Canada, *Canada's Residential Schools: The History Part 1, Origins to 1939*, 210–12.

47 Truth and Reconciliation Commission of Canada, *Canada's Residential Schools: The History Part 2, Origins to 1939*.

48 Ibid. Also see Miller, *Shingwauk's Vision*.

49 See Michael Coren, "On from Azusa Street," *National Post*, 21 November 2000, A17. Coren writes about Prime Minister Jean Chrétien's questioning of his political opponent Stockwell Day because he was a Pentecostal and how scary that might be for a political leader. Stockwell Day was a member of the Reform Party of Canada. Coren states: "Interestingly enough, Stockwell Day is not the only Canadian leader to be an active Pentecostal. Matthew Coon Come,

National Chief of the Assembly of First Nations, worships in a PAOC church." A number of Pentecostals served in Canadian politics at the provincial level in the 1950s and 1960s, including P.A. Gaglardi (Social Credit), Everet I. Wood (Social Credit), Raymond Edwards (New Democratic Party), and Ethel Wilson (Liberal Party). See Ronald A.N. Kydd, "The Pentecostal Assemblies of Canada and Society," 8–9.

50 Robert K. Burkinshaw, "Native Pentecostalism in British Columbia."

51 Ibid., 144.

52 Ibid., 153.

53 Gordon Upton, "Native Leadership in Canada," *The Pentecostal Testimony*, December 1986, 35.

54 Gordon Upton, "Canada's Forgotten People," *The Pentecostal Testimony*, November 1987, 4–5.

55 Ibid., 5.

56 Klaus Sonnenberg, "Native Church Leaders Confront the Issues of the 90s," *The Pentecostal Testimony*, November 1992, 16–17.

57 Peggy Kennedy, "Ottawa Sacred Assembly '95," *The Pentecostal Testimony*, March 1996, 24.

58 For an assessment on shamanism and Pentecostalism, see Laugrand and Oosten, *Inuit Shamanism and Christianity*. Allan Anderson has also made the link with his research on Africa in Anderson, *Spirit-Filled World*.

59 Westman, "Understanding Cree Religious Discourse"; Westman, "Pentecostalism among Canadian Aboriginal People."

60 McCleary, "An Ethnography of Pentecostalism among the Crow Indians of Montana." Also see Clatterbuck, ed., *Crow Jesus*.

61 Tarango, *Choosing the Jesus Way*.

62 Gibson, "Native Theological Training within Canadian Evangelicalism."

63 Canada, House of Commons Debates.

64 Ibid.

65 Evangelical Fellowship of Canada, "Letter to the Prime Minister."

66 Aldred, "Response to the Prime Minister's Apology to Aboriginal Peoples."

67 Ibid.

68 Coon Come, "I Choose to Forgive."

69 Yang and Abel, "Sociology of Religious Conversion."

70 See Robbins, "On the Paradox of Pentecostalism and the Perils of Continuity Thinking"; Engelke, "Past Pentecostalism."

71 Bosch, *Transforming Mission*.

CHAPTER SEVEN

1 Royal Commission on Bilingualism and Biculturalism, *The Cultural Contribution of the Other Ethnic Groups*. For a discussion of the controversy, see Driedger, *Multi-Ethnic Canada*, 106–8; and Fleras, *Unequal Relations*.

2 Fleras and Elliott, *Engaging Diversity*.

3 PAOC Archives, General Conference fonds, Pentecostal Assemblies of Canada, General Constitution, 1968: Article XI.

4 Cumbo, "'Your Old Men Will Dream Dreams'"; Di Giacomo, "Identity and Change."

5 Miller, *Canadian Pentecostals*, 201.

6 Drewitz, *History of the German Branch of the Pentecostal Assemblies of Canada*; Doberstein, *Grace and Glory*; Doberstein, *Alberta District*; Schatkowski, *Rev. Julius Schatkowski*.

7 Drewitz, *History of the German Branch of the Pentecostal Assemblies of Canada*.

8 Ibid.

9 Ibid., 8.

10 Ibid., 9.

11 See MacRobert, *The Black Roots and White Racism of Early Pentecostalism*; Kidd, *The Forging of Races*, 216; Espinosa, *William J. Seymour and the Origins of Global Pentecostalism*, ch. 6.

12 Dupree, "Church of God in Christ"; Alexander, *Black Fire*.

13 McIntyre, *Black Pentecostal Music in Windsor*, 1–18.

14 McGee and Pavia, "Church of God of Prophecy in Canada."

15 PAOC Archives, General Conference fonds, General Conference minutes, 1934.

16 PAOC Archives, General Secretary-Treasurer fonds, The Pentecostal Assemblies of Canada Year Book, 1941, 46.

17 Rosenior, "The Rhetoric of Pentecostal Racial Reconciliation."

18 Posterski, *Reinventing Evangelism*.

19 Wilkinson, *The Spirit Said Go*; Reimer and Wilkinson, *A Culture of Faith*; Bibby, "Canada's Mythical Religious Mosaic"; Statistics Canada, "Religions in Canada"; Guenther, "Ethnicity and Evangelical Protestants in Canada."

20 Aechtner, "Standing at the Crux."

21 Anderson, *To the Ends of the Earth*.

22 Reimer and Wilkinson, *A Culture of Faith*, 74.

23 Wilkinson, "Religion and Global Flows."

24 Medina, "Discerning the Spirit in Culture: Toward Pentecostal Interculturality"; Medina, "Hybridity, Migration, and Transnational Relations."

25 For example, in the BC/Yukon District, Edgar Lapeciros is the PAOC ministry leader for International and Ethnic Ministries/Cultural Ministry. "The Ethnic Ministries exists to reach non-believing multicultural people groups and to connect them with our existing churches, teaching them as they grow in faith, and to challenge them to discover their gifts and honour God with their lives. The Executive Director of Missions and Church Development, under the direction and guidance of the district executive / district officers, will seek to develop relationship and functioning models to help Canadian congregations work with existing congregations and to promote strong relationship/coordination with the district." Pentecostal Assemblies of Canada, "Cultural Ministry."

26 Wilkinson, *The Spirit Said Go.*

27 Wilkinson, *The Spirit Said Go*; Levitt, *God Needs No Passport.*

28 Lee, "Ethnic Korean Migration in Northeast Asia"; Lee, "Korean-Chinese Migration into the Russian Far East."

29 Moon, "The Recent Korean Missionary Movement."

30 Wilkinson, "The 'Many Tongues' of Global Pentecostalism."

31 1.5 refers to those young adults who arrived in Canada as youth and have lived roughly half their lives in Canada and the other half in Korea. For a discussion, see Beyer and Ramji, *Growing up Canadian.*

32 Interview with Michael Wilkinson, 2007.

33 Ibid.

34 Ibid.

35 Ibid.

36 Ibid.

37 Ibid.

38 See Beaman, *Reasonable Accommodation*; and Beaman, *Deep Equality in an Era of Religious Diversity* for a discussion about the limits of tolerance, religious differences, and equality.

39 Bibby, *Unknown Gods*, 22.

40 Beyer, *Religion and Globalization*; Beyer, *Religions in Global Society.*

41 Wilkinson discussed the various debates among Pentecostals over orthodoxy and orthopraxy and has added to Beyer's work by pointing out that for Pentecostals, there are also debates about orthopathy, or the ways in which Pentecostals experience and embody their faith. Wilkinson, "Pentecostals and the World."

42 Robertson, *Globalization.*
43 Roland Robertson, "Global Millennialism."
44 Whitt and Craig, "A Philosophy of Missions for the Pentecostal Assemblies of Canada," 4.
45 Ibid., 22.
46 Ibid., 107.
47 Ibid., 26.
48 Ibid., 30.
49 Ibid.
50 Ibid., 46–8.
51 Ibid., 57–8.
52 Ibid., 64–5.
53 Irving Whitt, "Rethinking Religion?" *The Pentecostal Testimony*, October 2001, 27.
54 Randy Sohnchen, "What Priority One Means," *The Pentecostal Testimony*, October 2001, 5.
55 Bill Morrow, "Is Anybody Answering?" *The Pentecostal Testimony*, October 2001, 26.
56 William Griffin, "I Do Not Want You to Be Ignorant," *The Pentecostal Testimony*, October 2001, 22.
57 Ibid.

CONCLUSION

1 Weber, *Economy and Society, vol. 1*, 241–54.
2 Anderson. *Spreading Fires.*
3 Airhart, *A Church with the Soul of a Nation*; Flatt, *After Evangelicalism*; Clarke and Macdonald, *Leaving Christianity.*
4 Finke and Stark, *The Churching of America.*
5 Reimer and Wilkinson, *A Culture of Faith.* A 2020 study from the Evangelical Fellowship of Canada estimated evangelicals to be 6 per cent of the Canadian population, a decline from 9 per cent in 2015. See https://www.faithtoday.ca/Magazines/2020-Jan-Feb/Not-Christian-anymore, accessed 5 March 2020.
6 Bibby, *Fragmented Gods*; Bibby, *Unknown Gods*; Bibby, *Restless Gods.*
7 Reginald Bibby describes the new cultural context using the language of polarization between the pro-religious, low-religious, and no-religious in *Resilient Gods: Being Pro-Religious, Low-Religious, or No-Religious in Canada*. For another interpretation, see Thiessen, *The Meaning of Sunday.*

References

PRIMARY SOURCES

Archives of the Pentecostal Assemblies of Canada

Aboriginal Advisory Committee fonds
C.B. Smith fonds
Canadian Pentecostal College Correspondence fonds
Central Pentecostal College fonds
Chaplains Committee fonds
Committee on Mission fonds
Credential Holders collection
Eastern Ontario and Quebec District fonds
Eastern Ontario District fonds
Eastern Slavic Branch fonds
Education Standards Committee fonds
Executive Committee fonds
Executive Officers Committee fonds
Finnish Branch Conference fonds
French Conference fonds
General Conference fonds
General Executive fonds
General Secretary-Treasurer fonds
General Superintendent fonds
German Branch Conference fonds
Institut Biblique Beree fonds [*sic*]
James E. Purdie fonds
James Montgomery fonds

Men's Ministry Committee fonds
Ministre Multilangue fonds
Ministries Division fonds
Missions in Canada Committee fonds
National Bible College Committee fonds
National Home Missions Committee fonds
Pentecostal Crusaders Committee fonds
Pentecostal Crusaders fonds
Pentecostal Oral Histories Project fonds
Quebec District fonds
R.E. McAlister fonds
Research collection
Saskatchewan District fonds
Social Concerns Committee fonds
Social Concerns Department fonds
Spiritual Life and Evangelism Department fonds
The Pentecostal Testimony Magazine fonds
Walter E. McAlister fonds
Western Bible College fonds
Women's Ministries Committee fonds
World Missions Committee fonds

Flower Pentecostal Heritage Center

Correspondence: McAlister, R.E. (1949–1950)
Personal Papers – McAlister, R.E.
Secretariat – Executive Files

Summit Pacific Library & Archives

Bernice Gerard collection

Published Magazines and Newspapers

Dominion Outreach
Real Living
The Good Report
The Latter Rain Evangel
The Pentecostal Evangel
The Pentecostal Testimony

The Promise
The Vancouver Courier
Truth Advocate
Vancouver Sun

SECONDARY SOURCES

Aechtner, Thomas H. "Standing at the Crux: Pentecostalism and Identity Formation in an African Diaspora Christian Community," in Wilkinson, ed., *Global Pentecostal Movements*, 171–94.

Airhart, Phyllis D. *A Church with the Soul of a Nation: Making and Remaking the United Church of Canada*. Montreal and Kingston: McGill-Queen's University Press, 2013.

Aldred, Ray. "Response to the Prime Minister's Apology to Aboriginal Peoples." Evangelical Fellowship of Canada, http://bbnc.evangelicalfellowship.ca/page.aspx?pid=5885, accessed 9 February 2019.

Alexander, Estrelda. *Black Fire*. Downer's Grove, IL: InterVarsity Press, 2011.

Allen, Richard. *The Social Passion: Religion and Social Reform in Canada, 1914–28*. Toronto: University of Toronto Press, 1973.

Althouse, Peter. "Apocalyptic Discourse and a Pentecostal Vision of Canada," in Wilkinson, ed., *Canadian Pentecostalism: Transition and Transformation*, 58–78.

– "Canadian Pentecostal Pacifism." *Eastern Journal of Practical Theology* 4, 2 (1991): 32–43.

– "The Influence of Dr. J.E. Purdie's Reformed Theology on the Formation and Development of the Pentecostal Assemblies of Canada." *Pneuma: The Journal of the Society for Pentecostal Studies* 19, 1 (1996): 3–28.

– "Waxing and Waning of Social Deprivation as a Model for Understanding the Class Composition of Early American Pentecostalism," in Wilkinson and Studebaker, eds, *A Liberating Spirit*.

– and Robby Waddell, eds. *Perspectives in Pentecostal Eschatologies: World without End*. Eugene, OR: Wipf and Stock, 2010.

Ambrose, Linda M. "Establishing a Gendered Authority through Pentecostal Publications: The Writings of Zelma Argue, 1920–1969." *Historical Papers: Journal of the Canadian Society of Church History* (2009): 69–80.

– "Zelma and Beulah Argue: Sisters in the Canadian Pentecostal Movement," in Wilkinson and Althouse, eds, *Winds from the North*, 99–127.

Anderson, Allan H. *An Introduction to Pentecostalism: Global Charismatic Christianity*. Cambridge, UK: Cambridge University Press, 2013.

– "Signs and Blunders: Pentecostal Mission Issues at 'Home and Abroad' in the Twentieth Century." Paper presented at the 29th annual meeting of the Society for Pentecostal Studies, 16–18 March 2000.

– *Spirit-Filled World*. Cham, Switzerland: Springer International Publishing, 2018.

– *Spreading Fires: The Missionary Nature of Early Pentecostalism*. Maryknoll, NY: Orbis Books, 2007.

– *To the Ends of the Earth: Pentecostalism and the Transformation of World Christianity*. Oxford: Oxford University Press, 2013.

Artibise, Alan F.J. *Winnipeg: A Social History of Urban Growth, 1874–1914*. Montreal and Kingston: McGill-Queen's University Press, 1975.

Atter, Gordon F. *The Third Force*, 3rd edn. Caledonia, ON: Acts Books, 1970.

Beaman, Lori G. *Deep Equality in an Era of Religious Diversity*. Oxford: Oxford University Press, 2017.

– ed. *Reasonable Accommodation*. Vancouver: University of British Columbia Press, 2012.

Bean, Lydia, Jason Kaufman, and Marco Jesus Gonzalez. "Why Doesn't Canada Have an American-Style Christian Right? A Comparative Framework for Analyzing the Political Effects of Evangelical Subcultural Identity." *Canadian Journal of Sociology* 33, 4 (2008): 899–944.

Berger, Peter. *The Desecularization of the World: Resurgent Religion and World Politics*. Grand Rapids, MI: Eerdmans, 1999.

Beyer, Peter. "Movements, Markets and Social Contexts: Canadian Pentecostalism in Global Perspective," in Wilkinson, ed., *Canadian Pentecostalism*, 264–76.

– *Religion and Globalization*. London: SAGE Publications, 1994.

– *Religions in Global Society*. London: Routledge, 2006.

– and Lori Beaman, eds. *Religion, Globalization, and Culture*. Leiden, Netherlands: Brill, 2007.

– and Rubina Ramji, eds, *Growing up Canadian*. Montreal and Kingston: McGill-Queen's University Press, 2013.

Bibby, Reginald. "Canada's Mythical Religious Mosaic: Some Census Findings," *Journal for the Scientific Study of Religion* 39 (2000): 235–9.

– *Fragmented Gods: The Poverty and Potential of Religion in Canada*. Toronto: Irwin, 1987.

– *Resilient Gods: Being Pro-Religious, Low-Religious, or No-Religious in Canada*. Vancouver: University of British Columbia Press, 2017.
– *Restless Gods: The Renaissance of Religion in Canada*. Toronto: Stoddart, 2002.
– *Unknown Gods*. Toronto: Stoddart, 1993.
Blumhofer, Edith. *Restoring the Faith: The Assemblies of God, Pentecostalism and American Culture*. Champaign, IL: University of Illinois Press, 1993.
Bosch, David J. *Transforming Mission: Paradigm Shifts in Theology of Mission*. Maryknoll, NY: Orbis Books, 1991.
Bothwell, Robert, Ian Drummond, and John English, *Canada 1900–1945*. Toronto: University of Toronto Press, 1987.
Bourdieu, Pierre. *Outline of a Theory of Practice*. Cambridge, UK: Cambridge University Press, 1977.
Bowen, Kurt. *Christians in a Secular World*. Montreal and Kingston: McGill-Queen's University Press, 2004.
Bradford, Tolly, and Chelsea Horton, eds. *Mixed Blessings: Indigenous Encounters with Christianity in Canada*. Vancouver: University of British Columbia University Press, 2016.
Bramadat, Paul, and David Seljak, eds. *Christianity and Ethnicity in Canada*. Toronto: University of Toronto Press, 2008.
– *Religion and Ethnicity in Canada*. Toronto: Pearson Longman, 2005.
Brock, Peter. *Pacifism in Europe to 1914*. Princeton, NJ: Princeton University Press, 1972.
Bruce, Steve. "Christianity in Britain, R.I.P." *Sociology of Religion* 2 (2001): 191–203.
– *God Is Dead: Secularization in the West*. Oxford: Wiley-Blackwell, 2002.
– *Secularization: In Defence of an Unfashionable Theory*. Oxford: Oxford University Press, 2013.
Brumback, Carl. *Suddenly from Heaven: A History of the Assemblies of God*. Springfield, MO: Gospel Publishing House, 1961.
Bumsted, J.M., and Michael C. Bumsted. *A History of the Canadian Peoples*, 5th edn. Don Mills, ON: Oxford University Press, 2016.
Burgess, Stanley M, and Eduard M. van der Maas, eds. *The New International Dictionary of Pentecostal and Charismatic Movements*. Grand Rapids, MI: Zondervan, 2002.
Burkinshaw, Robert K. "Native Pentecostalism in British Columbia," in Wilkinson, ed., *Canadian Pentecostalism*, 142–70.

Butler, Ewen H. *Canadian Winds of the Spirit: Holiness, Pentecostal and Charismatic Currents*. Lexington, KY: Emeth Press, 2018.

Canada. House of Commons. *Debates* (11 June 2008), number 110, 39th Parliament, 2nd Session. http://www.parl.gc.ca/HousePublication.aspx.Docid=3568890&Language=E.

Canada. The Truth and Reconciliation Commission. *Canada's Residential Schools: The History Part 1, Origins to 1939*. Montreal and Kingston: McGill-Queen's University Press, 2015.

Canada. The Truth and Reconciliation Commission. *Canada's Residential Schools: The History Part 2, 1939 to 2000*. Montreal and Kingston: McGill-Queen's University Press, 2015.

Cerillo, A., Jr, and G. Wacker. "Bibliography and Historiography of Pentecostalism in North America," in Burgess and van der Maas, eds, *The New International Dictionary of Pentecostal Charismatic Movements*, 397–405.

Chaves, Mark. *Congregations in America*. Cambridge, MA: Harvard University Press, 2004.

– "Denominations as Dual Structures: An Organizational Analysis." *Sociology of Religion* 54, 2 (1993): 147–69.

– "Religious Organizations: Data Resources and Research Opportunities." *American Behavioral Scientist* 45, 10 (2002): 1,523–49.

Clarke, Brian, and Stuart Macdonald. *Leaving Christianity: Changing Allegiances in Canada since 1945*. Montreal and Kingston: McGill-Queen's University Press, 2017.

Clatterbuck, Mark, ed. *Crow Jesus: Personal Stories of Native Religious Belonging*. Norman, OK: University of Oklahoma Press, 2017.

Comacchio, Cynthia R. *Nations Are Built of Babies: Saving Ontario's Mothers and Children, 1900–1940*. Montreal and Kingston: McGill-Queen's University Press, 1993.

Cook, Sharon Anne. *'Through Sunshine and Shadow': The Woman's Christian Temperance Union, Evangelicalism, and Reform in Ontario, 1874–1930*. Montreal and Kingston: McGill-Queen's University Press, 1995.

Cook, Tim. *The Secret Life of Soldiers: How Canadians Survived the Great War*. Toronto: Penguin Random House Canada, 2018.

Coon Come, Matthew. "I Choose to Forgive." http://archives.algomau.ca/main/?q=node/18835, accessed 9 February 2019.

Courtney, Caleb. "The 1909 and 1910 Canadian Pentecostal Camp Meetings in Markham, Ontario." http://calebcourtney.com/blog/?p=1159#en-1159-7, accessed 29 January 2019.

Craig, James D. "'Out and Out for the Lord': James Eustace Purdie, an Early Anglican Pentecostal." Unpublished MA thesis, University of St. Michael's College, Toronto, 1995.

Cumbo, Enrico Carlson. "'Your Old Men Will Dream Dreams': The Italian Pentecostal Experience in Canada, 1912–1945." *Journal of American Ethnic History* 3 (2000): 35–81.

Curtis, Heather D. "Houses of Healing: Sacred Space, Spiritual Practice, and the Transformation of Female Suffering in the Faith Cure Movement, 1870–90." *Church History* 3 (2006): 598–611.

Dayton, Donald. "The Rise of the Evangelical Healing Movement in Nineteenth Century America." *Pneuma: Journal of the Society of Pentecostal Studies* 4, 1 (1982): 1–18.

– *Theological Roots of Pentecostalism*. Peabody, MA: Hendrickson Publishers, 1987.

Dempster, Murray. "The Canada–Britain–USA Triad: Canadian Pentecostal Pacifism in WWI and WWII." *Canadian Journal of Pentecostal-Charismatic Christianity* 4 (2013): 1–26.

Di Giacomo, Michael. "Aimee Semple McPherson: 'Shot in the Arm' for French-Canadian Pentecostalism," in Wilkinson and Althouse, eds, *Winds from the North*, 160.

– "FLITE: Religious Entrepreneurship in Quebec in the 1970s and 1980s." *Journal of the Canadian Church Historical Society* xlvi, 1 (2004): 49–88.

– "Identity and Change: The Story of the Italian-Canadian Pentecostal Community." *Canadian Journal of Pentecostal-Charismatic Christianity* 2, 1 (2011): 83–130.

Doberstein, Horst. *Alberta District: Our Heritage*. Kitchener, ON: German Branch, 1992.

– ed. *Grace and Glory: The Story of the German Branch of the Pentecostals Assemblies of Canada*. Kitchener, ON: German Branch, 1990.

Drewitz, Arthur. *History of the German Branch of the Pentecostal Assemblies of Canada*. Kitchener, ON: German Branch, 1986.

Driedger, Leo. *Multi-ethnic Canada: Identities & Inequalities*. Toronto: Oxford University Press, 1996.

Dupree, S.S. "Church of God in Christ," in Burgess and van der Maas, eds, *The New International Dictionary of Pentecostal and Charismatic Movements*, 535–7.

Edgell, Penny. "A Cultural Sociology of Religion: New Directions." *Annual Review of Sociology* 38 (2012): 247–65.

Engelke, Matthew. "Past Pentecostalism: Notes on Rupture, Realignment, and Everyday Life in Pentecostal and African Independent Churches." *Africa: Journal of the International African Institute* 80 (2010): 177–99.

Espinosa, Gastón. *William J. Seymour and the Origins of Global Pentecostalism*. Durham, NC: Duke University Press, 2014.

Evangelical Fellowship of Canada. "Letter to the Prime Minister." http://www.evangelicalfellowship.ca/NetCommunity/Page.aspx?pid=5349, accessed 13 October 2009.

Finke, Roger, and Rodney Stark. *The Churching of America, 1776–1990: Winners and Losers in Our Religious Economy*. New Brunswick, NJ: Rutgers University Press, 1993.

Flatt, Kevin. *After Evangelicalism: The Sixties and the United Church of Canada*. Montreal and Kingston: McGill-Queens University Press, 2013.

Fleras, Augie. *Unequal Relations: An Introduction to Race, Ethnic and Aboriginal Dynamics in Canada*. Toronto: Pearson, 2011.

– and Jean Leonard Elliott. *Engaging Diversity: Multiculturalism in Canada*, 2nd edn. Toronto: Nelson Thomson, 2002.

Gerard, Bernice. *Bernice Gerard: Today and for Life*. Vancouver: Sunday Line Communications, 1988.

Gerson, Carole. "Publishing by Women," in Carole Gerson and Jacques Michon, eds, *History of the Book in Canada: Volume III, 1918–1980*, 319. Toronto: University of Toronto Press, 2007.

Gibson, Graham. "Native Theological Training within Canadian Evangelicalism: Three Case Studies." MA thesis, Wilfrid Laurier University, 1994.

Goode, Erich, and Nachman Ben-Yehuda. "Moral Panics: Culture, Politics, and Social Construction." *Annual Review of Sociology* 20 (1994): 149–71.

Grant, John Webster. *Moon of Wintertime: Missionaries and the Indians of Canada in Encounters since 1534*. Toronto: University of Toronto Press, 1984.

Gray, James H. *Booze: The Impact of Whiskey on the Prairie West*. Toronto: Macmillan, 1972.

Griffin, William. "1919: Ninety-Nine Years and Counting," in Wells, ed., *Picture This!* 24–42.

Guenther, Bruce L. "Ethnicity and Evangelical Protestants in Canada," in Bramadat and Seliak, eds., *Christianity and Ethnicity in Canada*, 365–414.

– "Pentecostal Theological Education: A Case Study of Western Bible College, 1925–50," in Wilkinson, ed., *Canadian Pentecostalism*, 99–122.

Haskell, David M. "'What We Have Here is a Failure to Communicate': Same-Sex Marriage, Evangelicals, and the Canadian News Media." *The Journal of Religion and Popular Culture* 23, 3 (2011): 311–29.

Hayday, Matthew, and Mary-Ellen Kelm, "Reconsidering 1969: A 'Turning Point' for Canada?" *Canadian Historical Review* 100, 2 (June 2019): 202–7.

Hiemstra, Rick. "Not Christian Anymore." *Faith Today*, 8 January 2020. https://www.faithtoday.ca/Magazines/2020-Jan-Feb/Not-Christian-anymore, accessed 6 March 2020.

Hocken, P.D. "Chambers, George Augustus (1879–1957)," in Burgess and van der Maas, eds, *The New International Dictionary of Pentecostal and Charismatic Movements*, 472.

Hogan, Brian. "Print and Organized Religion in English Canada," in Carole Gerson and Jacques Michon, *History of the Book in Canada: Volume III 1918–1980*, 283–7. Toronto: University of Toronto Press, 2007.

Hollenweger, Walter J. "Roman Catholics and Pentecostals in Dialogue." *The Ecumenical Review* 51, 2 (1999): 147–59.

Holm, Randall. "I'm Still There! Ronald A.N. Kydd's Influence on Canadian Pentecostalism." *Canadian Journal of Pentecostal-Charismatic Christianity* 1 (2010): 65–85.

Humphries, M. "War's Long Shadow: Masculinity, Medicine, and the Gendered Politics of Trauma, 1914–1939." *Canadian Historical Review* 91, 3 (2010): 503–31.

Hutchinson, Don, and Rick Hiemstra. "Canadian Evangelical Voting Trends by Region, 1996–2008." *Church and Faith Trends* 2, 3 (2009): 1–25.

Hutchinson, Mark, and John Wolffe. *A Short History of Global Evangelicalism*. Cambridge, UK: Cambridge University Press, 2012.

Hutchinson, Roger. "Focusing, Framing, and Discerning: The United Church of Canada and the Same-Sex Marriage Debate," in Rayside and Wilcox, eds, *Faith, Politics, and Sexual Diversity in Canada and the United States*.

Jennings, Mark. "A Silence Like Thunder: Pastoral and Theological Responses of Australian Pentecostal-Charismatic Churches to LGBTQ Individuals," in Wilkinson and Althouse, eds, *Pentecostals and the Body*.

Kärkkäinen, Veli M. "An Exercise on the Frontiers of Ecumenism: Almost Thirty Years of Roman Catholic–Pentecostal Dialogue." *Exchange* 29, 1 (2000): 156–71.

Kee, Kevin. *Revivalists: Marketing the Gospel in English Canada, 1884–1957*. Montreal and Kingston: McGill-Queen's University Press, 2007.

Keshen, Jeffrey A. *Saints, Sinners, and Soldiers: Canada's Second World War*. Vancouver: University of British Columbia Press, 2004.

Kidd, Colin. *The Forging of Races: Race and Scripture in the Protestant Atlantic World, 1600–2000*. Cambridge, MA: Cambridge University Press, 2006.

Kulbeck, Gloria G. *What God Hath Wrought: A History of the Pentecostal Assemblies of Canada*. Toronto: The Pentecostal Assemblies of Canada, 1958.

Kydd, Ronald A.N. "Canadian Pentecostalism and the Evangelical Impulse." In G.A. Rawlyk, ed., *Aspects of the Canadian Evangelical Experience*, 289–302. Montreal and Kingston: McGill-Queen's University Press, 1997.

– "Buntain, Daniel Newton (1888–1955)," in Burgess and van der Maas, eds, *The New International Dictionary of Pentecostal and Charismatic Movements*, 449–50.

– "The Pentecostal Assemblies of Canada and Society." Paper presented at the meeting of the Canadian Society of Church History, Queen's University, 1 June 1973.

– "Roman Catholic/Pentecostal Dialogue in Italy." *Journal of Ecumenical Studies* 33, 3 (1996): 444.

Laugrand, Frédéric B., and Jarich G. Oosten. *Inuit Shamanism and Christianity: Transitions and Transformations in the Twentieth Century*. Montreal and Kingston: McGill-Queen's University Press, 2010.

Lee, Jeanyoung. "Ethnic Korean Migration in Northeast Asia." In Tsuneo Akaha, ed., *Proceedings, International Seminar: Human Flows across National Borders in Northeast Asia*, 118–40. Monterey, CA: The Center for East Asian Studies, Monterey Institute of International Studies, 2002.

– "Korean-Chinese Migration into the Russian Far East: A Human Security Perspective." In Iwashita Akihiro, ed., *Siberia and the Russian Far East in the 21st Century: Partners in the "Community of Asia": Crossroads in Northeast Asia*, vol. 1, 67–93. Sapporo, Japan: Slavic Research Center, Hokkaido University, 2005.

Lefebvre, Solange, and Jean-François Breton. "Roman Catholics and Same-Sex Marriage in Quebec," in Rayside and Wilcox, eds, *Faith, Politics, and Sexual Diversity in Canada and the United States*.

Levitt, Peggy. *God Needs No Passport: Immigrants and the Changing American Landscape*. New York and London: New Press, 2007.

Lyon, David, and Marguerite Van Die, eds. *Rethinking Church, State, and Modernity*. Toronto: University of Toronto Press, 2000.

McAlister, R.E., "Called to Suffer for Jesus." *The Good Report*, May 1911, 6.
– "Healing in the Atonement." *The Good Report*, May 1911, 8.
McCleary, Timothy P. "An Ethnography of Pentecostalism among the Crow Indians of Montana." *Wicazo Sa Review* 15, 1 (2000): 117–35.
McDonnell, Killian. "Pentecostals and Catholics on Evangelism and Sheep-Stealing." *America* 180, 7 (1999): 11–14.
McGee, Gary B. *Miracles, Missions, & American Pentecostalism.* Maryknoll, NY: Orbis Books, 2010.
– and B.A. Pavia. "Church of God of Prophecy in Canada," in Burgess and van der Maas, *The New International Dictionary of Pentecostal and Charismatic Movements*, 542–3.
McGinnis, Janice P. "The Impact of Epidemic Influenza: Canada, 1918–1919." *Historical Papers/Communications historiques* 12, 1 (1977): 120–40.
McIntyre, Paul. *Black Pentecostal Music in Windsor.* Ottawa: Canadian Centre for Folk Culture Studies, National Museum of Man Mercury Series, Paper no. 15, 1976.
McKenzie, Stacey. "A Timeless Story," in David Wells, ed., *Picture This! Reflecting on 100 Years of the PAOC.*
MacRobert, Iain. *The Black Roots and White Racism of Early Pentecostalism.* London: MacMillan, 1988.
Malloy, Jonathan. "Between America and Europe: Religion, Politics and Evangelicals in Canada." *Politics, Religion & Ideology* 12, 3 (2011): 317–33.
– "Canadian Evangelicals and Same-Sex Marriage," in Rayside and Wilcox, eds., *Faith, Politics, and Sexual Diversity Canada and the United States.*
Marks, Lynne. *Revivals and Roller Rinks: Religion, Leisure, and Identity in Late-Nineteenth-Century Small-Town Ontario.* Toronto: University of Toronto Press, 1996.
Martin, David. *A General Theory of Secularization.* New York, NY: Harper & Row, 1978.
– *Pentecostalism: The World Their Parish.* Oxford, UK: Blackwell, 2002.
– *Tongues of Fire: The Explosion of Protestantism in Latin America.* Oxford, UK: Blackwell, 1990.
Medina, Néstor. "Discerning the Spirit in Culture: Toward Pentecostal Interculturality." *Canadian Journal of Pentecostal-Charismatic Christianity* 2 (2011): 131–65.
– "Hybridity, Migration, and Transnational Relations: Re-thinking Canadian Pentecostalism from a Latina/o Perspective," in Wilkinson, ed., *Global Pentecostal Movements*, 211–26.

Miller, Donald E., and Tetsunao Yamamori. *Global Pentecostalism: The New Face of Christian Social Engagement*. Berkeley, CA: University of California Press, 2007.

Miller, James R. *Shingwauk's Vision: A History of Native Residential Schools*. Toronto: University of Toronto Press, 1996.

– "The State, the Church, and Indian Residential Schools in Canada," in Marguerite Van Die, ed., *Religion and Public Life in Canada: Historical and Comparative Perspectives*, 109–29. Toronto: University of Toronto Press, 2001.

Miller, Thomas William. "The Canadian 'Azusa': The Hebden Mission in Toronto." *Pneuma: Journal of the Society of Pentecostal Studies* (1986): 5–29.

– *Canadian Pentecostals: A History of the Pentecostal Assemblies of Canada*. Mississauga, ON: Full Gospel Publishing House, 1994.

Mittelstadt, Martin. "'Canada's First Martyr': The Suspicious Death of David Wells, Winnipeg's First World War Pentecostal Conscientious Objector." *Manitoba History* 87 (2018). http://www.mhs.mb.ca/docs/mb_history/87/index.shtml.

Moberg, David O. *The Church as a Social Institution*, 2nd edn. Grand Rapids, MI: Baker Book House, 1984.

Moon, Steve. "The Recent Korean Missionary Movement: A Record of Growth, and More Growth Needed." *International Bulletin of Missionary Research* 27, 1 (2003): 11–17.

Murphy, Karen. *Pentecostals and Roman Catholics on Becoming a Christian: Spirit-Baptism, Faith, Conversion, Experience, and Discipleship in Ecumenical Perspective*. Leiden, Netherlands: Brill, 2018.

Nicholas, Jane. *The Modern Girl: Feminine Modernities, the Body, and Commodities in the 1920s*. Toronto: University of Toronto Press, 2015.

O'Dea, Thomas. "Five Dilemmas in the Institutionalization of Religion." *Journal for the Scientific Study of Religion* 1 (1961): 30–9.

Opp, James. *The Lord for the Body*. Montreal and Kingston: McGill-Queen's University Press, 2005.

– "Re-imaging the Moral Order of Urban Space: Religion and Photography in Winnipeg, 1900–1914," in James Opp and John C. Walsh, *Home, Work, and Play: Situating Canadian History, 1840–1980*, 33–46. Don Mills, ON: Oxford University Press, 2006.

Owram, Doug. *Born at the Right Time: A History of the Baby Boom Generation*. Toronto: University of Toronto Press, 1996.

Palmer, Bryan. *Canada's 1960s: The Ironies of Identity in a Rebellious Era*. Toronto: University of Toronto Press, 2009.

Pentecostal Assemblies of Canada. "Cultural Ministry." British Columbia and Yukon District. http://www.bc.paoc.org/international-ethnic-ministries/cultural-ministry, accessed 26 November 2018.

– "What is the 2020 Initiative?" https://paoc.org/events/2020, accessed 19 September 2017.

Pierson, Ruth Roach. *They're Still Women after All: The Second World War and Canadian Womanhood*. Toronto: McClelland & Stewart, 1986.

Poloma, Margaret. *The Assemblies of God at the Crossroads: Charisma and Institutional Dilemmas*. Knoxville, TN: University of Tennessee Press, 1989.

– *Main Street Mystics: The Toronto Blessing and Reviving Pentecostalism*. Lanham, MD: Altamira Press, 2003.

Posterski, Don. *Reinventing Evangelism*. Downers Grove, IL: InterVarsity Press, 1989.

Rambo, Lewis R., and Charles E. Farhadian, eds. *The Oxford Handbook of Religious Conversion*. Oxford and New York: Oxford University Press, 2014.

Ramirez, Daniel. *Migrating Faith: Pentecostalism in the United States and Mexico in the Twentieth Century*. Chapel Hill, NC: University of North Carolina Press, 2015.

Rayside, David, and Clyde Wilcox, eds. *Faith, Politics, and Sexual Diversity in Canada and the United States*. Vancouver: University of British Columbia Press, 2011.

"Reclaiming Power and Place: The Final Report of the National Inquiry into Missing and Murdered Indigenous Women and Girls." https://www.mmiwg-ffada.ca/final-report, accessed 21 June 2019.

Reed, David A. "Denominational Charismatics – Where Have They All Gone?" in Wilkinson, ed., *Canadian Pentecostalism*, 197–213.

– *"In Jesus' Name": The History and Beliefs of Oneness Pentecostals*. Blandford Forum, Dorset: Deo Publishing, 2008.

Reimer, Sam. "'Civility without Compromise': Evangelical Attitudes towards Same-Sex Issues in Comparative Context," in Rayside and Wilcox, eds, *Faith, Politics, and Sexual Diversity in Canada and the United States*.

– *Evangelicals and the Continental Divide*. Montreal and Kingston: McGill-Queen's University Press, 2003.

– and Michael Wilkinson. *A Culture of Faith: Evangelical Congregations in Canada*. Montreal and Kingston: McGill-Queen's University Press, 2015.

Riss, R.M. "Faith Homes," in Burgess and van der Maas, eds., *The New International Dictionary of Pentecostal Charismatic Movements*, 630–2.

Robbins, Joel. "On the Paradox of Pentecostalism and the Perils of Continuity Thinking." *Religion* 3 (2003): 221–31.

Robertson, Roland. *Globalization: Social Theory and Global Culture*. London: SAGE, 2000.

– "Global Millennialism: A Postmortem on Secularization," in Beyer and Beaman, eds., *Religion, Globalization, and Culture*, 9–34.

Rosenior, Derrick. "The Rhetoric of Pentecostal Racial Reconciliation: Looking Back to Look Forward," in Wilkinson and Studebaker, eds, *A Liberating Spirit*, 53–84.

Ross, Brian. "James Eustace Purdie: The Story of Pentecostal Theological Education." *Journal of the Canadian Church Historical Society* 17, 4 (1975): 94–103.

Royal Commission on Bilingualism and Biculturalism. *The Cultural Contribution of the Other Ethnic Groups*, vol. iv. Ottawa: Queen's Printer, 1970.

Rudd, Douglas. *When the Spirit Came upon Them: Highlights from the Early Years of the Pentecostal Movement in Canada*. Mississauga, ON: The Pentecostal Assemblies of Canada, 2002.

Schatkowski, Julius. *Rev. Julius Schatkowski: Autobiography, 1889–1974*. Alberta District, German Branch, n.d.

Scheitle, Christopher P., and Kevin D. Dougherty. "The Sociology of Religious Organizations." *Sociology Compass* 2, 3 (2008): 981–99.

Simpson, J. "The Politics of the Body in Canada and the United States," in Lyon and Van Die, eds., *Rethinking Church, State, and Modernity*.

Sloos, William. "The Story of James and Ellen Hebden: The First Family of Pentecost in Canada." *Pneuma: Journal of the Society of Pentecostal Studies* 32 (2010): 181–202.

Sneath, Robyn. "Imagining a Mennonite Community: The *Mennonitische Post* and a People of Diaspora." *Journal of Mennonite Studies* 22 (2004): 217–18.

Stackhouse, John G. "Bearing Witness: Christian Groups Engage Canadian Politics since the 1960s," in Lyon and Van Die, eds, *Rethinking Church, State, and Modernity*.

– *Canadian Evangelicalism in the Twentieth Century*. Toronto: University of Toronto Press, 1993.

Stark, Rodney. "Secularization, R.I.P." *Sociology of Religion* 3 (1999): 249–73.
– and Roger Finke. *Acts of Faith: Explaining the Human Side of Religion*. Berkeley, CA: University of California Press, 2000.
Statistics Canada. "Religions in Canada." 2001 Census. https://www150.statcan.gc.ca/n1/en/catalogue/96F0030X2001015, accessed 10 February 2019.
Stephen, Jennifer Anne. *Pick One Intelligent Girl: Employability, Domesticity, and the Gendering of Canada's Welfare State, 1939–1947*. Toronto: University of Toronto Press, 2007.
Stephenson, Lisa. *Dismantling the Dualisms for American Pentecostal Women in Ministry*. Leiden, Netherlands: Brill, 2012.
Stewart, Adam. "A Canadian Azusa? The Implications of the Hebden Mission for Pentecostal Historiography," in Wilkinson and Althouse, eds, *Winds from the North*.
– *The New Canadian Pentecostals*. Waterloo, ON: Wilfrid Laurier University Press, 2015.
– "Re-visioning the Disinherited: Pentecostals and Social Class in North America," in Wilkinson and Studebaker, eds, *A Liberating Spirit*, 136–57.
– Andrew Gabriel, and Kevin Shanahan. "Changes in Clergy Belief and Practice in Canada's Largest Pentecostal Denomination." *Pneuma: Journal of the Society of Pentecostal Studies* 39 (2017): 457–81.
Swenson, Donald S. "The Canadian Catholic Charismatic Renewal," in Wilkinson, ed., *Canadian Pentecostalism*, 214–32.
Tarango, Angela. *Choosing the Jesus Way: American Indian Pentecostals and the Fight for the Indigenous Principle*. Chapel Hill, NC: University of North Carolina Press, 2014.
Thiessen, Joel. *The Meaning of Sunday: The Practice of Belief in a Secular Age*. Montreal and Kingston: McGill-Queen's University Press, 2015.
Thietart, Raymond. "Chaos Theory and Organization." *Organizational Science* 6, 1 (1995): 19–31.
Thomas, Jerry. "Pentecostal Predominance in French Evangelicalism in Quebec, 1921–1963." *Historical Papers: Canadian Society of Church History* (2015): 63–73.
Ustorf, Werner. "Protestantism and Missions," in Alister E. McGrath and Darren C. Marks, eds, *The Blackwell Companion to Protestantism*, 392–402. Malden, MA: Blackwell Publishing, 2004.
Vance, Jonathan. *Memory, Meaning, and the First World War*. Vancouver: University of British Columbia Press, 1997.

Vondey, Wolfgang. *Pentecostal Theology: Living the Full Gospel*. London: Bloomsbury T&T Clark, 2017.

Wacker, Grant. *Heaven Below: Early Pentecostals and American Culture*. Cambridge, MA: Harvard University Press, 2001.

Wakefield, Gavin. *Alexander Boddy: Pentecostal Anglican Pioneer*. Milton Keynes, UK: Paternoster, 2007.

Weber, Max. *Economy and Society, Vols. 1 & 2*. Berkeley, CA: University of California Press, 1978.

– *The Protestant Ethic and the Spirit of Capitalism*. New York: Charles Scribner's Sons, 1958.

Wells, David, ed. *Picture This! Reflecting on 100 Years of the PAOC*. Mississauga, ON: The Pentecostal Assemblies of Canada, 2018.

Westman, Clinton. "Pentecostalism among Canadian Aboriginal People: A Political Movement?" in Wilkinson and Studebaker, eds, *A Liberating Spirit*, 85–110.

– "Understanding Cree Religious Discourse." PhD diss., University of Alberta, 2008.

Whiteley, Marilyn. *Canadian Methodist Women, 1766–1925: Marys, Marthas, Mothers in Israel*. Waterloo, ON: Wilfrid Laurier Press, 2005.

Whitt, Irving Alfred. "Developing a Pentecostal Missiology in the Canadian Context: The Pentecostal Assemblies of Canada." Unpublished D.Miss. thesis, Fuller Theological Seminary, 1994.

– and James D. Craig. "A Philosophy of Missions for the Pentecostal Assemblies of Canada." Mississauga, ON: PAOC, 2004.

Wilkinson, Michael. "Canadian Pentecostal Diversity: Incorporating the Many Voices." *Canadian Journal of Pentecostal-Charismatic Christianity* 2 (2011): 41–82.

– ed. *Canadian Pentecostalism: Transition and Transformation*. Montreal and Kingston: McGill-Queen's University Press, 2009.

– "Charles W. Chawner and the Missionary Impulse of the Hebden Mission," in Wilkinson and Althouse, eds, *Winds from the North*, 39–54.

– ed. *Global Pentecostal Movements*. Leiden, Netherlands: Brill, 2012.

– "History of English-Speaking Sociology of Religion in Canada," in Anthony Blasi and Giuseppe Giordon, eds, *National Survey of Histories of Sociology of Religion*, 35–51. Leiden, Netherlands: Brill, 2015.

– "The 'Many Tongues' of Global Pentecostalism," in Wilkinson, ed., *Global Pentecostal Movements*, 1–14.

– "Pentecostalism, the Body, and Embodiment," in Wilkinson and Althouse, eds, *Pentecostals and the Body*.

– "Pentecostals and the World: Theoretical and Methodological Issues for Studying Global Pentecostalism." *Pneuma: Journal of the Society of Pentecostal Studies* 38, 4 (January 2016): 373–93.
– "Religion and Global Flows," in Beyer and Beaman, eds, *Religion, Culture, and Globalization*, 375–89.
– "Sociological Narratives and the Sociology of Pentecostalism," in Amos Yong and Mel Robuck, eds, *The Cambridge Companion for Pentecostal Studies*, 215–34. Cambridge, UK: Cambridge University Press, 2014.
– *The Spirit Said Go: Pentecostal Immigrants in Canada*. New York: Peter Lang, 2006.
– "The Transformation of Religion and the Self in the Age of Authenticity." *Pneuma: The Journal of the Society for Pentecostal Studies* 40, 1–2 (2018): 91–108.
– and Peter Althouse. "Like a Mighty Rushing Wind: Innovation and the Transnational Character of Pentecostalism," in Wilkinson and Althouse, eds, *Winds from the North*.
– eds. *Pentecostals and the Body*. Leiden, Netherlands: Brill, 2017.
– eds. *Winds from the North: Canadian Contributions to the Pentecostal Movement*. Leiden, Netherlands: Brill, 2010.
Wilkinson, Michael, and Steven Studebaker, eds. *A Liberating Spirit*. Eugene, OR: Wipf and Stock, 2010.
Wilson, Bryan. *Religion in Secular Society*. London: Penguin, 1966.
Wilson, E.A. "McAlister, Robert Edward," in Burgess and van der Maas, eds, *The New International Dictionary of Pentecostal Charismatic Movements*, 852.
Wright, Donald. "20th Century Belongs to Canada." In Gerald Hallowell, ed., *The Oxford Companion to Canadian History*, 625. Don Mills, ON: Oxford University Press, 2004.
Wuthnow, Robert. *Cultural Analysis*. New York: Routledge, 1984.
– *Meaning and Moral Order: Explorations in Cultural Analysis*. Berkeley, CA: University of California Press, 1987.
Yang, Fenggang, and Andrew Abel. "Sociology of Religious Conversion," in Rambo and Farhadian, eds, *The Oxford Handbook of Religious Conversion*, 140–63.
Yong, Amos, and Estrelda Y. Alexander, eds. *Afro-Pentecostalism: Black Pentecostal and Charismatic Christianity in History and Culture*. New York: New York University Press, 2011.
Young, Pamela. "It's All about Sex: The Roots of Opposition to Gay and Lesbian Marriages in Some Christian Churches," in Rayside and Wilcox, eds, *Faith, Politics, and Sexual Diversity in Canada and the United States*.

Ziefle, Joshua. *David du Plessis and the Assemblies of God: Struggle for the Soul of a Movement*. Leiden, Netherlands: Brill, 2013.

Zuidema, Jason, ed. *French-Speaking Protestants in Canada*. Leiden, Netherlands: Brill, 2011.

Index

Note: Page numbers in bold indicate a table.